MIND YOUR WORDS

Master the Art of Learning and Teaching Vocabulary

DR. PRUDENT INJEELI

For book orders, email orders@traffordpublishing.com.sg

Most Trafford Singapore titles are also available at major online book retailers.

Cover concept conceived by Byron Injeeli

Printed in Singapore.

ISBN: 978-1-4669-9131-6 (sc)
ISBN: 978-1-4669-9133-0 (e)

Trafford rev. 05/23/2013

 www.traffordpublishing.com.sg
Singapore
toll-free: 800 101 2656 (Singapore)
Fax: 800 101 2656 (Singapore)

A word fitly spoken is like apples of gold in settings of silver

Proverbs 25:11 (the Bible)

Dedicated

To

the loving memories of my father

Like flowers that wither, you're gone for ever

CONTENTS

Part I

Part II

FOREWORD

I consider this a great privilege to write a forward to Dr. Prudent's book "Mind Your Words". I firmly believe that this book was long due for the benefit of the students wishing to understand the many complexities of English vocabulary and its usage. Additionally, it will be a great resource of valuable information and a guide for the teachers of English.

I have known Dr. Prudent Injeeli for over a decade now both as a lecturer and a person. We have been teaching together at various universities as colleagues and co-professors for graduate and some post-graduate courses. I first met Dr,Injeeli at Norton University, Phnom Penh, where I was the Dean of the college of Arts, Humanities and Languages at that time. I still remember once telling Dr. Injeeli that I usually did not look too carefully for any mistake or even a typo in his exam papers before signing and approving them. This was because I always had a strong confidence and firm belief that he would not make any such mistake or leave any room for me to make any necessary correction. Even though he always insisted that I thoroughly go over to make sure that he had left no error or even a typo anywhere in the papers. This simply tells how much regard I had for Dr. Injeel's competency in English language. Dr. Injeeli is also highly esteemed by the students of PUC where he has taught various English subjects such as, English literature, creative writing, and advanced writing etc.

With regards to his work "Mind Your Words", I am delighted to see Dr. Injeeli's initiative in compiling this valuable resource book as it will undoubtedly be of a great help to the students worldwide. Dr. Injeeli has finally committed his immense knowledge and expertise of the language particularly in the areas of linguistics and semantics into a book. He has taken pains to lay bare the intricacies and complexities of English vocabulary in an effort to show the ways and means to master the art of both learning and teaching vocabulary. This book is a vital document for a novice as well as an already well- versed user of English language.

The book offers a wide range of topics and themes that are of monumental importance and significance in understanding how words are "born"; how they get their meaning; how they should be correctly pronounced, how they make more words and finally how they should be correctly used. Dr. Injeeli has not only added essential chapters on English etymology, word formation, word families, word origins etc. but has also supplemented this valuable information with a wide range of enormously important stock of vocabulary that will certainly aid the user of this book to augment and enhance his/her vocabulary in a most effective and powerful way. To conclude, I would say that this work by Dr. Injeeli is a ground-breaking step in teaching English particularly in teaching English vocabulary and it is of great worth both for teachers and students of English language. I congratulate Dr. Injeeli on producing this immensely valuable book and wish him success in his further endeavors.

Sok Uttara Ph.D
Associate Dean and Professor
Paññāsāstra University of Cambodia (PUC)

A WORD OF GRATITUDE

I have been in the field of teaching for over twenty years now, and during all these years I have endeavored to impart my acquired knowledge and learning to my students in the most conscientious and devoted manner. I have taken pains to explore and research the mysteries and mazes of the wonderful world of learning and scholarship. Fortunately, I have had the privilege of being taught by some of the most dedicated and compassionate teachers throughout my academic career and I owe them so much gratitude that it cannot be expressed in words. However, all that can be said in this regard is, to quote an Indian axiom, "if you ever meet God and teacher together, bow down to the teacher first… ". And I firmly believe in this. So that says all with regard to my admiration and appreciation for my teachers and mentors for making and shaping my scholastic career.

Apart from my highly esteemed and revered teachers, I most certainly owe a lot my parents and my elder brother, Dr. Akhtar Injeel and my elder sister Baji Fehmida Waiz whose incessant guidance and assistance in every thick and thin of life has been a great source of inspiration and motivation that has kept me going on in life with all its challenges, trials and tribulations. Also, I cannot fail to mention my brother-in-law Mr. Naeem Waiz who himself being a journalist and a writer passionately encouraged me in my literary pursuits. Also, my uncles, Mr. Asif Raza, Mr. Yaqub Khan, my dear aunt Khalla Rakhil who have all contributed to my learning and growth, especially during my high school and college days. I owe them all.

Not to forget my school-days friend, my confidant and my soul-mate, Lawrence Francis, the sincerity and warmth of whose camaraderie and friendship has been a great source of inspiration that has always helped me in believing in myself and pulling it through even in the face of grim adversity and uncertainty.

They say that one's immediate family always has the biggest share in one's successes and failures, joys and miseries, pains and pleasures, expectations and despairs. I have been blessed with a most wonderful family who has given a purpose and meaning to my life, with their love being the driving force in all my ventures and endeavors, I am able to accomplish this and hope to do more. Thanks for putting up with me, Taskeen, Byron and Sheridan. All I can say, heaven without you will have no pleasure and hell with you, will have no pain.

Dr. Prudent Injeeli

The task of producing this book would have never been accomplished, had it not been for my brother, Dr. Akhtar Injeeli's persistent exhortations to publish it. Thanks Dr. Sahib.

WHY WORDS MATTER?

"Wait a minute, let me think of the right word", or "just give me a second, I can't think of the right word". How many times we hear people say such things, and how many times even we ourselves get strangled in a similar dilemma when we struggle to come up with the appropriate words to express our thoughts, feelings, perspectives or point of view. We dress our thoughts in words. We yearn in desperation to grasp the right word to put it exactly the way it is inside our mind or heart but words fail us because they are just not there to pop up at the right moment. So what does that prove? Yes, it does prove something, something very significant and substantial.

Word, words, words, it's all in words, we think in words; we live in words, we feel in words, we are delighted by words and we are shattered by words. We win new friends with words and we lose our longstanding old friends because of our words. Words can rip our hearts and words can soothe our wounded egos, words can be hard as stones and words can be soft as petals or a puff of air. Words make us laugh, words make us weep, with words we bless and with words we curse. Words cause partings that could have easily been averted with the right words at the right moment.

Words, words, words, take words not lightly, weigh them before you utter them, know them before you use them and understand them before you react or respond to them. Words are the most powerful devices at our disposal that can make a world of difference to individuals, groups, families, factions, nations and even to the whole world. Pacts are framed in words, negotiations are carried out in words, and promises are made in words. Yet the very words break those promises and bring talks, dialogues and discourses to a deadlock and the very words turn disputes into conflicts and conflicts into wars. Thus, at the bottom of everything we say or do, are words. Harsh and ill-spoken words haunt us all our lives while soft and pacifying words lift up our souls even when we are at our lowest. So, take words seriously, because words may seem to be lifeless and listless, just shapes and lines, rounded here and twisted there but words breathe, they live and they cry out and make their presence felt. Words deserve respect and reverence; they demand care and caution and require precision and preciseness, Treat words as you would treat a person and they won't desert you. On the contrary, they will be there to assist you, in time of sorrow and in time of triumph. We come to this world without words but we depart, leaving behind our words. The great ones leave them in books and the common lot to the memories of their loved ones. Words may help us win an argument but words not spoken wisely may cost us a friendship that once lost may bring a bitter remorse for the rest of our life. So take your words back before that friend has turned the corner and may never be seen again. Words are sharp weapons; don't play with them if you are not skilled at their use.

PART I

1 WHAT'S IN A WORD...?

("What's in a name?" Shakespeare – Romeo and Juliet)

I. General Overview

1.1 The status of English

> "Remember that you are a human being with a soul and the divine gift of articulate speech; that your native language is the language of Shakespeare and Milton and the Bible; and don't sit there crooning like a bilious pigeon.
>
> Look at her-a prisoner of the gutters; Condemned by every syllable she utters. By right she should be taken out and hung for the cold-blooded murder of the English tongue".

The above passage shows Professor's Henry Higgins' (My Fair Lady) utter disgust and annoyance with the way people speak and use English language. English, no doubt rules the world because of its grandeur, elegance, and universality. Above all its capacity to grow, adapt and adopt new words from numerous other sources. No other language of the world has had such a profound and enormous impact in science, technology, arts, humanities, religion and social sciences as has English. English is the most widely spoken and written language on Earth. Although, about one-fifth of the world's population, (or over one billion people), speaks some variety of Chinese as their native language, but you are more likely to find someone with some measure of knowledge of English than Chinese almost anywhere on the planet.

English was first spoken in Britain by Germanic tribes in Fifth Century AD also known as the Old English (Anglo-Saxon) period. During the Middle English period (1150-1500 AD), a lot of the Old English word endings were replaced by prepositions like by, with, and from. We are now in the Modern English period which started in the

Sixteenth Century. English, today without a shadow of doubt is the most predominant language in almost all walks of life, ranging from science, medicine, technology, research, computer science, news, media, entertainment, internet, travel-tourism and even sports. A good knowledge of English is almost synonymous to being the key to success in the contemporary fast-paced and rapidly developing world.

1.2 The Number Game

The number of words in English has grown from 50,000 odd (old English words) to about 1,000,000 today. About 80% of the entries in any English dictionary are borrowed, mainly from Latin.

New words keep coming up by combining words into one word such as housewife, greenhouse, overdue, and laptop etc.

The addition of prefixes and suffixes to words also increases the immense vocabulary of the English language.

Today, more than 750 million people use the English language.

An average educated person knows about 20,000 words and uses about 2,000 words in a week.

Despite its widespread use, there are only about 350 million people who use it as their mother tongue.

English is the official language of the Olympics.

More than half of the world's technical and scientific periodicals as well three quarters of the world's mail, and its telexes and cables are in English.

About 80% of the information stored in the world's computers is also in English.

English is also communicated to more than 100 million people every day by 5 of the largest broadcasting companies (CBS, NBC, ABC, BBC, CBC CNA).

1.3 How many words are there in the English language?

There is no single realistic answer to this question. As it's impossible to count the number of words in a language, because it's so hard to decide what actually counts as a word. A word may be generally considered a noun but it may also be used as a verb. Then, how should it be counted or what should it be considered in this regard? Should we count it only once as one word or consider it as two words. For example, table, generally refers to a piece or article of furniture, thus a noun, but it also could be used as a verb, meaning to *to table* (a motion / undecided issue) (1) to hold something back until a later time; (2) to remove from consideration. Similarly, should the plural of chair, **chairs** be considered another word apart from the main entry- chair? Again, take for example, laptop, which is a combination of **lap** and **top,** which already exist as two separate words. So, should it be taken as another "new" word in its own right or should it be ignored in the reckoning as a new word?

This argument leads us to suggest that there are, at the very least, a quarter of a million distinct English words, excluding inflections, **(s, es, ed, ing** etc. forms.) and words from technical and regional vocabulary not covered by any standard up-to-date dictionary. If distinct senses were counted, the total number of words would amount to approximately 750,000 that is, three quarters of a million.

The Oxford English Dictionary contains full entries for 171,476 words in current use, and 47,156 obsolete (out-of-date, no more in active use) words. To this may be added around 9,500 **derivative** words included as subentries. (**derivative** from **derivation** -the formation of a word from another word or from a root in the same or another language. such as **electricity** from **electric**.) Over half of these words are nouns, about a quarter adjectives, and about a seventh verbs; the rest is made up of exclamations, conjunctions, prepositions, suffixes, etc. And these figures don't take account of entries with senses for different word classes (such as noun and adjective).

The statistics of English are astonishing. Of all the world's languages (which now number about 2,700), it is arguably the richest in vocabulary. The compendious *Oxford English Dictionary* lists about 500,000 words; and a further half-million technical and scientific terms remain uncatalogued.

Standardized Result: 500,000 words, 1,000,000 words
(including scientific words)

All in all, about 750,000 words if we include professional terms not in general use, otherwise it would be about 250,000. However, in December 2010 a joint Harvard/ Google study found that English language contains 1,022,000 words and is expanding at the rate of 8,500 words per year. That means about 23- 25 words per day are added to the English language. The findings came from the computer analysis of 5,195,769 digitized books.

> **About 8,500-10,000 new words are added to English language every year, so, on the average 23-25 new words come up every day.**

2 What is a word?

According to *thefreedictionary.com* a word (wûrd / , [wɜːd] is:

1. A sound or a combination of sounds, or its representation in writing or printing that symbolizes and communicates a meaning and may consist of a single morpheme or of a combination of morphemes.
2. Something said; an utterance, a remark, or a comment:

A single distinct meaningful element of speech or writing, used with others (or sometimes alone) to form a sentence.

In language, a word is the smallest element that may be uttered in isolation with literal or practical meaning.

In linguistics, a word is one of the units of speech or writing that native speakers of a language usually regard as the smallest meaningful element of the language, although linguists would analyze these further into morphemes and lexical units.

In addition, a word may suggest a few more meanings or senses. Such as, take my word, here, word, suggests an assurance and guarantee. He gave me his word / He kept his word. Here it means a solemn promise. Word may also refer to the scriptures (the Bible – the word of God) or the teachings of Jesus.

3 What is Vocabulary?

A *vocabulary* is defined as "all the words known and used by a particular person". However, the words known and used by a particular person do not include all the words a person is exposed to or comes in contact with. By definition, a vocabulary includes the ability to use a word even if one cannot clearly explain it and the second step is, being well acquainted with the word, both, in its usage and meaning.

Generally "vocabulary" means "all the words known and used by a particular person. *Knowing* a word, however, is not just being able to recognize a word or use it, there is much more to it than just that. There are several aspects of word-knowledge which are used to assess the knowledge of a word or words.

Note: Some material in this section has been adapted from the works of I. S. P. Nation

4 The Size of Vocabulary: How many words does a native speaker know?

A native speaker is expected to add roughly 1000 word families a year to his/her vocabulary size of around 20,000 word families. That means a five year old school-beginning child will have a vocabulary of around 4000 to 5000 word families. A university graduate will have a vocabulary of around 20,000 word families (Goulden, Nation and Read, 1990). These figures are roughly estimated and there is likely to be very large variation between individuals. Moreover, these figures exclude proper names, compound words, abbreviations, and foreign words. A word family is taken to include a base word, (*e.g. go*) its inflected forms, (*goes, going*) and a small number of reasonably regular derived forms (Bauer and Nation, 1993). Some researchers suggest vocabulary sizes larger than these but in the well conducted studies (for example, D'Anna, Zechmeister nad Hall, 1991) the differences are mainly the result of differences in what items are included in the count and how a word family is defined. We will look at the word families and how they work, in proceeding pages.

> The English language contains about 616500 word forms, in addition, another 400,000 technical terms. This is the highest number in any language. But hardly does an individual use up to 60,000 words. A British native speaker, who has gone through a full length of sixteen years of education, may use up to 5000 words in speech and up to 10, 000 words in writing. The membership of the international Society for Philosophical Enquiry, where no admission is possible for individuals with an IQ below 148, requires an average vocabulary of 36250 words. Remember, Shakespeare employed (used) 33,000 different words in his plays.
>
> *The Guinness Book of World Records*

5 Ogden's word research and vocabulary lists:

Charles K. Ogden, (1889–1957), British linguist and philosopher, discovered that if we were to take the 25,000 word Oxford Pocket English Dictionary and take away the redundant words that can be made by putting together simpler words, we find that 90% of the concepts in that dictionary can be achieved with just 850 words.

Charles K. Ogden the developer of this technique called this simplified language **Basic English,** and it was released in 1930 as a book, entitled, *Basic English: A General Introduction with Rules and Grammar.* His most famous associate, I.A. Richards, led the effort in the Orient, which uses the techniques to this day.

II. Types of vocabulary

1. Reading vocabulary

A person's reading vocabulary is all the words he or she can recognize when reading. This is the largest type of vocabulary, simply because it includes the other three.

2. Listening vocabulary

A person's listening vocabulary is all the words he or she can recognize when listening to speech. This vocabulary is supported in size by context and tone of voice.

3. Writing vocabulary

A person's writing vocabulary is all the words he or she can make use of in writing. Contrary to the previous two vocabulary types, the writing vocabulary is inspired and prompted by its user.

4. Speaking vocabulary

A person's speaking vocabulary is all the words he or she can use in speech. Due to the natural mode of the speaking vocabulary, words are often misused. This misuse – though slight and unintentional – may be balanced by facial expressions, tone of voice, or hand gestures and other *paralingual features*.

5. Focal vocabulary

"Focal vocabulary" is a specialized set of terms and distinctions that is particularly important to a certain group; those with particular focus of experience or activity. A lexicon, or vocabulary, is a language's dictionary, its set of names for things, events, and ideas.

III. Vocabulary growth

1. At early age

Initially, in the infancy (babyhood) stage, vocabulary growth requires no effort. Babies hear words and imitate them, eventually associating them with objects and actions. This is the listening vocabulary. The speaking vocabulary follows, as a child's thoughts become more dependent on its ability to express itself without gestures and mere sounds. Once the reading and writing vocabularies are attained – through questions and education – the irregularities and inconsistencies of language can be noticed, understood and reconciled.

In first grade, a privileged student (i.e. a literate student) knows about twice as many words as a disadvantaged or underprivileged student. Generally, this gap does not tighten. This converts into a wide range of vocabulary size by age five or six, at which time **an English-speaking child will know about 2,500–5,000 words. An average student learns 3,000 odd words per year, or approximately eight words per day.**

After leaving school or finishing formal education (college/university), vocabulary growth slows down and almost settles at a certain level and is most likely to remain at that level. However, people may then expand their vocabularies by reading, playing word games, participating in vocabulary programs, etc.

2. Passive vs. active vocabulary

Even if we learn a word, it takes a lot of practice and context connections for us to learn it well. A rough grouping of words we understand when we hear them encompasses our "passive" vocabulary, whereas our "active" vocabulary is made up of words that come to our mind immediately when we have to use them in a sentence, as we speak. In this case, we often have to come up with a word in the timeframe of split seconds, so one has to know it well, often in combinations with other words in phrases, where it is commonly used.

3. The importance of learning / teaching vocabulary

No one can deny the importance of vocabulary in mastering language. According to a renowned linguist, Jeremy Harmer, "If language structures make up the skeleton of language, then it is vocabulary that provides the vital organs and the flesh" *The Practice of English Language Teaching, Longman Pub.*

Harmer goes on to stress the importance of vocabulary by asserting the supremacy of vocabulary even over grammar, structure and syntax. This is what Harmer has to say in this regard, "... where vocabulary is used correctly it can cancel out structural accuracy."

Most of the pedagogical strategies and training focus on teaching teachers how to teach structure, grammar, syntax and composition. Very little attention is given to the area of teaching vocabulary. Whereas, teaching vocabulary should be considered as vital a skill as teaching structure.

Why Teach / Learn Vocabulary?

   a. An extensive vocabulary aids expressions and communication
   b. Vocabulary size has been directly linked to reading comprehension
   c. Linguistic vocabulary is synonymous with thinking vocabulary
   d. A person may be judged by others based on his or her vocabulary

---

Native speakers' vocabulary:

**20,000 for undergraduate (add 1000-2000 words per year
or 3-7 words per day)**

IV. Second Language Vocabulary Acquisition

Learning vocabulary is one of the first steps of learning a second language, yet one never reaches the final step in getting a full hold on vocabulary and of course on language itself. Whether in one's native language or a second language, the acquisition of new vocabulary is a continuous process. Several methods can help one learn new vocabulary.

1. Memorization

Although memorization can be seen as dull or boring, associating one word in the native language with the matching word in the second language until memorized is still one of the best methods of vocabulary acquisition. By the time a student reaches adulthood, he or she generally gathers a number of personalized memorization methods. However, the drawback of this method is that a student tends to learn words in isolation, without seeing them in context. Words exist in relation with other words; therefore, students need to see words placed with other words to understand their purpose, their place, their function and their particular meaning in the context they occur.

2. The Keyword Method

One useful method to build vocabulary in a second language is the keyword method. When additional time is available or one wants to emphasize a few key words, one can create **mnemonic** (memory-aid) strategies or word associations. Although these strategies tend to take longer to put in practice and may take longer in disposing to memory or calling to mind, they create new or unusual connections that can increase preservation. As students advance and grow older, they tend to rely less on creating word associations to remember vocabulary. The key word method can work in two ways. The teacher may introduce the important or target words before going through a text or focus on them after having read the text once or even twice.

3. Basic English vocabulary

Several word lists have been developed to provide people with a limited vocabulary either quick language proficiency or an effective means of communication. In 1930, Charles Kay Ogden created Basic English (850 words). Other lists include Simplified English (1000 words) and Special English (1500 words). The General Service List, 2000 high frequency words compiled by Michael West from a 5,000,000 word corpus, has been used to create a number of adapted reading texts for English language learners. Knowing 2000 English words, one could understand quite a lot of English, and even read a lot of simple material without any problem.

4. Headword

A **headword/ head word / lemma**, or sometimes **catchword** is the word under which a set of related dictionary or encyclopedia entries appear. The headword is used to locate the entry, and orders its alphabetical position. Depending on the size and nature of the dictionary or encyclopedia, the entry may include different meanings of the word, its etymology and pronunciation, compound words or phrases that contain the headword, and encyclopedic information about the concepts represented by the word.

For example, the headword bread may contain the following (simplified) definitions:

Bread *(noun)* A common food made from the combination of flour, water and yeast

Money *(slang)*

to know which side your bread is buttered to know how to act in your own best interests.

(verb) To coat in breadcrumbs

Similarly, *dust (soil, dirt)* is a *noun* and *to dust* is verb, meaning *to wipe away dust.*

The Academic Dictionary of Lithuanian contains around 500,000 headwords. The Oxford English Dictionary has around 300,000 headwords, while Merriam-Webster's Third New International Dictionary has about 470,000. Both of these values are as claimed by the dictionary makers, and may not be using exactly the same definition of a headword. Also, the Oxford English Dictionary covers each word much more exhaustively than the Third New International.

V. Linguistics Terms in Teaching Vocabulary

1. **Phonetics**, the study of the physical properties of speech (or signed) production and perception
2. **Phonology**, the study of sounds (or signs) as discrete, abstract elements in the speaker's mind that distinguish meaning
3. **Morphology**, the study of internal structures of words and how they can be modified
4. **Syntax**, the study of how words combine to form grammatical sentences
5. **Semantics**, the study of the meaning of words (lexical semantics) and fixed word combinations (phraseology), and how these combine to form the meanings of sentences

6. **Pragmatics**, the study of how utterances are used in communicative acts, and the role played by context and non-linguistic knowledge in the transmission of meaning

7. **Discourse analysis**, the analysis of language use in texts (spoken, written, or signed)

8. **Inflection** *n* : the change of form that words undergo to mark such distinctions as those of case, gender, number, tense, person, mood, or voice; a form, or suffix etc.

9. **Morpheme:** *n* the smallest unit of meaning in a word or a part of a word

10. **Word** *n* : A speech sound or series of speech sounds that symbolizes and communicates a meaning, capable of independent use and without necessarily being divisible into smaller units

VI. Why build vocabulary?

> **Polonius: What readeth thou my Lord?**
> **Hamlet: Words, words, words**
>
> *Shakespeare*

"It's all in words" Anne Sullivan to Helen Keller (The Miracle worker)

1. The Significance of Vocabulary

We think in words, that is to say, words assist us in reaching conclusions that ultimately aid us in our decisions and actions. **Words are the dresses of our thoughts, the better words we use, the better dressed up our thoughts appear.** We are surrounded by words that are at work within us and all around us. So, why take words lightly?

Words are powerful devices that can change the whole meaning of what a person may be trying to say. It's the power of words behind the arguments in a courtroom that persuade a judge to proclaim his verdict; it's the choice of words that can affect a change in another person's views, political inclinations, philosophical ideals and even religious beliefs.

2. Choice of Words

2.1 Beware of Synonyms: Just like no two human beings are exactly the same in every way, features or nature (even twins) likewise, no two words mean exactly the same thing. Thus, take heed; synonyms are words that mean only approximately the same thing. They are words with similar meanings, not exactly the same meaning. Therefore, the choice of a synonym must be made very prudently. The word *sad* has a fairly long list of synonyms but each of the word (synonym) shows a slightly different shade of meaning. Let's look at the synonyms of *sad.* Here we go: *Unhappy, miserable, depressed, gloomy, blue, wretched, dejected,* and the list can go on and on. But each word in the list has a distinct intensity, shade and mood of its own that the others do not express. Novice or inexperienced writers may be too quick to consult the list of synonyms or even antonyms to find the right or appropriate words to express a particular idea or just to make their writing more impressive, but they fail to recognize the dangers and disadvantages of doing so. Their choice of a synonym may actually damage or even completely ruin their "creativity" or even convey a very different meaning or message than the one they had intended. Synonyms are not substitute words or even "better sounding" words; they are the words that help you say what you exactly want to say or are trying to say. And by the way, mind your antonyms too, as they can prove even worse. At the heart of this whole argument is the idea, that synonyms are out there to help you match your thoughts with the right words, they are by no means, substitute words.

2.2 Accuracy of Meaning: Having just the right word that closely expresses your idea enables you to communicate more effectively and clearly. Was the smell a scent / an aroma / perfume / fragrance or a stench? Or, Titanic was a big / huge / large, massive / colossal / gigantic / ship.

2.3 Shade and degree: Words have shades of meaning (denotations) together with connotations. A denotation is the formal definition of a word or a regular and generally recognized dictionary meaning: "A *fox* is any of various flesh-eating mammals of the species related to the dogs and wolves." A connotation is the extensional (extended) quality that a word has gained over time. The connotation of a fox is a cunning, crafty, or clever person, somebody who is good at cheating others to achieve his own goal and interests. Connotation and denotation work together to construct meaning and allow a writer to create the shades and tones of meaning--the slight but subtle differences--that create an impact in expression.

2.4 Clarification of a concept: Sometimes a single word does not present the exact idea you have in mind. One way to clarify what you are thinking is to use more than one word--here again we touch on synonyms that are approximate in meaning--to describe the idea. Each time you refer to the idea or thing with a different word, your reader's understanding of it gets more exact and clearer.

The use of right word
is more important than the
right argument

---

2 TO KNOW A WORD

> *Know a man me before you accuse him*
> *Know a word before you use it*

I. Word Knowledge

1.1 How do we "know" a word?

Knowing a word is like knowing a person. That is to say, how well you know a word is just as how well you know a person. As (really) knowing a person is not just knowing his /her name or who he / she is or where he/she lives or works but actually knowing his / her characteristics, behavior , nature and personality and even much more than that. Likewise, knowing a word includes, being able to recall its meaning when we come across it. Also, being able to see which shade of meaning (connotation) is most suitable for the context that it is seen in. In addition, knowing the meaning of a word also includes, being able to make various associations with other related words. Because, words, like human beings tend to go along or get along with some words better than others. Therefore, we just can't dump word randomly in a sentence without realizing their feasibility or "rapport" with other words in the sentence or in a paragraph.

> *A man is known by the company he keeps and a*
> *word is known by the collocations it makes.*

1.2   Receptive Knowledge of a word:

Knowing a word involves being able to recognize it when it is heard (what it sounds like) or when it is seen (what it looks like i.e. its spelling) This also includes, being able to distinguish it from words with a similar form and being able to judge if the word form sounds right. E.g., to **make a party**, neither sounds right nor looks right. Whereas, to **arrange a party, have a party, give a party**, are the accepted forms and usages.

1.3 Productive Knowledge of a word:

Productive knowledge of a word includes receptive knowledge, plus, the right / correct spellings and its accurate usage in various grammatical patterns and its possible collocations.

II. Vital steps in knowing a word:

	Form:		
1	*Written form*	What does the word look like?	How is the word written and spelled?
	Spoken form	What does the word sound like?	How is the word pronounced?
	Position:		
2	*Grammatical patterns*	In what patterns does the word occur?	In what patterns must we use the word?
	Collocations	What words or types of words can be expected before or after the word?	What words or type of words must we use with this word?
3	**Function:**		
	Frequency	How common is the word?	How often should the word be used?
	Appropriateness	Where would we expect to meet or come across this word?	Where can this word be used?
4	**Meaning:**		
	Concept	What does the word mean?	How should the meaning be explained?
	Associations	What other words does this word make us think of?	What other words could we use instead of this?

	Connotation	What connotative meaning can the word suggest	E.g., *Fox* - an animal (denotative meaning) *Fox* – a clever and cunning person, particularly a woman. (connotative meaning)
5	**Syntax:** *Grammatical Function*		
	Part of speech	What is the grammatical status of the word as a part of speech?	Can it be used as more than one part of speech like, a noun and verb etc. E.g. rebel (n) rebel (v)
	Pronunciation	How would the pronunciation (syllable stress) of the word change when used as a noun, verb or an adjective? *Sometimes a word (or a name) may have come into English language from another language, thus may contain some unusual way of pronouncing certain parts or syllables in that word.	E.g. **RE**bel (n) re**BEL** (v) **RE**cord (n) re**CORD (v)** **DIS**count (n) dis**COUNT** (v) E.g., Echelon - **(ĕsh'ə-lŏn')** **Che Guvera** is pronounced Chay (the ch as in cherry) Gay VAH rah. A variation would be Cheh (as the first syllable in cherry) Geh VAH rah.
6	**Phonetic construction:**	How to write the phonetic notation of the word	E.g. The **"Ch"** sound can be /**ch/ /k/ , /sh/** Church /t͡ʃ/ Chemistry /**k**/ Champagne /ʃ/

7	**Silent letters**	A word may have certain silent letter(s) that could prove embarrassing if not heeded by leaving them alone (mute) when speaking the word	"**a**" in boat , "**e**" in people "**b**" in comb, tomb, bomb, debt "**g**" in gnarl, gnaw, gnome, sign "**m**" the first "**m**" in mnemonics "**n**" in column "**p**" in pneumonia
	for more on this, please see unit "Silent Letters"		
8	**Usage:**	How to use the word correctly in writing or speech	Literal/Denotation vs. Connotation (positive / negative connotation E.g. clever vs. intelligent, stupid vs. naive)
9	**Linguistic Patterns:**		
	Root and derivation	What is the origin of the word	E.g. **Television**, Tele – far , Vision from Vidi (Latin) to see, thus, television or TV is a device that shows things that are happening far away **Musician** derived from the word **music**
	Affixation	What affixes (prefix, suffix etc.) can be used with the word	**in**correct not **un**correct **dis**respectful not **un**respectful
10	**Idiomatic usage:**	What would the word mean when used in an idiomatic or metaphorical sense	E.g. to call someone a pig, to describe a place like heaven or hell, a nightmare (a terrible experience)

11	**Synonym / Antonym**	What other words are close to the meaning of the word or are the direct opposites of the word	**Amazing:** (synonyms) astonishing - astounding - wonderful – surprising **Amazing:** (antonyms) usual, ordinary , average , dull, regular
12	**Etymology** /ˌetəˈmäləjē/	The history of a **linguistic form** (as a word) shown by tracing its development since its earliest recorded existence in the language where it is found, by tracing its transmission from one language to another, by analyzing it into its component parts. A *definition* tells us what a word means and how it's used in our own time. Whereas, an *etymology* tells us where a word came from (often, but not always, from another language) and what it *used to* mean. *Good bye* comes from "God b with you", *Gossip* from "God siblings", *history* from "His story"., vision or video from 'vidi' , "to see" or "I can see"	Etymology of two words, astronomy and astrology. **Astronomy:** c.1200, from Old French astrenomie, from Latin astronomia, from Greek astronomia, literally "star arrangement," from astron "star" + nomos "arranging, regulating," related to nemein "to deal out" **Astrology (n.)** late 14c., from Latin astrologia "astronomy, the science of the heavenly bodies," from Greek astrologia "telling of the stars," from astron "star" + -logia "treating of"

13	**Morphology (study of parts of a word)**	A morpheme is the smallest linguistic unit that has a *semantic* meaning. *Semantics* is the study of meaning that is used to understand human expression through language	The word unbreakable has three morphemes. Each one having its own distinct meaning, **un + break + able**
14	**Register**		
	Register is concerned with the overall tone of a text or conversation and the relationship that is built between the speaker and listener in a given context	In linguistics, a **register** is a variety of a language used for a particular purpose or in a particular social setting. For example, we would not speak to a 5-year-old child, a close friend, a professor or a priest using the same style of speech.	Other half (for husband or wife) Better half (wife) Husband or wife (formal) Hubby (very informal, almost slang) Bloke – for boyfriend
15	**Polysemy**	An area of linguistics that is concerned with the way words may have a number of different meanings	**Fair**: not dark skin, (white) **Fair**: just , impartial **Fair**: a kind of festival **Bank**: a place to deposit and withdraw money **Bank**: the edge or boundary of a river **Bank:** (verb) to take advantage of a situation **Condition:** situation, circumstances state **Condition:** specification , rules, terms

---

Babu English

Highly embellished and sophisticated form and style of English intended to make a strong impression. A negative term for a variety of South Asian (Indian & Pakistani) English marked in speech and writing by indirectness, stylistic ornamentation, and extreme formality and politeness. **"A thousand apologies for failing to comprehend the gist of your meaning"** Ranjeet Singh of Mind Your Language, BBC series; with due respect I beg to state…

Typical abbreviations used to indicate the language from which a word originated

OE – Old English , the language spoken in England from the years 700 – 1100

ME – Middle English, the language spoken in England from 1100 – 1500

OF – Old French, the language spoken in France from 800 – 1200

F – The language spoken in France today

Lat. - Latin, spoken by Romans approximately 2, 500 years ago

GK – Ancient Greek, spoken in Greece approximately 2, 500 years ago

---

II. Degree of knowledge

Words do not become part of a person's mental dictionary at very first sight or single contact, that is to say, it is hardly a case of first sight-love when it comes to learning words. Words gradually enter a person's vocabulary over a period of time as more aspects of word knowledge are learnt. Roughly, these stages could be described as follows:

1. Never encountered the word.
2. Heard the word, but cannot define it.
3. Recognize the word due to context or tone of voice.
4. Able to use the word and understand the general and/or intended meaning, but cannot clearly explain it.
5. Fluent with the word – meaning and usage

Degrees of word-knowledge

1. **orthography**   - written form
2. **phonology**   - spoken form
3. **reference**   - meaning
4. **semantics**   - concept and reference
5. **register**   - appropriateness of use
6. **collocation**   - lexical neighbors
7. **word associations** - closely related words: e.g. **tree** ⇨ branch ⇨ leaf
                                                    animal ⇨ skin ⇨ fur ⇨ coat
8. **syntax**   - grammatical function / sentence structure
9. **morphology**   - word parts

The receptive vocabulary size range of college-educated native English speakers is 13,200 - 20,700 base words (Goulden, Nation, & Read, 1990), with an average of 17,200 base words.

The receptive size of a college-educated native English speaker is about 17,000 word families, about 40% more than the first year college students, who know about 12,000 word families. A word family consists of a base word and its *inflected* forms and derivations (Nation, 2001, p. 8).

> **Inflection:** inflected forms of a word are any changes in the form of a word while keeping its base form intact in all the subsequent forms, as, **go** ⇨ goes ⇨ going ⇨gone (but not went)

The average receptive vocabulary size of highly proficient university-educated non-native English speakers ranges between 13,500 and 20,000 base words, being comparable to that of university-educated English native speakers which may range from 35,000 to 50,000 words.

2000 most frequent word families of English make up 79.7% of the individual words in any English text, the 3000 most frequent word families represent 84%, the 4000 most frequent word families make up about 86.7%, and the 5000 most frequent word families cover 88.6%.

By knowing the 2000 most frequent word families of English, readers can understand approximately 80% of the words in any text. Therefore, the goal of an English learner should be to acquire these 2000 word families first, since this relatively small number of words is recycled in any piece of writing and consolidates the basis for reading comprehension.

However, knowing only the 2000 most frequent word families or 80% of the words in a written text gives a second language learner only a general idea of what is being said in a text, without ensuring deep reading comprehension. A much better reading comprehension power is ensured if a reader knows the meanings of at least 90% of the words in a text.

> If a reader has to pause and look up the meanings of five or more words per page (on average) in the dictionary, then that text or book is certainly too high and unsuitable for the reader of that level. Thus, reading that text or book will not be of any great help to the reader in building vocabulary or language skills.

By knowing the 2000 most frequent word families, plus the Academic Word List (AWL), a second language reader would understand about 90% of the words encountered in any academic text.

Second language learner has about 260 to 300 words in the productive vocabulary after 7 months of exposure to English. (i.e. Contact with English, 2-3 hours per day) His/her Receptive Vocabulary, however, is 2.2 times more than the productive vocabulary, which adds up to about 1000 words in a year.

A **sight word** is a word whose spellings are not straightforward and, therefore, does not enable a learning reader to determine what spoken word it represents just by sounding it out according to the rules. Learning readers recognize sight words from having memorized them or by drawing their meaning from context.

In more linguistic terms a sight word lacks a complete one-to-one correspondence between its *graphemes* and *phonemes*. Some examples of sight words are done, eight, today, together, try, squirrel, stick, street, warm etc.

How many words are just enough to get around?

Every individual's working vocabulary varies, but it seems that most people use only about 2,000 to 3,000 different words to get around with daily life activities and with their work. A college graduate might use 5,000 to 6,000, while both those with and without a college degree can recognize and understand at least twice as many words as they normally use. Imagine, then, how much of an addition 1,062 more words will be to a working vocabulary of 2,000 to 3,000 or even to a words-recognized-and-understood vocabulary of twice that.

> **Webster's 3rd edition has a vocabulary of around 54,000 word families.**

With a vocabulary bulk of around 20,000 word families, we should expect that a native speaker will add roughly 1000 word families a year to his / her vocabulary bank. That means that a five year old beginning school will have a vocabulary of around 4000 to 5000 word families. A university graduate will have a vocabulary of around 20,000 word families

The gap between their vocabulary size and that of native speakers is usually very large, with many adult foreign learners of English having a vocabulary size of much less than 5000 word families in spite of having studied English for several years.

From the frequency point of view, the word _**the**_ is a very significant word in English. It occurs so frequently that about 7% of the words on a page of written English and the same proportion of the words in a conversation are repetitions of the word _**the.**_

Here are some figures showing what proportion of a text is covered by certain numbers of high frequency words.

Table 1: Vocabulary size and text coverage in the Brown corpus

Vocabulary size	Text coverage
1000	72.0%
2000	79.7%
3000	84.0%
4000	86.8%
5000	88.7%
6000	89.9%
15,851	97.8%

Word types and text coverage

Types of words	No. of Words	Proportion of text
High-frequency words	2.000	87%
University word list	800	8%
Technical words	2,000	3%
Low frequency words	123,200	2%
Total	128,000	100%

Problems with Frequency counts

a. Certain useful and important words are not enlisted in the first or the second 1000 words

b. Some words that are not suitable for a beginners' vocabulary are found in the first 100 words list

c. Word-frequency list are not standardized and often differ

d. Usually the order of the words in a frequency list is not the best order in which to teach words

e. Word-frequency words are not reliable above a certain level.

III.   Linguistics: Word Categories and types of Nyms

No.	Category	Meaning / Definition	Example
1.	Synonym	Words with similar or same meaning	Jump – hop
2.	Antonym	Words with opposite or dissimilar meaning	Fat – thin
3.	Antagonym / Autoantonyms	A word that can mean the opposite of itself	Clip – to cut Clip – to join, to attach Bound – tied Bound- ready to go, to spring
4.	Homonym Homograph	**Homonym**: A word that is written and pronounced the same way as another , but has a different meaning **Homograph:** A word that is spelled / written in the same way as another word but is different part of speech and is therefore, explained in a separate entry Spare – (adj.) extra Spare – (verb) to leave somebody or something, particularly for another time	Lie – to say or tell something that is not true Lie – to lie in bed Right- correct Right (right side or right hand)

5.	**Hyponym 1**	A word that represents different categories covered by superordinate	Animal: cat, horse, dog
6.	**Metonym** **(Metonymy)**	A word or phrase that is used to represent something that is closely associated with something else.	Bench – a panel or group of judges, White house – American government Crown: monarch (king/ queen)
7.	**Synecdoche**	A word that refers to a part of something to mean the whole	All hands on the deck. Hand or hands here refer to people (laborers, workmen)
8.			
9.	**Entry**	Any word or phrase that has been listed (entered) in a dictionary	
10.	**Headword**	One of the list of words in a dictionary that is followed by an explanation	
11.	**Red word**	A word that is written in red in the dictionary and is one of the 7,500 most frequent words in the language	
12.	**Transitive** **(vs. Intransitive)**	A word describing a verb that is always used with a direct object	Tom **_broke_** the **glass.** (transitive) Jerry **_laughed_** (intransitive)
13.	**Neologism**	A completely new word	**Glitch** (sudden failure, error, breakdown, problem, fault)
14.	**Loanword**	A word that is borrowed from another language	Caravan – from Arabic cliché - from French
15.	**Poly words**	A small group of word used together to suggest a single meaning	Inside out , by the way
16.	**Stem word**	The main Word or the base word from which other forms and variants of the same word can be made	**Wait = stem** wait (infinitive) wait (imperative waits (pr. simple) waited (past, past participle) waiting (continuous)

17.	Content words / Lexical words / Open class	A word that conveys the main information in a text, it is *open classes* of words because it is open to adding new word members	Nouns, lexical verbs, adjectives, and adverbs (mostly, nouns keep adding in the open class)
18.	Function words Grammatical word Closed class	A word that expresses a grammatical relationship or purpose. It is closed category of words because it does not easily accept new words. Its members are fixed and do not usually change	determiners, conjunctions, and prepositions etc.
19.	Part to whole	A piece or portion of something related to the total object	toe: foot sole: shoe leaf : plant wall: room
20.	Whole to part	The whole is related to one of its parts	tree : trunk house: room coat: sleeve
21.	Age or size	An animate (living) or inanimate (nonliving) object is related to a younger or older object of the same type	fawn: deer freshman: senior calf: cow child: mother
22.	Rhyme	Although items do not begin with the same sound/letter, the ending sounds are the same	goat: boat trouble: bubble slow : toe light: kite
23.	Person to location	A person is related to the place with which he is associated	sailor : ship criminal : jail King: Palace
24.	Object to use	Something is related to its function	oven: bake soap: clean broom: sweep
25.	Source to object	The place from which an item is taken and the item are compared	pound: stray dog bakery : cookies mind: thought

26.	**Palindrome**	A word, that may be read the same way in both directions	madam, racecar, deed, level, civic, pop, eye, nun, radar
27.	**Acronym**	Abbreviations that can be read as words (mostly written in capitals)	NASA, UNICEF, ASEAN UNO is not an Acronym
28.	**Heteronym**	Words that have the same spelling (**homographs**) but different pronunciation and meaning	Polish – from Poland Polish – to shine shoes Wind – strong air Wind – to turn the knob of watch or a toy , to tighten
29.	**Capitonym**	A word that you will find in the dictionary, but it has been used to describe words that change their pronunciation and meaning when **capitalized**. They are thus a form of **heteronym**	**Ares**: God of War **ares**: Plural of metric unit of area **Said**: Egyptian port **said**: spoken/ past tense of say
30.	**Accent Heteronyms**	Infrequent **foreign words** accepted into use in English, keep their **diacritical marks** (accents). However, as English does not make use of diacritical marks, it is generally considered acceptable to omit them.	**attachés** and **attaches** **exposé** and **expose** **resumé** and **resume** **rosé** and **rose**
31.	**Homophones** **Oronyms**	Words which sound the same. Generally the word **homophone** is used to describe one of a pair or group of words that have the same sound while **oronyms** are normally strings of words (phrases)	**prince** and **prints** **Some others** I've seen. **Some mothers** I've seen.

32.	**Anagrams**	Words or phrases made by jumbling up or rearranging the letters of other words	dear – read ; dormitory - dirty room **Mother-in-law =Woman Hitler**
33.	**Oxymoron**	Two opposite words suggesting a unique idea or meaning	Pretty ugly, open secret , clearly confused, deafening silence , tragic comedy , bad luck, sick joke , dark comedy
34.	**Spoonerisms**	Words or phrases in which letters or syllables get, misplaced, confused or swapped	A lack of pies (A pack of lies)
35.	**Tautonyms** (in linguistics)	Words in which the second half of word repeats the first, both in words or in names, as parts of the name	Baba, nana , mama , Lu Lu , yoyo, bulbul, Tin Tin , Tun Tun, To To , chu chu , meow meow, papa , booboo Yo Yo, Ma , win win , sera sera , wo wo

Tautonyms; a scientific name consisting of two terms, in which the generic name and specific name are the same (Ex.: *Vulpes vulpes*, the red fox): this kind of name is no longer used in botany, but is common in zoology

36.	**Toponym** *From Greek **topos** (topos = place)*	A word (or name) coined in association with the name of a place or thing	1. A place name; e.g. **London**, **Mount Everest**. 2. A word derived from a place name; e.g. **champagne** from Champagne in France, **cashmere** from Kashmir in India. **Ireland**: name of a place, also name of a person, as Paul **London**, Chris **Jericho**
37.	**Eponym** *From Greek **epo** (=on)*	Name from which another name or word is derived	**Romulus** giving rise to **Rome**, the word **sandwich** coming from the **Earl of Sandwich**. **Pasture** from **Louis Pasture, TaTa** (from Ratan Tata- an industrial tycoon of India) **Honda, Suzuki, Mercedes**

38.	**Hypernym** *From Greek **hyper** (hyper=over)*	A word that has a more general meaning than another, or a word that suggests a category under which other words or items can fall	In the relationship between chair and furniture, **furniture** is a hypernym; in the relationship between horse and animal, **animal** is a hypernym
39.	**Hyponym 2** *From Greek **hypo** (hypo =under)*	A word that has a more specific meaning than another; thus suggesting a sub category	In the relationship between chair and furniture, **chair** is a hyponym; in the relationship between horse and animal, **horse** is a hyponym
40.	**Meronym** *From Greek **meros** (mero=part)*	A word that refers to a part of what another word refers to:	1. In the relationship between leg and ankle, **ankle** is a meronym; in the relationship between edge and stick, **edge** is a meronym 2. A term midway between two opposites; e.g. **present** between **past** and **future**.
41.	**Metonym** (Metonymy) *From Greek **meta** (meta=change)*	A word describes something by the name of something associated with it	**The Crown** referring to the monarchy, **the bottle** referring to alcohol, **the White House** for the US executive branch, The **Pentagon** referring to US security agency
42.	**Paronym** *From Greek **para** (para=beside)*	A word from the same root, and usually (but not always) a similar pronunciation, as another	**beautiful** and **beauteous**
43.	**Patronym** *From Greek **pater** (pater=father)*	A name derived from the name of one's father, or another male ancestor Many races mentioned in the Old Testament of the Bible are typical examples of Patronym	**Jackson from** Jack, **Younason** from Younas **Peterson** from Peter **Israelites** from Israel **Ishmaelite** from Ishmael, **Moabites** (Moab)

44.	**Retronym** *From Greek **retro** (retro=backward)*	An adjective-noun pairing generated by a change in the meaning of the base noun, usually as a result of technological advance	Watch became **pocket-watch** due to introduction of wrist watch; pen became **fountain pen** due to introduction of ball-point pen.
45.	**Pseudonym** *From Greek **pseudo** (pseudo=false)* *Also called **pen name***	An false name, especially adopted by an author	Eric Arthur Blair wrote many stories / novels under the pseudonym **George Orwell** Alfred George Gardiner (1865–1946) wrote under the pen name or pseudonym **- Alpha of the Plough**
46.	**Backronym** [Compound of **back + acronym**] *backward* and *acronym,* or a "**reverse acronym**	A backronym is a word derived from the first letters of the words of a phrase. Sometimes longer movie names or TV shows are shortened by turning them into *backronyms*	In "Wikipedia", *wiki* stands for "**what I know is**" The movie **Men in Black is** also commonly known as **MIB.** One popular Indian reality TV show, **Dance India Dance** is also known as **DID**

A Comparative Chart
(some feature may overlap)

Term	Spelling	Meaning	Pronunciation	Example
Homonym	Same	Different	Same	**Fair:** reasonable, just, honest **Fair:** festival
Homograph	Same	Different	Same or different ⟶	**Fine:** very good **Fine:** money paid for breaking law, or damaging something **Bow:** [boh] crossbow **Bow:** [bou] to bend one's head or / and upper body in respect **Row:** [roh] noisy disorder, quarrel **Row:** [rəʊ] queue, line (to row a boat) **Live:** [laɪv] adj. livr telecast **Live:** [lɪv] to live in … **Wind:** [wahynd] v. to turn **Wind:** [wĭnd] n.
Homophone	Same or different	Different	Same	ate – eight ; fair - fare
Heteronym	Same	Different	Different	**Present** (verb) to offer , to give **Pre**sent (adj.) to be at a place – not absent **Pre**sent (noun) – a gift
Heterograph	Different	Different	Same ⟶	**Pair:** two, couple **Pare:** cut, trim, clip **You:** [yū] pronoun **Yew:** [yū] a tree **Ewe:** [yū] A female sheep, especially when full grown.

Polyseme Polysemy: The coexistence of several meanings in one word	Same	Different but could be related	Same or different $\longrightarrow$	Cricket: (n) an insect Cricket: (n) a sport Book: (n) a book to read Book: (v) to reserve sth. in advance , to book a seat, a ticket etc.
Capitonym	Same except for capitalization	Different when capitalized	Same or different	Polish (v) [pä-lish] to shine shoe, furniture, etc. Polish: _[poʊlɪʃ]_ sb. or sth. from or related to Poland

IV.   Word Relationships

Synonyms, Antonyms, Homonyms, Analogies

Words, like human beings appear to make up tribes and families. Some words tend to go along other words with similar meanings or shades of meanings. Words that mean the same thing but look different are called synonyms. Their meanings are very similar (e.g., attractive – charming, pretty - cute). An antonym is a word that has the opposite meaning of another word (e.g., pretty/ugly). A homonym is a word that sounds like another word but has a different meaning.

Because these terms are often confused, here is an easy way to keep them straight.

Heard alike	Similar meaning	An opposite
O	Y	N
M	N	T
O	O	O
N	N	N
Y	Y	Y
M	M	M

Words are related in many other ways as well. When thinking about the relationship between two words, you must examine those words for ways in which they are different, alike, or related to each other.

3 WORD STRESS

I. What is Word Stress?

As in any other language of the world, words are made up of smaller units called syllables which determine both the written and the spoken structure of the word. If words are not uttered with their due syllable stress, we would sound like a robot. All syllables in a word are not uttered with the same force or strength. In one word, there is ONE syllable that carries a higher or stronger stress. We say **one** syllable rather **loudly** and all the other syllables relatively with a softer tone.

Let's look at three words: **photograph**, **photographer** and **photographic**. Do they sound the same when spoken? No. Because we accentuate (stress) ONE syllable in each word. And it is not always the same syllable.

Word	Total Syllables	Stressed Syllable	Sound Trajectory (graph)
PHO TO GRAPH	3	#1	
PHO TO GRAPH ER	4	#2	
PHO TO GRAPH IC	4	#3	

This happens pretty much with ALL the words with two or more syllables:

TEACHer, JaPAN, CHINa, aBOVE, converSAtion, INteresting, imPORtant, deMAND, etCETera.

The syllables that are not stressed are **weak** or **small** or **quiet**. A good listening activity or drill involves listening for the STRESSED syllables, not the weak syllables. Use of word stress in speech, instantly and automatically improves pronunciation and even listening comprehension. Right stress on the right syllable makes words come alive, otherwise they'd sound like a robot producing (not speaking) the programmed words.

Follow the stress in individual words each time you listen to English – while talking or listening to native speaker or on the radio in films or a tape script / audio recording.

II. Rules of Word Stress in English

There are two very simple rules about word stress:

a. **One word has only one stress.** (One word cannot have two stresses. If you hear two stresses, you hear two words. Two stresses cannot be one word. It is true that there can be a **"secondary"** stress in some words. But a secondary stress is much smaller than the main **"primary"** stress, and is only used in long(er) words.)

b. **We can only stress vowels, not consonants.**

Here are some guidelines for word stress. But don't forget, that as English language works, not all rules apply all the time. Many times you just have to rely on the music, rhythm and sense of the stress in a word.

By sense of a word stress, we mean to say, words such as **small** and **tiny** would carry a *"sense"* suggesting lower stress whereas, words such as **big, huge, tall**, would suggest a *"sense"* of stronger and louder stress. Also, remember a syllable receives its stress because of the vowels in it, and not because of the consonants in it.

1. Stress on first syllable

Rule	Example	
Most **2-Syllable Nouns**	PRESent, EXport, CHIna, TAble	Nouns in most cases
Most **2-Syllable Adjectives**	PRESent, SLENder, CLEVer, HAPpy	

2. Stress on last syllable

Rule	Example
Most **2-syllable verbs**	to preSENT, to exPORT, to deCIDE, to beGIN

There are many two-syllable words in English whose meaning and class change with a change in stress. The word **present**, for example is a two-syllable word. If we stress the first syllable /'pre-zᵃnt/ it is a noun (gift) or an adjective (opposite of absent). But if we stress the second syllable /pri-'zent/ it becomes a verb (to offer). Here are a few more examples of such words, **export**, **import**, **contract, discount** and **object**. These words can all be used as nouns or verbs depending on the syllable stress. If the stress is placed on the first syllable, the word will be spoken as a noun and if on the second syllable, it will be a verb.

3. Stress on the second-last syllable (second from the end)

Rule	Example
Words ending in **-ic**	GRAPHic, geoGRAPHic, geoLOGic
Words ending in **-sion** and **-tion**	teleVIsion, reveLAtion

For a few words, native English speakers don't always "agree" on where to put the stress. For example, some people say **teleVIsion** and others say **TELevision**. Another example is: **CONtroversy** and **conTROversy**.

4. Stress on the third-last syllable (third from end)

Rule	Example
Words ending in **-cy**, **-ty**, **-phy** and **-gy**	deMOcracy, dependaBIlity, phoTOgraphy, geOLogy
Words ending in **-al**	CRItical, geoLOGical

5. Compound words (words with two parts)

Rule	Example
For compound **nouns**, the stress is on the **first** part	BLACKbird, GREENhouse
For compound **adjectives**, the stress is on the **second** part	bad-TEMpered, old-FASHioned
For compound **verbs**, the stress is on the **second** part	to overTAKE, overrun, overDO to overFLOW

6. Verb Stress

If the verb has 3-syllables, you can follow the 2-syllable verb rule, which says the verb is stressed on the second syllable. So, ConFIRM becomes conFIRMing

In compound nouns, both components (both words) are stressed, and primary stress is on the first component (the first word) even if the two words are written separately. The second component is usually a noun. The first component can be a noun, a gerund, an adjective, a verb.

7. Compound Words (Noun + Noun) the stress on the first word or the component shows a strong connection or relationship with the second word, thus making it a compound word - suggesting a single idea.

FOOTball, ARMchair, MAILbox PHOtograph, TELegram, TELescope WRITing desk, SWIMming pool

HIGH school, HIGHway, HOT dog , CRYbaby, PUSHcart, , GREENhouse , WHITEboard, DARKroom , WALKing stick , STONE Age

Exceptions:

(1) manKIND, well-BEING , self-aNALysis , afterNOON –
(2) Stress in the following words falls on the second component in speech.
good WILL, easy MONey , evening STAR (Venus), flying SAUCer

If one of the components in a two-word adjective is a noun, primary stress may fall on the noun, irrespective of whether it is the first or second component. (Both components are stressed.) Always check such cases in the dictionary.

COLor-blind, WATerproof , high-CLASS, low-COST , LAW-abiding, EARsplitting , off-COLor

off-BALance , AIRsick, SEAsick

8. Compound numerals

In compound numerals consisting of several words, all components are stressed, and the strongest stress is on the last component. **Compound numerals from twenty-one**

to ninety-nine are hyphenated. Fractions in the meaning of nouns may be written with or without a hyphen.

thirTEEN , seventeen , fifTEENTH, eighteenth , twenty-THREE, forty-SIX , fifty-SEVen , ninety-EIGHT

sixty-SECond , seventy-FIFTH , five HUNdred and thirty-TWO , three hundred THOUsand , one-HALF / one HALF

two-THIRDS / two THIRDS , one twenty-FIFTH , twenty-three HUNdredths.

Simple Rules to remember

a. For compound nouns, the stress is on the first part
Examples: BLACKbird, GREENhouse

b. For compound adjectives, the stress is on the second part
Examples: bad-TEMpered, old-FASHioned

c. For words that can be used both as Nouns and Verbs, stress the first syllable when used as a Noun and stress the second syllable when used as a Verb.

E.g., REbel (N) and reBEL (V) , DIScount (N) and disCOUNT (V) , CONvert (N) and conVERT (V)

What's the difference between a "DANCING teacher" and a "dancing TEACHER"?

4 WORD FAMILIES

1. Word families are groups of words that are sufficiently in close relationship to each other to form a 'family'. Words can be grouped into families in two main ways:

1. They are similar in form
2. Their meanings are related.

Look at the following two examples of **form-based** word families:

World - worldly - worldwide (adj.)
Family - familiar - unfamiliar - familiarity – familiarize
Receive – reception, receptionist, receiver, receipt

Each of these families is attached to a common root word, although the resultant connections of meaning are also an important bonding or connecting feature.

Here are two examples of **meaning-based** word families:

blue , red = **color** ; big - little = **size**

1.1 Significance of word families

A knowledge of Word Families help learner identify the connection of one word with another which further helps in building vocabulary without being nervous about learning more new words. Students must learn to recognize how one word is actually connected to another word in its form, meaning and even usage. A fair knowledge of suffixes and prefixes will further prove helpful in identifying the meanings of the words in their respective families.

A sound understanding of word classes is important for the study of both kinds of word families.

2.Form-based families

In the form-based word family, for example the word **teach - teacher**, is most easily explained by recognizing two morphemes in "teacher". A root word which is *teach;* and a derivational suffix *er* which is also found in other words such as lectur*er*, driv*er*, and learn*er*.

The family link can be shown through definitions: one word provides material out of which the other's definition is built (a teacher is 'a person who teaches'). Similarly, a duckling is 'a small duck'; replaying is 'playing again', and so on.

2.1 Compound Words

A more complicated kind of similarity is found in compound words. In this case the derived word is formed by combining two root words, as in *classroom.*

In terms of word families, compounds represent a union of two families, so classroom unites the families of *class* (lesson) and *room* word. The word class can make more of its own "class" words, as classwork, classmate, classless, etc. and room can make more words in its own class or group, as roommate, roomful, roomette, /rü-'met/ (a small private single room on a railroad sleeping car)

2.2 Meaning-based families

Some words are closely related in meaning but not in form. For example, a female lion is a lioness, but a female dog is a bitch, while a male sheep is a ram and a female sheep is a ewe. The word families dog – bitch and sheep – ram – ewe are based solely on meaning, without the additional link provided by similarity of form as with **lion –** *lioness*

Links that are based on meaning are far richer and more extensive than those based on form. Even the most straightforward-looking word, such as book, has a multitude of meaning-based links to other words:

Book
page, volume, journal, publication, author, publisher, title, edition, paper, cover, index, chapter, contents, novel, textbook, literature, literacy, bookseller, bookshop, bookshelf, library, read, write, consult, collect, bookworm (both meanings), bibliomania, bibliophile

As can be seen from this list in the box above, similarity of form supports a few of these links, namely those in which the related word also contains the root word book: textbook, bookseller, bookshop, bookshelf, and bookworm. The remaining links are no less clear or accessible for having no equivalent (partner) in form.

Meaning-based links are important for vocabulary growth, not just as an aid when guessing the meanings of new words, but also when improving upon existing vocabulary.

2.3 Specific meaning relations

Specific meaning relations are helpful in developing reasoning skills, since they include such features as:

Classification:	**man** – cow – monkey – mammal
	flower – violet – daffodil – rose
Range / Scale:	stout – fat – plump , slim – thin – skinny
Opposites:	hard – easy; sensible – foolish

3. Common word families (by form)

Skilled readers recognize patterns in words rather than sound words out, letter by letter. Word families, also known as phonograms, rimes, or chunks, are letter patterns that are more stable than individual vowel sounds. Readers can use word families to decode by analogy-use what they know about one word to decode another. If a reader knows the word, tack, for example, it's likely that he/she will be able to read other -*ack* words, such as *snack* and *jacket.* Recognizing word families helps students build large reading vocabularies.

 Common Word Families Part II, Unit 4

5 WORD FORMATION

I. Parts of a Word

Do new words just come into existence rather randomly or is it that they keep appearing because there are some linguists busy at work putting together words through various letter-combinations as *anagrams.* Interestingly nothing of this sort happens in the origin of new words. Most words are simply made from other words or from parts of other words. These parts are generally classified as affixes, morphemes, roots or the base form of the words.

1.1 Base Words:

A *base word* **is** a word that does not have a prefix or suffix added to it. Some examples from thousands of *base words* are: write, month, normal, and cover, read etc.

A base word (also called a "root word") is a word that has nothing added either to its beginning or ending. A *base word* is a morpheme or a group of morphemes that have one complete meaning. Base words can be short, such as "**door**" or much longer as "**environment**". These are the parts of language that are used to communicate, but are also used to build more complicated words with more complex meanings. From the base word, **door,** we can make, *doormat, doorstep, doorbell, do-to-door, doorway, outdoor, doorman, doorkeeper,* etc. Similarly, with the word *"environment"* we can make, *environmental, environmentalist,*

1.2 Morphemes

A **Morpheme** is the smallest unit of meaning in language. Morpheme(s) may or may not be a complete word in a language, but they are the building blocks for creating new words by adding affixes (prefixes, suffixes, infixes, circumfixes etc.) and other parts of words.

1.3 Units (components) of a word:

Graphemes are the smallest units in a writing system capable of causing a contrast in meaning. In the English alphabet, the chnage from *cat* to *bat* introduces a meaning change; therefore, *c* and *b* represent different graphemes. It is usual to transcribe graphemes within angle brackets, to show their special status: <c>, <b>. The main graphemes of English are the twenty-six units that make up the alphabet. Other graphemes include the various marks of punctuation: <.>, <;>, etc., and such special symbols as <@>, <&>, and (£). . . .

Graphemes . . . may signal whole words or word parts--as with the numerals, where each grapheme <1>, <2>, etc. is spoken as a word that varies from language to language (a *logogram*). . . . And several of the relationships between words are conveyed by graphology more clearly than by phonology: for example, the link between *sign* and *signature* is very clear in writing, but it is less obvious in speech, because the *g* is pronounced in the second word, but not in the first."

Phoneme

The smallest sound unit in a language that is capable of conveying a distinct meaning, such as the *s* in *sing* and the *r* in *ring*. The /f/ sound represented by the letter **"ph"** in the word **"pho**neme" is also a phoneme. There are approximately **44 phonemes** or sound units in English E.g. **a** in c**a**t

1.4 Vowel Phonemes:

PHONEME	EXAMPLES				
a	c<u>a</u>t				
e	p<u>e</u>g	br<u>ea</u>d			
i	p<u>i</u>g	want<u>e</u>d			
o	l<u>o</u>g	w<u>a</u>nt			
u	pl<u>u</u>g	l<u>o</u>ve			
ae	p<u>ai</u>n	d<u>ay</u>	g<u>a</u>t<u>e</u>	st<u>a</u>tion	
ee	sw<u>ee</u>t	h<u>ea</u>t	th<u>ie</u>f	th<u>e</u>s<u>e</u>	
ie	tr<u>ie</u>d	l<u>igh</u>t	m<u>y</u>	sh<u>i</u>n<u>e</u>	m<u>i</u>nd
oe	r<u>oa</u>d	bl<u>ow</u>	b<u>o</u>n<u>e</u>	c<u>o</u>ld	
ue	m<u>oo</u>n	bl<u>ue</u>	gr<u>ew</u>	t<u>u</u>n<u>e</u>	
oo	l<u>oo</u>k	w<u>ou</u>ld	p<u>u</u>t		

ar	c*ar*t	f*a*st (regional)			
ur	b*ur*n	f*ir*st	t*er*m	h*ear*d	w*or*k
or	t*or*n	d*oor*	w*ar*n (regional)		
au	h*au*l	l*aw*	c*a*ll		
er	wood*e*n	c*ir*cus	sist*er*		
ow	d*ow*n	sh*ou*t			
oi	c*oi*n	b*oy*			
air	st*air*s	b*ear*	h*are*		
ear	f*ear*	b*eer*	h*ere*		

1.5 Consonant Phonemes:

PHONEME	EXAMPLES				
b	*b*aby				
d	*d*og				
f	*f*ield	*ph*oto			
g	*g*ame				
h	*h*at				
j	*j*u*dge*	*g*iant	bar*ge*		
k	*c*oo*k*	*q*ui*ck*	mi*x*	*Ch*ris	
l	*l*amb				
m	*m*onkey	co*mb*			
n	*n*ut	*kn*ife	*gn*at		
p	*p*aper				
r	*r*abbit	*wr*ong			
s	*s*un	mou*se*	*c*ity	*s*cien*ce*	
t	*t*ap				
v	*v*an				
w	*w*as				
wh	*wh*ere (regional)				
y	*y*es				
z	*z*ebra	plea*se*	i*s*		
th	*th*en				
th	*th*in				

ch	_**ch**_ip	wa_**tch**_			
sh	_**sh**_ip	mi_**ss**_ion	_**ch**_ef		
zh	trea_**s**_ure				
ng	ri_**ng**_	si_**n**_k			

1.6 Prefixes and Suffixes

According to Merriam-Webster Online Dictionary, prefixes and suffixes are morphemes that are added to **base words** to change their meaning. Many of the prefixes and suffices that are used in the English language are borrowed from Latin or Greek.

A prefix is a morpheme that is added to the beginning of a base word to alter the base word's meaning. These prefixes usually have their own meaning that enriches the definition of the base word, such as adding the prefix "a-" to the base word "sleep" to create the word "asleep"

A suffix is a morpheme that is added to the end of a word and usually changes what part of speech the word is classified as. For example, the suffix "-ly" can be added to the adjective "brave" to become the adverb "bravely."

II. Word Formation through Derivation:

2.1 Derivation is the process, system or method of forming new words out of existing words.

Primary Derivation

Primary Derivation is made by making certian changes in the body or structure of a simple word as **bond** from bind

Verb ——→ Noun		Verb ——→ Noun	
Advise	Advice	Gape	Gap
Bind	Bond	Grieve	Grief
Bless	Bliss	Live	Life
Break	Breach	Lose	Loss
Choose	Choice	Prove	proof
Receive	Receipt	Sing	Song
Chop	Chip	Sit	Seat
Float	Fleet	Speak	Speech

Give	Gift	Strike	Stroke
Sit	Seat (n-sitting)	Strive	Strife
Adjective ⟶ Noun		**Verb ⟶ Adjective**	
Hot	Heat	Attract	Attractive
Proud	Pride	Destroy	Destructive
Noun ⟶ Verb		**Noun ⟶ Adjective**	
Belief	Believe	Grass	Grassy
Breath	Breathe	Sleep	Sleepy
Drop	Drip	Breeze	Breezy
Food	Feed	Knot	Knotty
Adjective ⟶ Verb			
Full	Fill		
Fool	Fool / befool		

2.2 Secondary Derivation:

This type of derivation depends on the addition of suffixes and prefixes or any other affixes. Secondary Derivation may use the following stalk of affixes.

1. English Prefixes:

No.	Prefix	Meaning	Example
1	**A**	On, in	Asleep, ashore, ajar
2	**A**	Out, from	Awake, arise, alight
3	**Be**	By, do	Beside, betimes (bewitch, bemoan)
4	**For**	Thoroughly	Forgive, forbear
5	**Fore**	Before	Foretell, forecast
6	**In**	In, inside	Inland, income, inlay, inborn, inbuilt
7	**Over**	Above, beyond	Overflow, overcharge, overrun, overtake
8	**To**	This	Today, tonight
9	**Un**	Not, reverse	Untrue, unkind (undo, untie, unfold)
10	**Under**	Beneath, lower	Underground, undergo, underestimate
11	**With**	Against	Withhold, withdraw, withstand

2. Latin Prefixes:

No.	Prefix	Meaning	Example
1	**Ab**	Away (negative / opposite)	Abnormal , abuse
2	**Ad**	**(ac, ag, al, an, ap, ar , as , a)** all give the meaning of **"to"**	Adjoin, accord, affect, aggrieve, allege, announce, appoint, arrest, assign, attach, avail
3	**Ambi (amb, am)**	On both sides, around	Ambivert, ambiguous, ambivalence
4	**Ante**	before	Antedate , antiseptic
5	**Bene**	Well, advantage , blessing	Benediction, benefit, beneficent
6	**Bi, bi, bin**	Two, twice,	Bicycle, bisect, binocular
7	**Circum, ciru**	Around, circular	Circumference , circumfix, circumspect
8	**Contra, counter**	Against	Contradict , counteract
9	**Post**	After	Postscript, postdate, postmortem
10	**Re**	Again, back	Redo. Reclaim,. Refund

3. Greek Prefixes:

No.	Prefix	Meaning	Example
1	**A (an)**	Without, not	Atheist, apathy , anarchy
2	**Amphi**	On both sides, around	Amphibian, amphitheater
3	**Anti (ant)**	Against	Antipathy , antagonist
4	**Auto**	Self	Autobiography , automatic , autocrat
5	**Ex, ec,**	Out, out of	Exodus, eccentric
6	**Hemi**	Half	Hemisphere
7	**Meta**	Causing a change	Metamorphosis , metonymy
8	**Mono**	Single, alone	Monopoly , monorail, monotony
9	**Pan**	All	Panorama , pantheism
10	**Para**	Besides, additional	Paramedic, Paralingual ,
11	**Phil**	Love	Philosophy , philanthropy, Philomena
12.	**Syn (sysm, syl, sy)**	With, together	Synonym, sympathy, syllable, system

4. English Suffixes:

Suffixes indicating an agent or doer or performer of an action	
Suffix	**Example**
1 **Er, ar, or , yer**	Teacher, sailor, beggar, lawyer,
Suffixes indicating state, action, condition , being etc.	
2 **dom**	Kingdom
3 **hood**	childhood
4 **lock**	wedlock
5 **lege**	knowledge
6 **ness**	darkness
7 **red**	hatred
8 **ship**	friendship
9 **th**	Growth, health
Suffixes forming Diminutives or the suffixes indicating smallness in size, shape or age	
Suffixes	**Example**
10 **let**	piglet
11 **en**	kitten, maiden
12 **ie**	birdie (bird)
13 **Kin, ling**	napkin, starling, lambkin, yearling
14 **el / le**	satchel, kernel
15 **ock**	bullock , hillock
16 **ling**	duckling, weakling

Suffixes forming Adjectives		
Suffixes	**Meaning**	**Example**
17 **ed**	having, possessing	talented, gifted
18 **en**	made of	wooden, golden, earthen
19 **ful**	full of	hopeful, merciful
20 **ish**	somewhat like, about	boyish, reddish, bluish, twentyish
21 **less**	free from, without	hopeless, careless, sleeveless
22 **ly**	like, in manner of	softly, manly, godly, gently
23 **some**	having the quality or tendency of	quarrelsome, troublesome
24 **ward**	having the tendency or leaning to, inclining to , in the direction of	forward, eastward, backward
25 **y**	with the quality of , having sth.	lucky (having luck) wealthy, healthy

	Suffixes forming Verbs		
26	**en**	causative, forming transitive verbs	weaken, sweeten, harden
27	**se**	to make, to do, affect	cleanse (from clean)
28	**er**	showing seriousness or insensitivity	chatter, glitter , glimmer
	Suffixes forming Adverbs		
29	**ly**	Like, as	nicely, carefully, wisely , gently
30	**long**	toward, in the direction of	headlong
31	**hood**	condition, rank	childhood, monkhood, priesthood
32	**ness, ship, th**	madness, friendship, truth , health (from heal) dearth from dear (dear – not easily available, rare, expensive)	

5. Latin Suffixes: Suffixes making Nouns

	Suffixes	**Meaning / Usage**	**Example(s)**
33	**ain, (an, en, on)**	agent or doer of an action or thing →	chieftain, artisan, citizen, surgeon
34	**eer, ier, ary, ar, er**		engineer, financier, missionary, scholar (school, schol(astic) preach(er) teach(er)
35	**ate (ee, ey, y)**		Advocate, employee, trustee, trainee, attorney, deputy
36	**or (our, eur, er)**		Sailor, savior, amateur, interpreter
37	**age**	state, action or result of an action →	bondage, hostage, breakage, wreckage, leakage,
38	**ance, ence**		assistance, excellence, innocence
39	**cy**		Accuracy, bankruptcy, hypocrisy, democracy, leniency (lenient) fluency (fluent)
40	**ion**		opinion, action

41	ice, ise		service, cowardice
42	ment		development, improvement
43	mony		matrimony, testimony
44	tude		magnitude , fortitude
45	ty		obesity, cruelty, frailty,
46	ure		seizure, pleasure,
47	y		injury, victory

6. Latin Suffixes: Suffixes forming Diminutives

	Suffix	Meaning / Usage	Example(s)
48	cule	being small in size →	molecule (from diminutive of Latin *moles* ("a mass") meaning, small mass
49	sel		damsel
50	el		**chapel** (from French- *chapelle* Medieval Latin cappella (cape)
51	le		from French *cerclet*, diminutive of *cercle*
52	et , ette		**cigarette** (from cigar) , owlet,
53	let		piglet, leaflet
54	ule		globule
55	ary		**aviary** (from avian – bird) library – (Latin librāria, from Latin librārius (adj.) of books, equivalent to lib (e) r book + -ārius <u>-ary</u>
56	ery		nunnery
57	ry		treasury
58	ter , tre		**theatre**, from Latin *theatrum*, from Greek *theatron*

7. Latin Suffixes: Suffixes forming Adjectives

	Suffix	Meaning / Usage	Example(s)
59	al		manual , national, parental
60	an	having the qualities or features of ⟶	human (n , adj)
61	ane		arcane , mundane
62	ar		molecular, familiar
63	ary		revolutionary, honorary
64	ate		fortunate, considerate

Pls. Note that ...*ate* as a suffix when used as a verb denotes the meaning of **to do, act, perform, as in, demonstrate, activate, advocate. In this case the pronunciation of the word for example that of advoc*ate* is v [ˈædvəˌkeɪt] compared to ...*ate* used as a noun: advoc*ate* - n [ˈædvəkɪt]**

	Suffix	Meaning / Usage	Example(s)
65	ble		feeble
66	ible	⟶	sensible
67	able		workable, eatable , suitable
68	esque		picturesque , burlesque
69	id		humid, lucid
70	ile		juvenile, servile,
71	ine		divine, feminine, canine
72	lent		turbulent , indolent
73	ose		verbose
74	ive		creative, active, selective
75	ous		courageous, advantageous, dangerous

8. Latin Suffixes: Suffixes forming Verbs

	Suffix	Meaning / Usage	Example(s)
76	ate		terminate, advocate, relocate
77	fy	to do, to carry out, to perform ⟶	verify, simplify, terrify
78	ish		nourish, punish, furnish

9. Greek Suffixes

	Suffix	Meaning / Usage / Function	Example(s)
78	**ic (ique)**	adjective	angelic , phonetic, dramatic
79	**ist**	Noun / common noun (doer of an action)	pianist, chemist, artist
90	**isk**	Noun	asterisk, obelisk (pillar)
81	**ism**	Noun (system)	communism, nationalism
82	**asm**	Noun (quality / condition / feature)	enthusiasm
83	**ize**	The act or process of doing sth.	Nationalize, standardize
84	**sis**	Noun (quality / condition / feature)	crisis , analysis
85	**sy**	Noun (quality / condition / feature)	heresy, poesy
86	**e**	Noun (quality / condition / feature)	catastrophe
87	**y**	Noun (quality / condition / feature)	monarchy, philosophy

III. Word Compounding

3.1 Compounding or Word-compounding *refers to the faculty and device of language to form new words by combining or putting together old words. In other words,* **compound**, **compounding** *or* **word-compounding** *occurs when a person joins two or more words together to make them one word. The meanings of the words interconnect in such a way that a new meaning comes out which is very different from the meanings of the words when they are seen or read alone. Examples,* **earth***quake,* **in***take,* **sky***scraper,* **wall***paper,* **class***room etc.*

3.2 Methods of Compounding:

No	Type	Description	Examples
1	**endocentric**	A+B denotes a special kind of B	darkroom
2	**exocentric**	A+B denotes a special kind of an unexpressed semantic head	paleface
3	**copulative**	A+B denotes 'the sum' of what A and B denote	bittersweet, sleepwalk
4	**appositional**	A and B provide different descriptions for the same referent	actor-director, maidservant

3.3 Formal classification

(1) **Closed form**, where two or more separate words (mostly **noun + noun)** are joined together to create a new word, such as **notebook** or **keyboard**

(2) **Hyphenated form**, such as **six-pack**, or **son-in-law**, where a hyphen / dash joins the words together.

(3) **Open form,** such as **post office** or **half sister**, where there is a space between the words, but they are considered to be a compound word.

(4) **Verb + Noun:**   breakfast, cutthroat, pickpocket,

(5) **Gerund + Noun:**   drawing-room, writing-desk, walking-stick

(6) **Verb + Adverb:**   drawback , lockup

(7) **Adverb + Verb**:   upkeep, outcry, outcome

3.4 Compound Nouns:

Noun + Noun: newspaper , classroom

3.5 Compound Adjectives, may be formed from:-

(1) **Adjective + Adjective**:   red-hot , dull-gray

(2) **Noun+ Adjective**:   sky-blue, lifelong

(3) **Adverb + Participle**:   everlasting, outspoken

(4) **Adjective + Noun**:   sweetheart , nobleman

3.6 Compound Verbs, may be formed from: -

(1) **Noun + Verb:**   backbite, waylay, browbeat

(2) **Adjective + Verb:**   fulfill, whitewash, safeguard

(3) **Adverb + Verb**:   overtake, undergo, overdo, overhear

3.7 Compounds with Prefixes

With a few of exceptions, compounds created by the addition of a prefix are not hyphenated: a few examples are given below:

biochemistry, coordinate, extraordinary, infrastructure, interrelated, macroeconomics, metaphysical, microeconomics, minibike, multicultural, nonviolent, overanxious, postwar, transatlantic, unnatural, underdeveloped

3.8 Exceptions include:

1. Compounds in which the second element is capitalized or a number:
   anti-Semitic, post-Freudian
2. Compounds which **need hyphens** to avoid confusion
   un-ionized (as distinguished from unionized)
3. Compounds in which a vowel would be repeated (especially to avoid confusion)
   co-op, semi-independent, anti-intellectual (but reestablish, reedit)
4. Compounds consisting of more than one word
   non-English-speaking, pre-Civil War
5. Compounds that would be difficult to read without a hyphen
   pro-life, pre-war, co-edited

3.9 Primary Words vs. Compound Words:

Words which are not derived or compounded or developed from other words are known as *Primary* words. These words have their own origin. When more words are formed from these original or base words, they are categorized into three classes.

(1) Compound words, formed by joining two or more simple words as, classroom, sunlight
(2) Primary Derivates, formed by making certain change in the structure of a simple word, as *bond* from *bind*; *receipt* from *receive*.
(3) Secondary Derivates, formed by an addition to the beginning (prefix) or to the end (suffix); as *dis*courage, *un*happy, agree*ment*, good*ness*

Most common compound words in everyday use:

IV. Most Common Compound Words

1	bulldozer	48	sunflower	95	strawberry	142	bedroom
2	bathroom	49	tablespoon	96	sunlight	143	sunglasses
3	cupcake	50	something	97	snowball	144	armchair
4	without	51	spotlight	98	sometime	145	breakfast
5	weekend	52	seaside	99	scrapbook	146	downstairs
6	upgrade	53	railway	100	seaweed	147	goldfish
7	teapot	54	sailboat	101	rainbow	148	underwear
8	standby	55	nothing	102	sandpaper	149	underground
9	Sunday	56	popcorn	103	piggyback	150	toothpaste

10	Sunday	57	overlap	104	pancake	151	suitcase
11	tablecloth	58	outline	105	overnight	152	background
12	somehow	59	nobody	106	outside	153	cupboard
13	spaceship	60	workbook	107	notebook	154	wildlife
14	seashell	61	wheelbarrow	108	keyboard	155	watermelon
15	surfboard	62	upset	109	homework	156	understand
16	roundabout	63	teaspoon	110	website	157	teammate
17	peppermint	64	starfish	111	freeway	158	toothpick
18	policeman	65	lookout	112	grapefruit	159	sunburn
19	Overhead	66	motorcycle	113	fortnight	160	sunshine
20	Outdoor	67	lifesaver	114	eyeball	161	somebody
21	newspaper	68	iceberg	115	timetable	162	somewhere
22	Ourselves	69	jellyfish	116	without	163	screwdriver
23	Meantime	70	herself	117	today	164	shipwreck
24	Leftovers	71	haircut	118	railway	165	raincoat
25	However	72	handwriting	119	supermarket	166	saucepan
26	Itself	73	grandfather	120	someday	167	pineapple
27	Hedgehog	74	footpath	121	mailbox	168	paperwork
28	Hairbrush	75	earring	122	kneecap	169	overseas
29	Handbag	76	fireman	123	lighthouse	170	neighborhood
30	goalkeeper	77	skateboard	124	income	171	nowhere
31	Football	78	forget	125	jigsaw	172	masterpiece
32	Earphone	79	whiteboard	126	highway	173	ladybug
33	Fingernail	80	postcard	127	hairdresser	174	lipstick
34	Driveway	81	airport	128	hardware	175	indoors
35	sometimes	82	brainstorm	129	grandmother	176	shoelace
36	bookmark	83	dishwasher	130	forecast	177	everything
37	Toolbox	84	yourself	131	earthquake	178	bookcase
38	Butterfly	85	wheelchair	132	fishbowl	179	jellybean
39	Bedtime	86	upstairs	133	afternoon		
40	Daylight	87	toenail	134	cannot		
41	Heartbeat	88	outcome	135	spaceman		
42	hopscotch	89	newsletter	136	seafood		
43	Hallway	90	otherwise	137	shopkeeper		
44	gingerbread	91	maybe	138	rattlesnake		
45	grasshopper	92	leapfrog	139	scarecrow		
46	Fourteen	93	horseshoe	140	playground		
47	Eyelash	94	inside	141	password		

To find a comprehensive list of Compound Words, see **2276 Compound Words** list prepared by **Rick Walton**, visit: **http://www.rickwalton.com/curricul/compound. htm**

Did You
Know?

According to a survey the most annoying word is "whatever"

V. Methods of word formation

5.1 Agglutination:

The process of forming new words from existing ones by adding affixes to the them, like shame + less + ness › shamelessness

5.2 Backformation:

Removing seeming affixes from existing words, like forming *edit* from **editor,** *air-condition* from *air conditioning,* *automate* from *automation* , *aviate* from *aviation,* *babysit* from *babysitter*

5.3 Blending:

Blending is a technique in which parts of two words are put together to create a new word, such as taking parts of "motor" and "hotel" to form "motel." and *smog* from **smoke** and **fog.** There are no overlapping parts in words that are formed from the blending method, which makes them different from compound words, which do share morphemes.

5.4 Conversion:

Forming a new word from an existing identical one, like forming the verb *green* from adjective *green* (verb green – to make or paint sth. green in color , party (noun) party or to party (verb)

5.5 Borrowing:

One of the more basic formation techniques, borrowing, involves borrowing an existing word from another language and introducing it into the English language without any change or modification to the existing word. Currently, **over 120 languages have influenced the English language throughout history**.

A loanword or a word borrowed from another language. *Pandit* **from Hindi (Indian)** meaning, an expert of a particular field.

For a list of the most commonly used words in English which are borrowed from other languages see, Part II, Unit 14

5.6 Neologism: from *Neo* – new, *Logism* –logos (speech or utterance) that is, new speech or new word Making a completely new word. New words keep coming up in every field of studies as, prolife, Islamophobia, omnishambles, google (verb) to search

5.7 Coinage: Another way of making new words. Sometimes the name of a product is selected by the name of its inventor e.g. pasture (v) from Louis Pasture, sandwich, even Suzuki

5.8 Truncation, also known as shortening or clipping, is the process of forming a word by shortening another word. An example would be forming "fridge" from "refrigerator", "flu" from "influenza." ad from advert - advertise – advertisement

5.9 Derivation: Making words by adding affixes (prefixes, suffixes, circumfixes, infixes) E.g., happy – happi**ness, un**happy ,happi**ly. Inflection** can be another method of creating more variants of the same word. E.g. *decide* – decid**es** – decid**ing** – decid**ed** (inflectional derivations) furthermore, **decisive, decisively**

Some more examples of English derivational suffixes:

i.	adjective to noun:	*ness*	(slow ⟶ slowness)
ii.	adjective to verb:	*ise/ize*	(modern ⟶ modernize)
iii.	noun to adjective:	*al*	(recreation ⟶ recreational)
iv.	noun to verb:	*fy*	(glory ⟶ glorify)
v.	verb to adjective:	*able*	(wash ⟶ bearable)
vi.	verb to noun:	*ance*	(**deliver** ⟶ deliverance)
vii.	with no change	**e.g., call**	(used as noun) **call** used as a verb to call

5.10 Unpaired Words

An **unpaired word** is one that, according to the usual rules of the language, would appear to have a related word (prefix) but does not, as, **intrepid** (fearless, courageous) - trepid is rarely used antonym **uncouth** (rude, uncivilized) – couth is hardly ever seen or heard.

A few more examples:

Unkempt (kempt), unruly (ruly),

The word **uncanny** may appear to be a combination of **un** and **canny, un seemingly** acting as a prefix meaning "not" or "the opposite" as in unfaithful, but that's not the case with this word. **Uncanny** means, strange, weird or unusual. And if we remove "un" we are left with the word **canny**, which interestingly is not the opposite of uncanny, but another (independent) word that means very clever, cunning, careful etc. So here we have: *Uncanny*, meaning- strange, weird or unusual, and *Canny*, meaning clever, cunning, shrewd, careful, etc. Thus, the word *uncanny* is a typical unpaired word, though it appears to be paired as **un + canny**. Also, it may be worth noting that the word *canny* is hardly ever used

---

VI. Affixation

Before we proceed with the process of affixation (fixing or attaching prefixes, suffixes etc.) to words, let's first look at the two main and important element or units of a word. See the box

6.1 Morphology: The study of morphemes or parts (meaningful components) of a word.

Morpheme: The smallest meaningful unit in a word e.g., the **"s"** in *cats* has a meaning, that of a plural form of the word *cat*. Cat is a free morpheme or an independent word. Free Morphemes can stand on their own as independent words, whereas bound morphemes cannot stand alone by themselves as they must connect with other words to make any sense or meaning. Examples of bound morphemes: *s, ous, im, re, ed, en* etc.

> **Bound morphemes** are meaning-bearing units of language, such as prefixes and suffixes, which are attached to unbound or free morphemes and cannot stand alone.
>
> **Unbound or free-standing** morphemes are individual elements or units that can stand alone within a sentence, such as dog, laugh, look, and box. Bound morphemes can turn the word, **dog** to dog*s*, laugh to laugh*s* / laugh*ing,* look to look*s* / look*ed* / look*ing* and box to box*es* etc.
>
> <u>**Stem**</u>: The main part of a word to which affixes are added, e.g., with **"look"** as the stem , *ed*, *ing* and *s* can be added to make words- look*ed*, look*ing* and look*s.*

An **affix** is a *morpheme* that is attached to a word *stem or* the base form of a word to create a new word.

6.2 Positional categories of affixes

Affixes are divided into several categories, depending on their position with reference to the stem (base word) Given below are different types of affixes.

No.	Affix/Ad fixes	Example	Description
1	**Prefix**	<u>un</u>clear	Appears before a stem (base word)
2.	**Suffix**	Enjoy**ment**	Appears after a stem (base word)
3	**Postfix**	look**ing**	Appears at the end of a stem (base word)
4	**Infix**	Son-**in**-law	Appears within a stem or a pair of stems
5	**Circumfix**	<u>Un</u>thank**ful**	One affix comes before and the other after the stem or the base word.
6	<u>**Interfix**</u>	speed-**_o_**-meter, Brian-O-Neil (name)	Links two stems together in a <u>compound</u>
7	<u>**Duplifix**</u>	t**ee**ny-w**ee**ny, tooty-frooty	Incorporates a <u>reduplicated</u> portion of a stem (may occur in front, at the rear, or within the stem)
8	**Transfix**	wr**_o_**te (compare root "write")	A discontinuous affix that is within a discontinuous stem

9	**Simulfix**	mouse → mice	Changes a segment of a stem
10	**Suprafix**	**pro**duce (noun) pro**duce** (verb)	Changes a <u>suprasegmental</u> phoneme of a stem
Prefix and *suffix* may be listed under the term *adfix* in contrast to *infix*.			

"ous" at the end of a word often means "full of".

e.g. famous: full of fame.

glorious; full of glory, gracious, ridiculous, furious, dangerous.

"al" at the end of a word often means "to do with".

E.g. **musical**: to do with music, **criminal**: to do with crime, **historical**: to do with history.

6.3 Onomatopoeic Formation of words:

What is Onomatopoeia? Pronounced: \ˌä-nə-ˌmä-tə-ˈpē-ə, -ˌma-\ or as, **on-o-mat-o-pee-a**

The noun **onomatopoeia** is thought to have been first used in around 1577 AD. According to the Oxford Dictionary, the word **onomatopoeia** originates from the Greek word *onomatopoiia* meaning 'word-making'. The Merriam-Webster Dictionary reports the onomatopoeia is derived from the Greek *onoma* 'name' and *poiein* 'to make'.

6.4 Definition of Onomatopoeia

Onomatopoeia is the formation of a word from a sound associated with what is named (e.g., cuckoo, sizzle).

Babies and little children learn better with the help of onomatopoeia method of making words. A baby may call a dog *bow wow,* identifying it from the sound or the 'voice' it produces. A toy that makes a sound like *chu chu* may be given the name *chu chu* by a baby. In Linguistics it is known as the *Bow Wow Theory* of the origin of languages.

Some more examples of <u>**Onomatopoeia words**</u>: *Cock-a-doodle-do*, (rooster), *tick tock. Of clock, moo of cow , click* of a mouse (computer) , *squeak* of a mouse (animal), *quack* of duck, *hiss* of a snake , *buzz* of bees , *twitter* of birds, *jingle / tinkle / ring* of bells, *clank* of chains, *jingle* of coins, *beat* of a drum, *roar* of a lion / guns, engine, thunder, *rustle* of leaves/ silk , *whistling* of winds, *clink* of steel, *ripple* of water, *bang* of a gun etc.

VII. Types of Word Origins

7.1 Etymological theory recognizes that words originate through a limited number of basic mechanisms, the most important of which are the following:

a. Borrowing, i.e. the adoption of loanwords from other languages.
b. Word formation such as derivation and compounding.
c. Onomatopoeia and sound symbolism, i.e. the creation of imitative words.

While the origin of newly emerged words is often more or less transparent, it tends to become obscured through time due to:

a. **Sound change:** for example, it is not obvious at first sight that English *set* is related to *sit* (the former is originally a causative formation of the latter), and even *less* so that bless is related to *blood* (the former was originally a derivative with the meaning "to mark with blood", or the like).
b. **Semantic change:** English *bead* originally meant *"prayer"*, and acquired its modern sense through the practice of counting prayers with beads.

The word *bless* has its traces in the word *blood*. As blood of a sacrificial animal was sprinkled on the altar and even on the garments of a person by the priest to anoint and bless him. This practice was carried out in the Old Testament times in Israel. Similarly, *gift* from *give; gait /gate* from *go, good bye* from *God be with you* and *gossip* from *god-siblings* etc.

7.2 English Etymology

As a language, English has been very receptive and accommodating as far as its capacity to expand its vocabulary is concerned. The Anglo-Saxon (a German tribal language) roots, which are the original source and the birthplace of English language, can be seen in the similarity of numbers in English and German, particularly *seven/sieben, eight/acht, nine/neun* and *ten/zehn*. Pronouns also show a strong similarity: *I/ich; thou/Du; we/wir; she/sie*. However, over time, language change has modified and revised many grammatical elements, such as the noun case system, which is greatly simplified in Modern English; and certain elements of vocabulary, much of which is borrowed from French. Though more than half of the words in English either come from the French language or have a French equivalent, most of the common words used are still of Germanic origin.

English words of more than two syllables are likely to come from French, often with modified endings. That is because the French endings are either pronounced in a different way or are not pronounced at all. Take for examples, *bou·quet* (bō-kā')*n.* *bon voyage* (bɔ̃ vwajaʒ)

Medical and scientific terminology in English relies heavily on words of Latin and Greek origin. Many Spanish words as buckaroo from vaquero or "cowboy" have also contributed to English vocabulary. Cuddle, eerie and greed come from Scots; , mosque, muslim, apricot, adobe, alcohol, algorithm, assassin, cotton, caliber, sherif, orange, julep, hazard, candy, cat, jar, jacket, safari, sofa and zero from Arabic; honcho, sushi, and tsunami from Japanese; dim sum, gung ho, kowtow, kumquat, ketchup, and typhoon from Cantonese Chinese; behemoth, hallelujah, Satan, jubilee, and rabbi from Hebrew; taiga, sable and sputnik from Russian; galore, whiskey, phoney and Tory from Irish; guru, karma, pandit from Sanskrit; kampong and amok from Malay; and boondocks from the Tagalog word bundok.

7.3 Morphology

Morphology is the branch of linguistics that is concerned with the internal structure of words as well as the formal relationships that exist among the words of a language. The words known to a speaker are recorded as *lexical entries* (meaningful words) in his/her *mental lexicon (mental dictionary)* When a word is learnt, it becomes a comprehensive entity of the memory as a noun, verb, adjective, determiner, auxiliary, etc. along with its phonological form and its distinct meaning.

7.4 Semantics

Semantics is the study of the meaning of words, phrases, and sentences in language. It explores the minimum of knowledge about a linguistic sign or combinations of signs such that the expression can convey a specific communicative content.

7.5 Word Roots (How words are made)

Many words are made up of a root (or base word) and a prefix. Some words also have a suffix. For example, the root word *port* means *to carry* or *to bear*. Attach the prefix *ex,* meaning *out* or *out of,* and you have the word *export, to carry out.* Attach the prefix *im,* meaning *in* or *into* and you have *import, to carry in.* Attach the prefix *trans,* meaning *across*, and you have *transport,* meaning *to carry across*. Now let's attach the suffix *able,* meaning *able to be,* and you have *importable, exportable,* and *transportable.*

The very words **prefix** and **suffix** are good examples, too. **Pre** means **before** and **fix** means *to* **fasten** or **attach,** so quite literally, a prefix is something attached to the beginning of something else. **Suf** is a alternative form of **sub, below or under,** so a suffix is something fastened underneath something else (in this case, behind the root).

By learning the common roots and prefixes (and a few suffixes) we can recognize the meaning of many new words almost immediately. (But do look them up for confirmation.) Take the word **abject,** for example. If you know that **ab** means **away** or **down** and **ject** means **to throw,** you can easily figure out that **abject** doesn't mean something happy. Rather **abject's** root meaning of **thrown down** is quite close to the dictionary defintion of **cast** *down in spirit* **or** *sunk into depression.*

Now since **ject** means **to throw,** think how many words you can define almost immediately: **reject, project, inject, subject, eject,** and so on. Note that some modern words are formed by using abbreviated forms of other words. Thus, we see the use of the letter **i** for **Internet** in **iPhone, iPod,** and **iTunes,** indicating that these items or services work with the Internet. Similarly, the use of **e** for **electronic** appears in words such as elearning (and various forms: **e-learning,** and so on), **e-commerce,** and **e-business.** The **"e-terms"** seem to have been coined before the **"i-terms"** became popular. And note that most of the **"i-terms"** are trademarks, while the others are general descriptors: "I'm going to download some **iTunes** from Apple's **e-commerce** site because I love **e-music.** At any rate, these abbreviated forms are not traditional prefixes, but because they are indeed attached to the front of what amounts to root words, they could be considered functional prefixes.

 Word Roots Part II, Unit 5

Let's face it -- English is a crazy language

There is no egg in the eggplant,
No ham in the hamburger
And neither pine nor apple in the pineapple.
English muffins were not invented in England,
French fries were not invented in France.

We sometimes take English for granted, but if we examine its paradoxes we find that:
Quicksand takes you down slowly,
Boxing rings are square,
And a guinea pig is neither from Guinea nor is it a pig.

If writers write, how come fingers don't fing?
If the plural of tooth is teeth,
Shouldn't the plural of phone booth be phone beeth?
If the teacher taught,
Why hasn't the preacher praught?

If a vegetarian eats vegetables,
What the heck does a humanitarian eat?
Why do people recite at a play,
Yet play at a recital?
Park on driveways and
Drive on parkways?
How can the weather be as hot as hell on one day
And as cold as hell on another?

You have to marvel at the unique lunacy of a language where a house can burn up as it burns down,
And in which you fill in a form
By filling it out
And a bell is only heard once it goes!

English was invented by people, not computers,
And it reflects the creativity of the human race
(Which of course isn't a race at all.)

That is why:
When the stars are out they are visible,
But when the lights are out they are invisible.
And why it is that when I wind up my watch
It starts,
But when I wind up this poem
It ends.

6 SOUND PATTERNS

I. The IPA Chart

Consonants		Vowels			
IPA	Examples	IPA	Full Vowels	Vowels	.... followed by R
b	buy, cab	ɑː	PALM, father	ɑr	START, bard, barn, snarl, star (also / ɑːr./)
d	dye, cad, do	ɒ	LOT, pod, John	ɒr	moral, forage
ð	thy, breathe, father	æ	TRAP, pad, shall, ban	ær	barrow, marry
dʒ	giant, badge, jam	aɪ	PRICE, ride, file, fine, pie	aɪər	Ireland, sapphire (/aɪr./)
f	phi, caff, fan	aʊ	MOUTH, loud, foul, down, how	aʊər	hour (/aʊr./)
g (g)	guy, bag	ɛ	DRESS, bed, fell, men	ɛr	error, merry
h	high, ahead	eɪ	FACE, made, fail, vein, pay	ɛər	SQUARE, scared, scarce, cairn, Mary (/eɪr./)
j	yes, yacht	ɪ	KIT, lid, fill, bin	ɪr	mirror, Sirius

k	sky, crack	iː	FLEECE, seed, feel, mean, sea	ɪər	NEAR, beard, fierce, serious (/iːr./)
l	lie, sly, gal	ɔː	THOUGHT, Maud, dawn, fall, straw	ɔr	NORTH, born, war, Laura (/ɔːr./)
m	my, smile, cam	ɔɪ	CHOICE, void, foil, coin, boy	ɔɪər	<u>loir</u>, <u>coir</u> (/ɔɪr./)
n	nigh, snide, can	oʊ	GOAT, code, foal, bone, go	ɔər	FORCE, boar, more, oral (/oʊr./)
ŋ	sang, sink, singer	ʊ	FOOT, good, full, woman	ʊr	couri r
ŋg	finger, anger	uː	GOOSE, food, fool, soon, chew, do	ʊər	boor, moor, tourist (/uːr./)
θ	thigh, math	juː	cued, cute, mule, tune, queue, you	jʊər	cure
p	pie, spy, cap	ʌ	STRUT, mud, dull, gun	ʌr	borough, hurry
r	rye, try, very			ɜr	NURSE, word, girl, fern, furry (/ɜˑ/)
s	sigh, mass	**Reduced vowels**			
ʃ	shy, cash, emotion	ə	Rosa's, a mission, comma	ər	LETTER, perceive (also /ɚ/)
t	tie, sty, cat, atom	ɨ	roses, emission (either ɪ or ə)	ən	button
tʃ	Church, catch	ɵ	omission (either oʊ or ə)	əm	rhythm
v	vie, have	ʉ	beautiful, curriculum ([jʉ]) (either ʊ or ə)	əl	bottle

w	wye, swine	i	HAPPY, serious (either ɪ or iː)	ə, i	(vowel is frequently dropped: nasturtium)
hw	why				
z	zoo, has				
ʒ	equation, pleasure, vision, beige				
Marginal consonants					
x	ugh, loch, Chanukah				
ʔ	uh-oh /ˈʌʔoʊ/				

II. So, what are the rules of the game?

Like many other languages, English too has its unique and sometimes even strange and weird characteristics and features. These oddities are most often seen in its spelling patterns and in silent letters. No matter how much research and study we may carry out to come up with some definite rules and systems, there is always some *exception* or *exemption* that spoils all our efforts to make things simple and practical. So, then are there any rules to govern these so called patterns? The answer is yes BUT these rules do not ALWAYS apply. They may apply often but never as a rule of the thumb in all cases.

As we know that English alphabet has 26 letters out of which 21 are consonants (19 hard consonants) and five vowels.

Vowels				
A	E	I	O	U

Semi Vowels		
	Y	W	

Y is also sometimes considered as a vowel because of the sound it makes in some words as **try, cry.** Here the sound of **y** is same as or similar to that of "**I**" as in wide, hide, while, etc.

Consonants							
B	C	D		G	H	J	K
L	M	N	P	Q	R	S	T
V	W	X	Y	Z			

ä sound	ë sound	e sound	ï sound		yü sound		
A	B	F	I	O	Q	R	Z
H	C	L	Y		U		
J	D	M			W		
K	E	N					
	G	S					
	P	X					
	T						
	V						

III.   Some facts about some letters:

1. Two letters of the alphabet can also be entire words by themselves: **A** and **I**, as in this example:
   Yesterday **I** met **a** famous movie star.
   (Some letters can sound like full words as, B = be , C = see, sea , Q = queue , R= are , T = tea , U = you , V = we, , X = ex (former) Y = why

2. In any English word, the letter *q* must always be followed immediately by the letter *u.*
   Examples: ***qu**ick, **qu**it, **qu**iet, **qu**ite, **qu**arry, **u**nique, **qu**est, **qu**estion, **qu**ench*

3. Most words in English begin with the letter **S**. The **S** section is always the largest in any English dictionary. Even most encyclopedias have two volumes of letter **S**.

4. The most often used vowel in English words is **E**.

5. The letter **X** begins the least number of English words. The **X** section in the dictionary or an encyclopedia is always the shortest.

6. All five vowels can make two sounds, a long and a short sound. If there is only one vowel in a word, it will make a short sound. If there are two vowels in a word, the first will make the long sound and the second will make the short sound or remain silent. For example, take the word "get" It has only one vowel "e" therefore, it makes a short sound. Whereas in word "read", the first vowel "e" makes a long **ee** sound and the second vowel "a" remains silent.

IV. PHONICS: Letters and their Sound Patterns

1. Sounds of "A"

Long **"a"** sound – e.g. date, way, bake, rail, aim , ape
Short "a" sound – e.g. Cap. The word *cape* has two vowels, therefore, the first one makes a long sound and the second remains silent (see point # 6 above)
In the word "all" the "a" sound is **/fôl/** or as /ɑ:/ in arm, father, palm In the word "regal" the "a" sound is unstressed (schwa) /'rēgəl/

The sound of "a" in noun is a short "a" /ə/ sound and it is a long "a" /eɪ/ sound when the word is used as a verb as shown below.

Advocate: *noun* /'ad-və-kət/ *verb* [transitive] /'ædvəkeɪt/

Five English letters have the capacity to make 2 sounds: These are **C, G, N, S, X**

1. **C** = /k/ – cat, cow	**C** = /s/ mice, cite
2. **G** = /j/ - general	**G** = /g/ go , game
3. **N** = /n/ - no, never	**N** = /ŋ/ sing , ring
4. **S** = /s/ - sale , sit	**S** = /z/ surprise
5. **X** = /s/ - sale , sit	**X** = /z/ xerox, xylophone

2. "C" followed by *e, i, y* generally produces /s/ sound, e.g. cell, city, cycle

Exceptions: ocean, special
The word **"Celtic"** originally pronounced /Seltik/ has now undergone a change to /Keltik/ especially in the American pronunciation. **"Celtic"** by default pronunciation should be pronounced as "Seltik" because according to common spelling rules, C followed by E gives the sound S and not K. For example, **ceiling, cent, century, precept, intercept etc.**

3. The sounds of "E"

There are three common sounds using the letter **E**
Sound "ee" meat week , beat
Sound "eh" bet , bread, fed, met
Sound "e" /û/ , /ɛ/ as in "earth" ,
Sound of "e"" as in effort" / ĕfʾərt/

4. **G** followed by *e, i , y* generally produces /dʒ/ "j" sound e.g. **g**iant, **ge**neral, **gy**mnasium

   Exceptions: get , girl, tiger, together, begin , gynecology /gī-nə-ˈkä-lə-jē, ˌji-/ , gill /gil/

5. The sound of **"I"**

   "I" as in "idea" /ī'dēə/ , /ī-ˈdē-ə/
   "I" as in "ill" /il/ , "ink" /iNGk/
   "I" /ə/ **as in "dirt" "flirt"** /flərt/

6. The sounds of **"O"**

   "O" as in old /ōld/ , goat /oʊ/
   "OO" uː: do, f**oo**d, f**oo**l, s**oo**n
   "O" in "form" /fôrm/
   "O" in "boy" /ɔɪ/
   "O" in "son" /sən/, in "occur" /əˈkər/ in "tractor" /ˈtraktər/ in "onion" /ˈənyən/
   Exceptional sounds of "O" **one** /wən/ **, once** /ˈwən(t)s/, **do** /dōo/ who, /hōo/

   Remember the rule: in case of two vowels in word, the first one makes the stronger or longer sound while the second one makes the weaker sound or almost no sound, e.g. **donor** /ˈdōnər/ More examples: power , done , solve, note , June
   ---

7. **The sounds of "Q"**

   The **"Q"** sound is a combination between the /k/ sound and the /w/ sound. Sometimes the "Q" Sound is at the end of a word and uses only the /k/ sound. UE followed by Q is generally silent, e.g., unique [yoo-neek], critique /kriˈtēk/ However, the vowel preceding the "Q" makes a long and strong sound.

8. **The "R" sounds (Rhotic and Non-Rhotic accents)**

   English pronunciation can be divided into two main accent groups: a **rhotic** ˈroʊtɪk/, sometimes /ˈrɒtɪk/) speaker pronounces a rhotic consonant in words like *hard* and *butter*; a **non-rhotic** speaker does not. Therefore, when pronounced by a non-rhotic speaker, the word *butter* would sound like *butta* / bʌtə/ . The rhotic speaker may utter the consonant sound *tt* in butter very low and soft almost as if skipping the sound and jumping to R as ButteR, similarly, letter may be pronounced as LetteR and WAteR

9. S as "s" or ""z"

SS always produces the /s/ sound e.g. glass, mass
S never makes the /ʒ/ "z" sound in the beginning of a word, e.g. sip, soap, sit
S when used somewhere in the middle or at the end of a word (generally) makes the "z" sound e.g. wise, close, season etc.
In these examples, the letter S is always pronounced as Z:
is was rise rose lose nose boys girls phase phrase noise tries he's she's his hers goes guys as fears reason result desert raise
S as "ZH" usual - *u·su·al* /'yo͞o ZHo͞o əl/

10. The sounds of "U"

"U" in **"union"** /'yü-nyən/ , **"unity"** /'yo͞onətē/
"U" in **"cup"** (kŭp) or murmur, (mûr'mər) more examples: urge, urn , nurse , curse , urban
"U" in **"full"** /'fu̇l/

11. The "X" sounds

X followed by a consonant (generally) produces its original sound of /ks/, e.g., text,
X at the end of a word also produces its original **/ks/** sound, e.g. box, tax, fix
X followed by a vowel (a, e , i , o , u) generally produces /gz/ e.g., exist, example, exam
X hardly comes at the beginning of a word; fewer than 200 words begin with "x"
When "x" comes at the beginning of a word, it mostly produces the sound of "z" /ʒ/
A few common words beginning with "x" are – **Xerox** /'ziː(ə)ɹ.ɑks/, **Xylem** / zī'ləm/ , **Xylophone** - /'zaɪləˌfəʊn/
The word x-ray is pronounced in parts as "x" and "ray" and Xmas is a shortened form of Christmas

12. The sounds of "Y"

At the end of a word, **"y"** can make a strong **"e"** sound as in "baby," or a long "i" sound as in "spy." , and **"Y"** /j/ in yellow /'ye-lō,/. Also "Y" can make the / **ai**/ sound as in cr**y**

More examples of the "Y" sounds

1. as /j/ at the beginning of a word: yes
2. as /j/ after vowel: play, Dmitriy, grey
3. as /i/ without stress at the end of multi-syllable word: baby, happy
4. as /ai/   under stress in an open syllable: my, type, rye, lying, pyre, tyre, typhoon
5. as /i/ in a closed syllable without stress and with stress: KYrgYzstan, myth, system, gymnastics
6. as /i/ in an open syllable under stress: typical, lyric, tyranny
7. as /i/ in an open syllable without stress: physique, pyjamas
8. as "i"   in "bird" under stress before "r": Kyrgyzstan, myrtle, myrrh
9. as /ai/   in a stressed closed syllable: hyphen, cycle, cyclone
10. as /ai/   in the following words: ally, hypothesis, psychology
11. as *shva* /ə/ in martyr /ˈmärtər/
12. as /i/ in money, key

---

13. **Sounds of "Z":** "Z" in zoo /ˈzü/

V. English Diphthongs:

5.1   Standard English diphthongs

	(British)	American
low	[əʊ̯]	[oʊ̯]
loud	[aʊ̯]	[aʊ̯]
lout	[ʌʊ̯]	
lied	[aɪ̯]	[aɪ̯]
light	[ʌɪ̯]	
lane	[eɪ̯]	[eɪ̯]
loin	[ɔɪ̯]	[ɔɪ̯]
loon	[uː]	[ʊʊ̯]
lean	[iː]	[iː]
leer	[ɪə̯]	[ɪɚ̯]
lair	[ɛə̯]	[ɛɚ̯]
lure	[ʊə̯]	[ʊɚ̯]

earth /ûrth/   juice /jo͞os/   few /ˈfyü/ ,

valley /valē/   they /T͟Hā/   toy /toi/

court /kôrt/   couch /kouCH/   crown /kroun/

coat /kōt/   law /lô/   cause /kôz/

day /dā/   choice /CHois/

The following spelling patterns may have the same sound, that is, a long **ee**

See /sē/   sea /sē/   seize /sēz/   chief /CHēf/

5.2 More same-sound diphthongs

OU and **OW**:   noun – crown , sound – town

OA and **OU**: coat - court , goal – soul

AW and **AU**: laws – cause , draw – pause

UE and **EW**: due , dew , blue , new

AY and **EY**: pray - prey – delay, convey

5.3 Three sounds of double "O" i.e. "OO"

(1) /ʊ/ book /ˈbu̇k/   (2) /uː/ cool /ko͞ol /   (3) door /**dôr / , /dōr/**

5.4 Two sounds of "IE"

(a) chief /CHēf/   (b) science /ˈsī-ən(t)s/

5.5 The sound of "IO": /ə/ region (rēˈjən) **union** (yo͞onˈyən) Junior (jo͞onˈyər)

5.6 The sound of "OI": /ɔɪˈ/   point /joint/ **oil**

5.7 The sounds of **"OU"** /aʊ/   (1) **cloud** (kloud)   (2) **couple** (kŭp'əl)   (3) **flour** (flou'ər,

(4) **hour** (/aʊr./)   (5) **soup** / uː/ (so͞op)

5.8 The sound of **"UE"** blue (blo͞o)

5.9 The sounds of **"UI"**   (1) /uː/ fruit (fro͞ot)   (2) /ɪ/ guilt (gĭld)   (3) /aɪ/ guide (gīd)

5.10 The sound of **"AW"**   (1) /ɒ/ saw (sô)

5.11 The sound of **"EW"**   (1) dew /'dyü/ , /'dü/

5.12 The sounds of **"OW"**   (1) /oʊ/ low   (2) /aʊ/ now   (3) flower /'flaʊ(-ə)r/

5.13 The sound of **"AY"**   (1) day /eɪ/

5.14 The sounds of **"EY"**   (2) key /'kē /

5.15 The **CH** and **TU** sound as /tʃ/

5.16 **CH: ch**arge , mar**ch** , **ch**air , **ch**eap , **ch**urch , **ch**ip

5.17 **TU:** ac**tu**al . for**tu**ne , punc**tu**al , pic**tu**re , na**tu**re

5.18 The **EXCE** and **ACCE** combination produces **"X"** sound

5.19 **EXCE: exce**pt , **exce**ss , **exce**llent , **exce**l , **exce**ption

5.20 **ACCE: acce**pt , **acce**ss, **acce**nt , **acce**ptance

5.21 **C, SC** as **"S"**

5.22 **C:** ceremony, certain, census, censor, center, cement

5.23 **SC:** scene, scissor, science, scenery scent

EXCEPTION: Sceptic is pronounced as **(skēp'tĭk)** also written as **skeptic**

PH , GH as "F"

5.24 **PH:** phone, physical, phobia, phase, philosophy, prophet atmosphere, physics

5.25 **GH:** laugh, cough, tough, rough, draught - *US*, **draft** [drɑːft]

5.26 **G, D, DG(E) as "J"** /dʒ/

5.27 **G as "J"** /dʒ/: **g**entle, **g**esture, **g**eometry, **g**eneric

5.28 **D as "J"** /dʒ/: sol**d**ier e**d**ucate, gra**d**ual, indivi**d**ual

5.29 **DG**E as "J" /dʒ/: e**dg**e, lo**dg**e, bri**dg**e, do**dg**e

5.30 **The sound of C , CK , CH , QU as "K"**

```
Remember "Q" is never seen in a word without "U"
e.g. queen , quilt, quack
```

5.31 **C as K**   car , **c**are , basi**c**,   **CK as K**   ba**ck** , pi**ck**

5.32 **CH as K**   **ch**emist , scheme,   **QU as K**   uni**que** , criti**que**

5.35 **The "SH" / ʃ / sounds:**

(a) **TIO as "SH"** / ʃ /   e.g. action , nation, emotion
(b) **SI, SSI as "SH"** / ʃ /   e.g. tension, impulsion (from impulse, desire, instinct)
        mission , discussion
(c) **CI as "SH"** / ʃ /   special , social , ancient , delicious

5.36 **SU, SSU as "SH"** / ʃ / sugar ,sure , issue , pressure

5.37 **SCH, SCI "SH"** / ʃ /   schedule (Br.) conscience

5.38 **"TI", "CI" and "SI"** most frequently produce **"sh"** at the beginning of all syllables except the first.

TI: national, patient, palatial, infectious
CI: gracious, ancient, musician, financial
SI: admission, mansion, division

7 SILENT LETTERS

The Dumb Guests

I. One of the most annoying features of any language is the existence of silent letters in its articulation and pronunciation system. The worst about this particular "feature" of language is that mostly there are no set hard and fast rules to direct and guide the learner specially the novice ones. English is no exception. However, with some measure of research and study we do see some method in the madness.

No.	Description	Example
1	**W** before **R** is silent	Write , writ, wrong , wrist , wrap
2	**K** before **N** is silent	Know, knife
3	**T** before **CH** is silent	Match, watch , catch
4	**GH** after **I , EI , AU, OU** is silent	Night, weight , aught , thought , though , plough , bough
5	**N** after **M** ,especially when the word ends at **N**	Autumn, column , solemn
6	**B** is silent after M (especially when the word ends at **B**) However, when the form of such word changes with **"ing"** or **"ed"** endings, the **B** sound is pronounced, merging it with the **M**	Comb, bomb , climb \'klīm\ However, combing, bombing, and climbing retain both sounds of M and B. But not so in **climbable** or such cases. **Climbable** will be pronounced- \'klīm\ + able
7	**P** is silent when it comes in the beginning of words that follow **P** with **S , N**	Psychology , pneumonia , pseudo
8	**G** in the middle or towards the end of some words is silent , especially before **N** and **TH**	Sign, resign, campaign, foreign, strength

9	G is silent in the beginning of words that follow G with N	Gnostic , gnome
10	H is silent (in most cases) after W	When, why, what, when (in "rhyme" , "h" is silent *Compare*: W is silent in "Who" and H is silent in "when"
11	L is silent (in most cases) before K, F, and M	Talk, folk, calf, half, balm , calm (also note silent L in could, should, would)
12	D is silent when it comes before J	Adjacent , adjust
13	D is silent when it comes before G	Judge, dodge, fridge
14	UE is silent when it comes at the end of words mostly preceded by G or Q	Vogue, unique , vague, critique
15	T is silent after F in some cases	Often (*often* is also pronounced with the "t" as in "after"
16	W is silent after S	Answer
17	B is silent before T	Doubt
18	P before T is silent in certain cases	Empty Ptolemy
19	E before U is silent	Europe , Euphrates
20	S before L is silent	Island , aisle (in some cases)
21	U after A is silent	Gauge, laugh,
22	U before E / I	Guess, guide
23	"W" before "or" often makes the sound "wer"	as, worm, worship, worst, worth, work. **Exceptions:** worry, worried, wore

II. Silent Vowels

Vowels	Words
a (in a digraph)	aisle, team, spread, boat
e (in a digraph)	great, heist, feud, pie, toe
e (ending vowel)	pale, scene, lime, stove, fuse
i (in a digraph)	pail, receive, believe, juice
o (in a digraph)	people, jeopardy
u (in a digraph)	gauge, laugh, guess, guide

II. Silent Consonants

Consonants	Words
b	comb, tomb, bomb, debt
c	black, scene, science
d	fudge, bridge, ledge
f	cliff, stuff, staff
g	gnarl, gnaw, gnome, foreign, sign
h	ghost, whistle; school, chord
k	knee, knife, knowledge
l	quilt, swell, tall
m	mnemonics
n	condemn, column, solemn
p	pneumonia, receipt
s	brass, fuss, press
t	depot, watch
w	window, shadow, answer
z	jazz, buzz

A **Diagraph** (also written "digraph" without the "a" after "i") is a pair of letters representing a single speech sound, such as the *ph* in **phase** or the *ea* in **heat,** whereas, a **blend** is a consonant cluster, like "bl" in **blue** , "cr" in **crow** , **"fl"** in flower, "sk" in **sky** and "tw"in **twenty**. Both elements are pronounced in these cases.

III. Silent Diagraph

3.1

Consonant Digraph	Words
gh	high, nigh, daughter

*Some silent letters do produce sound when other word forms are created

Base Words	Other Word Forms
sign (silent letter g)	signal, signature
bomb (silent letter b)	bombard, bombardment
solemn (silent letter n)	solemnity, solemnize

3.2 **"i"** comes before **"e"** when it is pronounced **"ee"**, e.g. brief, field, priest,

Except **"c"** – **"ei"** after **"c"** e.g., re**cei**ve, de**cei**ve, **cei**ling , re**cei**pt

3.3 EI or IE

"ei" (NOT **"ie"**) when sounding like **"a"** as in "neighbor, or weigh".
Exceptions: neither, foreign, sovereign, seized, counterfeit, forfeited, leisure
When a word ends at the suffix – *ent* , add **"i"** , as in: anc**ient** , suffic**ient** , pat**ient**, profic**ient** , effic**ient** , defic**ient**, quot**ient**

3.4 L or LL: One-syllable words (mostly) end in a double LL

E.g. will , shall, kill, bill, mill, sill
Two or more than two syllable words (mostly) end in one L
E.g. careful, doubtful, hopeful
A single syllable word that already will have a double LL ending, takes only one L at the end of the word if "full" has to be added to it, e.g. will + full = willful , skillful
However, if the second syllable is meant to be an adverb, it will take LL and Y, e.g. ski**llful**ly NOT skillfu**ly** thus, both words ski**ll** + fu**ll** retain their double **LL**s before adding a Y to make the adverb form.
"all" and **"well"** followed by another syllable(s) have only one **"L"**
E.g. also, although, welcome, welfare, already (all ready would mean everything is ready)
Note: we**lf**are but fare**well**
WELCOME has only one L
"full" and **"till"** when joined to another root syllable, drops one **"L"**
E.g. useful, cheerful, **un**til
For words ending in a single **"L"** after a single vowel, double the **"L"** before adding a suffix, regardless of accent.
E.g. cancel = cancelled, travel = traveller, metal = metallic, signal = signalling (also written as signaling AM) **AM = American , BR / Br. = British**

Almost no English words end in **"V"** and none in **"J"** (unless someone has coined one)

3.5 If a word of more than one syllable ends in a **"T"**, preceded by a single vowel, and has the accent on the last syllable, then double the final consonant.

E.g. permit; permitted, admit; admitted, regret; regretted.
But, if the accent is on the first syllable, don't double the **"t"**.
E.g. visit; visited, benefit; benefited

3.6 The same goes for most of the other consonants, as "G" lo**g** changes to lo**gg**ing, hug to hugging , set to setting , hit to hitting , man to manning

3.7 **"er"** or **"or"** endings. The most common everyday words end in "er".

E.g. baker, painter, teacher
If in doubt, use "or", when the meaning of the word is "one who" or "that which".
E.g. author, director, instructor, indicator, conveyor, escalator.

3.8 **"ery"** or **"ary"** endings. Words ending in "ery" are often obvious

E.g. very, brewery, flattery, bakery, nursery
If in doubt, use **"ary"**.
E.g. dictionary, secretary, commentary, stationary
Seven words ending in "ery" that might cause confusion
distillery, confectionery, millinery, cemetery, dysentery, monastery, stationery
(paper, pen etc.)

3.9 **"ise", "ize" or "yse" endings**

Most of these types of words end in **"ise"**.
E.g. sunrise, surprise, supervise, exercise, disguise, unwise, surmise, advertise
"ize" generally gives an idea of 'making' or "turning into" as, nationalize , Americanize, stabilize, dramatize etc.

3.10 **Only two common words end in "yse".or "yze"** viz. analyse (analyze) and paralyse (paralyze)

3.11 **Only two common words end in "ize"** prize and capsize
(others, only if they convey the idea of "making" or "turning into" as described above)

3.12 **"ceed", "sede" and "cede"**

There are only three **"ceed"** words: succeed, exceed, proceed
There is only one **"sede"** word: supersede
All others end **"cede"** E.g. intercede, antecede, and precede

3.13 **"able" or "ible" endings**

Use of **"able"**

- After root words, e.g. **avail**able, **depend**able
- **After root words ending in "e"** (drop the "e") E.g. desire - desirable, believable, usable
- After **"i"** E.g. reliable, sociable

Use of **"ible"**

- After non-root words, i.e. words / word parts that do not make any sense without **"ible"**. Word such as **"audi"** alone makes no sense **unless "ible"** is attached to it to make **audible. Similarly, horri**ble, **poss**ible.
- When the root has an immediate **"ion"** form. E.g. digest**ion** - digest**ible**, suggest**ion** - suggest**ible**, convers**ion** - convert**ible**
- After a root ending in **"ns"** or **"miss"** E.g. respo**nsible**, comprehe**nsible**, per**missible**
- After a soft **"c"** or **"g"** E.g. le**gible**, negli**gible**, for**cible**, invin**cible**

Exceptions: contemptible, resistible, collapsible, flexible

English is a Crazy Language

by Richard Leder

English is the most widely spoken language in the history of our planet, used in some way by at least one out of every seven human beings around the globe. Half of the world's books are written in English, and the majority of international telephone calls are made in English. Sixty percent of the world's radio programs are beamed in English, and more than seventy percent of international mail is written and addressed in English. Eighty percent of all computer texts, including all web sites, are stored in English.

English has acquired the largest vocabulary of all the world's languages, perhaps as many as two million words, and has generated one of the noblest bodies of literature in the annals of the human race. Nonetheless, it is now time to face the fact that English is a crazy language—the most loopy and wiggy of all tongues.

In what other language do people drive in a parkway and park in a driveway?

Why do we call it *newsprint* when it contains no printing but when we put print on it, we call it a *newspaper*?
Why are people who ride motorcycles called *bikers* and people who ride bikes called *cyclists*?
Why—in our crazy languagecan your nose run and your feet smell?

Why it is called a *TV set* when you get only one?

Why does the word *monosyllabic* consist of five syllables?

www.ojohaven.com/fun/crazy.html

8 SPELLING RULES

(or shall we say, Spelling Patterns)

Crazy English Spellings

I take it you already know
Of tough and bough and cough and dough?
Others may stumble but not you
On hiccough, thorough, slough and through.
Well done! And now you wish perhaps,
To learn of less familiar traps?

Beware of heard, a dreadful word
That looks like beard and sounds like bird.
And dead, it's said like bed, not bead-
for goodness' sake don't call it 'deed'!
Watch out for meat and great and threat
(they rhyme with suite and straight and debt).

A moth is not a moth in mother,
Nor both in bother, broth, or brother,
And here is not a match for there,
Nor dear and fear for bear and pear,
And then there's doze and rose and lose-
Just look them up- and goose and choose,
And cork and work and card and ward
And font and front and word and sword,
And do and go and thwart and cart-
Come, I've hardly made a start!
A dreadful language? Man alive!
I'd learned to speak it when I was five!
And yet to write it, the more I sigh,
I'll not learn how 'til the day I die.

I. Unreliable Patterns

As noted before, English spelling system is weird, odd and even creepy at times. English spelling patterns can easily freak out a new learner of the language. But let's face it and try to make some sense of all the oddities and twists of the writing system of this otherwise beautiful and bountiful language. The sounds of patterns are not always consistent. Just when you think you've figured out the sound of a particular pattern, one or more exceptions ring the alarm. At times one feels that there are more exceptions to the rules than the rules. Consider the patterns that follow: Note the pronunciation of the words in the third column.

ear	near	bear
son	ton	on
but	rut	put
bone	lone	gone
one	done	stone
gave	save	have
dough	though	tough
as	has	gas
there	where	here
hard	card	ward
bead	read	head
go	no	to
new	stew	sew
love	dove	move
down	town	own
harm	farm	warn
hand	sand	wand
care	dare	are
moose	goose	choose
form	storm	worm
road	toad	broad
hatch	catch	watch
good	hood	food
dome	home	come
boot	hoot	foot
how	now	low
hush	rush	push

ford	cord	word
toe	hoe	shoe
lost	cost	most
seen	green	been
speak	sneak	break
paid	raid	said
other	mother	bother
fork	pork	work
give	live	hive
hour	sour	pour
car	star	war
ease	tease	cease
ouch	pouch	touch
rose	those	whose
is	his	this
over	clover	mover

The poem that follows cleverly illustrates how unreliable patterns can be:

Our Peculiar Language

When the English tongue we speak
Why is **break** not rhymed with **freak**?

Will you tell me why it's true
We say **sew**, but likewise **few**?

And the maker of a verse
Cannot rhyme his **horse** with **worse**?

Beard sounds not the same as **heardCord** is different from **word.**

Cow is **cow,** but low is **low**
Shoe is never rhymed with **foe**

Think of **rose** and **close** and **lose**
And think of **goose** and yet of **choose**

Think of **comb** and **tomb** and **bomb**
Doll and **roll** and **home** and **some.**

And since *pay* is rhymed with *say*
Why not *paid* with *said* I pray?

We have *blood* and *food* and *good*
Cough is not pronounced like *could*

Wherefore *done* but *gone* and *lone*?
Is there any reason known?

And in short it seems to me
Sounds and letters disagree!

(Author Unknown)

II. English Spellings: Method in the Madness

In this otherwise madness of spelling chaos, let's try to determine some system and establish some sense of direction. Here we go!

1. "**Q**" is always followed by "**U**" - "**qu**" , that is, "**Q**" never stands by itself

    E.g. **quick, queen, quarrel**

2. "**l**" , "**f**" and "**s**" are doubled after a single short vowel at the end of a word.

    E.g. **call, tall, toss, miss, cliff, staff**

    Exceptions: us, bus, gas, if, of, this, yes, plus, nil, pal.

3. The sound of "**ee**" on the end of a word is nearly always "**y**"

4. Words ending in an "**o**" preceded by a consonant usually add "**es**" to form the plural.

    E.g. **potatoes, volcanoes Exceptions:** pianos, solos, Eskimos

5. Nouns ending in a single "**f**" change the "**f**" to a "**v**" before adding "**es**" to form the plural

E.g. **leaf – leaves**; **wolf – wolves Exceptions:** dwarfs, roofs, chiefs

6. If a word ending at **"y"** is preceded by a consonant, change the **"y"** to **"i"**, before adding any ending.

party – parties   marry – married;   carry – carriage;

heavy – heaviness   funny – funnily   pretty – prettier

Except: cry – crying, hurry – hurrying, worry - worrying

7. Words ending in both **a single vowel and a single consonant** always double their last consonant before adding an ending.

e.g. stop, stopped, stopping,   **flat,** flatter, flattest,   **swim,** swimmer, swimming.

Exceptions: fix, box, fox, mix. (**"x"** is the same as **"ck"**; that is it counts as a double consonant ending)

To form plurals of the words ending at **"s, x, z, sh**, and **ch"**, add **"es"**

E.g. buses, foxes, buzzes, wishes and churches

8. In most cases the last **"e"** drops before adding any ending, as receive receiving, **but when adding a suffix beginning with a consonant, retain (keep) the last "e" Example, achieve +ment =** achievement , hope + **full** = hopeful (but note the suffix **full** drops one **"L"** because no two syllable words take double **L** only one syllable words take double **L** (will, shall, smell kill, bell)

One More Exception to the dropping last "e" rule

The last **"e"** will drop even if the suffix begins with a consonant in the following cases:

True + **ly** = truly , due + **ly** = duly , whole + **ly** = wholly , nine + **th** = ninth

9. Words ending in **"ce"** or **"ge"** retain the **"e"** before a suffix beginning with, **a , o, u** to avoid changes in pronunciation. That is because **"ce"** has a soft sound which is **"s"**

and "ge" has a soft sound which is "J", so to retain these respective sounds, (ce = s and ge = j) the last "e" in both cases remains intact. **This is how it works:**

Replace + able (note the suffix *able* here is not beginning with a consonant but with the vowel *a*) **but we do not drop the last "e" so that we can retain the sound of "s" made by "*ce*".** Otherwise, the dropping of "e" would change the pronunciation of the word to something like **replacable = replakable.**

Similarly, let's take the case of the word **sing** and **singe**. If we add **ing** to sing it becomes sing**ing** but if we take the word **singe** and drop the last **e** before adding **ing,** it will again become **singing**. But if we keep the last **e** after **g** (as **ge = J) the pronunciation will change to sinjing instead of singing.** Thus we have two different words with different pronunciations and different meanings.

So, this is how it will work.

Sing + ing = singing (continuous form of the verb sing)

Singe + ing = singeing (continuous form of the verb **singe** which means to burn or cause a burning sensation)

So we can see the logic of the rule of dropping and / or maintaining the last **e** in case of *ce* and *ge*

The same would be the case with the word **change**

Change + able = changeable /'tʃeɪndʒəb(ə)l/ and if we drop the last **e,** we get changable (there is no such word)

Take another example, **courage + ous = courageous** /kəˈreɪdʒəs/ **(without the last e, it would be couragous** (again there is no such word)

-CEED, -CEDE, & -SEDE (make "*seed*" sound)

English has only 12 words ending with the "SEED" sound, yet they tend to cause a bit of a problem with spelling.

Let's look at each variation separately

-SEDE: Only one word in English ends in **–sede: SUPERSEDE**

-CEED: Only three words in the English language end in **–ceed: PROCEED, EXCEED, SUCCEED**

-CEDE: The other eight words end in **–cede: ACCEDE; INTERCEDE; ANTECEDE; CEDE; RECEDE; PRECEDE; CONCEDE; SECEDE**

What really does "OK" stand for?

Originally spelled with periods, (O.K) this term outlived most similar abbreviations owing to its use in President Martin Van Buren's 1840 campaign for reelection. Because he was born in Kinderhook, New York, Van Buren was nicknamed *Old Kinderhook,* and the abbreviation proved eminently suitable for political slogan.

OK[1] or **o·kay** (ō-kā') *Informal*
n. pl. **OK's** or **o·kays**
Approval; agreement: Get your supervisor's OK before taking a day off.
adj.

1. Agreeable; acceptable: Was everything OK with your stay?
2. Satisfactory; good: an OK fellow.
3. Not excellent and not poor; mediocre: made an OK presentation.
4. In proper or satisfactory operational or working order: Is the battery OK?
5. Correct: That answer is OK.
6. Uninjured; safe: The skier fell but was OK.
7. Fairly healthy; well: Thanks to the medicine, the patient was OK.
adv.
Fine; well enough; adequately: a television that works OK despite its age.
interj.
Used to express approval or agreement.
tr.v. **OK'ed** or **OK'd** or **o·kayed, OK'·ing** or **o·kay·ing, OK's** or **o·kays**
To approve of or agree to; authorize.

[Abbreviation of **oll korrect**, slang respelling of **all correct.**]

More Crazy Structure of English

The plural of box is boxes, but we couldn't possibly call a herd of ox, "oxes",
we have to say oxen.

One fowl can be a goose, and many geese,
but who could say the pural of moose is "meese"?

You may trap one mouse, or many mice,
but don't dare say "hice" for more than one house.

If the plural of man is men, why can't pan be "pen",
or fan "fen", or can "cen" ?

The shop-girl can help me try on a sandal on my foot, or both feet,
but if i want a boot, would a pair be "beet"?

"Doubt" is spoken one way, but "thought" in another,
though both have the same diphthong,
and "aught" rhymes with thought,
though the vowels are entirely different.
If masculine pronouns are he, his and him,
why aren't the feminine ones she, shis, and shim ?

9 COLLOCATION

And thou shall know a word by the company it keeps

The "father" of *collocation*, J.R. Firth, a British linguist, was the first one to use the term "collocation" in its linguistic sense. Words like human beings have a tendency to go along with some (other) words and they don't tend to associate with certain (other) words. It's like keeping company with some and avoiding others. So, in other words, we may say that words too have "friends" and even "enemies".

1. Definition:

The word **collocation** means, being at the same place, or existing together. The word "collocation" is made up of two words, **co** – meaning together, and **locat** (locate) from location or place. Thus, a collocation is an association of two or more words that are commonly used together (placed together) in English. There are strong collocations and weak collocations.

Note also (non-linguistic senses):

- **collocate (verb):** place side by side or in relation
- **collocation (noun):** the action of placing things side by side or in position
- **collocate / co-locate (verb):** share a location or facility with someone or something

2. Strong and weak collocation (the predictability factor)

If we look deeper into collocations, we find that not only do the words "go together" but there is a degree of probability in their association. Generally, in any collocation, one word will "call up" another word in the mind of the speaker of the language. In other words, if I give you one word, you can predict the other word, with varying degrees of success. This predictability is not 100%, but it is always **much** higher than with non-collocates.

Strong collocations are word pairings that are expected to come together in a more acceptable way than the weaker ones that may not sound too convincing or plausible. Good or strong collocations are the type of word-pairings that are mostly formed with **'make'** and **'do'**. You **make a cup of tea**, but **do your homework**. Collocations are very common in business settings when certain nouns are routinely combined with certain verbs or adjectives. For example, **draw up a contract, set a price, conduct negotiations and make a deal etc.**

The predictability factor may be **strong**: for example "auspicious" collocates with very few words, as in:

- auspicious occasion
- auspicious moment
- auspicious event

Weak collocation:

- auspicious meeting

In other words, the process works like a strong password or a weak password.

2.1 . Verb Collocations

verb + noun collocations used in everyday situations.

- to feel free
- to come prepared
- to save time
- to find a replacement
- to make progress
- to do the washing up

2.2. Business Collocations

There are a number of forms including adjectives, nouns and other verbs that combine with these key words.

- to key in a PIN
- to deposit a check
- hard-earned money

- protection money
- counterfeit money

2.3 Sport Collocations

- to score a goal (football / hockey)
- to save a goal (football / hockey)
- to take a run (cricket)
- to take a catch (cricket)
- to drop a catch (cricket)
- to knock (sb.) out (boxing)

3. Common Expressions

Collocations are often used as short expressions to describe how someone feels about a situation. In this case, collocations can be used in the adjective form, or as strong and forceful expressions using an intensifier and a verb. Here are a few examples using some of these collocations:

- I **deeply regret** the loss of your loved one.
- Tom's in an **utter fury** over the misunderstanding with his wife.
- He went to a **great length** to explain the situation.

4. When is a collocation NOT a collocation?

Within the area of ***corpus linguistics,*** **collocation** is defined as a sequence of words or ***terms*** which ***co-occur*** more often than would be expected by chance. The term is often used in the same sense as *linguistic government*.

Collocation comprises the restrictions on how words can be used together, for example which prepositions are used with ("***governed by***") particular verbs, or which verbs and nouns are used together. An example of this is the collocation *strong tea*. While the same meaning could be conveyed through the roughly equivalent (weaker collocation) as *powerful tea*, the fact is that English prefers to speak of tea in terms of being strong rather than in terms of being powerful. A similar observation holds for ***powerful computers*** which is preferred **over *strong computers.*** Compare, powerful drug – strong medicine.

5. Common features

Certain restrictions on the substitution of the elements of a collocation

We can say *highly sophisticated,* and we can say *extremely happy.* Both adverbs have the same lexical function, that is adding the degree, or magnifying the impact of the adjectives (sophisticated, happy), however, they are not interchangeable. Still, other adverbs can replace both *highly* and *extremely, very* is one of them.

Syntactic modifiability

Unlike the majority of idioms, collocations are subject to syntactic modification. For example, we can say *effective writing* and *write effectively.*

6. Types of Collocation

There are several different types of collocation made from combinations of verb, noun, adjective etc. Some of the most common types are:

- **Adverb + Adjective:** completely satisfied (NOT ~~downright~~ satisfied)
- **Adjective + Noun:** excruciating pain (NOT excruciating ~~joy~~)
- **Noun + Noun:** a surge of anger (NOT a ~~rush~~ of anger)
- **Noun + Verb:** lions roar (NOT lions ~~shout~~)
- **Verb + Noun:** commit suicide (NOT ~~undertake~~ suicide)
- **Verb + Expression with Preposition:** burst into tears (NOT ~~blow up in~~ tears)
- **Verb + Adverb:** drive fast (NOT drive ~~extremely~~)

7. Model Collocations

There are several different types of collocation. Collocations can be adjective + adverb, noun + noun, verb + noun and so on. Given below are seven main types of collocation in sample sentences.

7. 1 adverb + adjective

- Invading that country was an **utterly stupid** thing to do.
- We entered a **richly decorated** room.
- Are you **fully aware** of the implications of your action?

7. 2 adjective + noun

- The doctor ordered him to take **regular exercise**.
- The Titanic sank on its **maiden voyage**.
- He was writhing on the ground in **excruciating pain**.

7.3 noun + noun

- Let's give Mr Jones a **round of applause**.
- The **ceasefire agreement** came into effect at 11am.
- I'd like to buy two **bars of soap** please.

7.4 noun + verb

- The **lion** started **to roar** when it heard the **dog barking**.
- **Snow was falling** as our **plane took off**.
- The **bomb went off** when he started the car engine.

7.5 verb + noun

- The prisoner was hanged for **committing murder**.
- I always try to **do my homework** in the morning, after **making my bed**.
- He has been asked to **give a presentation** about his work.

7.6 verb + expression with preposition

- We had to return home because we **had run out of money**.
- At first her eyes **filled with horror**, and then she **burst into tears**.
- Their behaviour was enough to **drive anybody to crime**.

7.7 verb + adverb

- She **placed** her keys **gently** on the table and sat down.
- Mary **whispered softly** in John's ear.
- I **vaguely remember** that it was growing dark when we left.

8. Collocation Lists

Some Common Verbs		
have	**do**	**make**
have a bath	do business	make a difference
have a drink	do nothing	make a mess
have a good time	do someone a favor	make a mistake
have a haircut	do the cooking	make a noise
have a holiday	do the housework	make an effort
have a problem	do the shopping	make furniture
have a relationship	do the washing up	make money
have a rest	do your best	make progress
have lunch	do your hair	make room
have sympathy	do your homework	make trouble
take	**break**	**catch**
take a break	break a habit	catch a ball
take a chance	break a leg	catch a bus
take a look	break a promise	catch a chill
take a rest	break a record	catch a cold
take a seat	break a window	catch a thief
take a taxi	break someone's heart	catch fire
take an exam	break the ice	catch sight of
take notes	break the law	catch someone's attention
take someone's place	break the news to	catch someone's eye
take someone's	someone	catch the flu
temperature	break the rules	
pay	**save**	**keep**
pay a fine	save electricity	keep a diary
pay attention	save energy	keep a promise
pay by credit card	save money	keep a secret
pay cash	save one's strength	keep an appointment
pay interest	save someone a seat	keep calm
pay someone a	save someone's life	keep control
compliment	save something to a disk	keep in touch
pay someone a visit	save space	keep quiet
pay the bill	save time	keep someone's place
pay the price	save yourself the trouble	keep the change
pay your respects		

come	go	get
come close	go abroad	get a job
come clean	go astray	get a shock
come direct	go bad	get angry
come early	go bald	get divorced
come first	go bankrupt	get drunk
come into view	go blind	get frightened
come last	go crazy	get home
come late	go dark	get lost
come on time	go deaf	get married
come prepared	go fishing	get nowhere
come right back	go mad	get permission
come second	go missing	get pregnant
come to a compromise	go on foot	get ready
come to a decision	go online	get started
come to an agreement	go out of business	get the impression
come to an end	go overseas	get the message
come to a standstill	go quiet	get the sack
come to terms with	go sailing	get upset
come to a total of	go to war	get wet
come under attack	go yellow	get worried

9. Activities:

9.1 Find the verb which does not collocate with the noun in bold

1. **Shame:**   acknowledge, feel, express, make, hide, overcome, admit
2. **Job:**   apply for, catch, create, get, hold, hunt for, lose, take up
3. **Language:**   acquire, brush up, enrich, learn, pick up, tell, use
4. **Damage:**   assess, cause, mend, repair, suffer, sustain, take
5. **Prayer:**   beg, answer, kneel in, offer, say, utter
6. **Teeth:**   brush, cap, drill, fill, gnash, grit, wash
7. **Pleasure:**   derive, enhance, find, give, pursue, reach, savor,
8. **Silence:**   disturb, interrupt, maintain, observe, pierce, reduce to, suffer

9.2 Choose the noun from the list which collocates with each set of verbs (1-8). **Write answers from a-h**

Set 1: In the office

> (a) **your computer**   (b) **a letter**   (c) **a phone call**   (d) **a form**
> (e) **a computer file**   (f) **a message**   (g) **a report**   (h) **your e-mail**

1 _____ You can make it. You can take it. You can receive it. You can return it. What is it?

2 _____ You can crash it. You can shut it down. You can play on it. You can reboot it. What is it?

3 _____ You can complete it. You can draft it. You can file it. You can submit it. What is it?

4 _____ You can get it. You can send it. You can address it. You can mail it. What is it?

5 _____ You can sign it. You can make a copy of it. You can send it off. You can fill it in. What is it?

6 _____ You can open it. You can delete it. You can create it. You can back it up. What is it?

7 _____ You can send it. You can take it. You can leave it. You can listen to it. What is it?

8 _____ You can reply to it. You can check it. You can go through it. You can delete it. What is it?

Set 2: On the road

> (a) **your flight**   (b) **an appointment**   (c) **a meeting**   (d) **your office**
> (e) **a presentation**   (f) **an agreement**   (g) **lunch**   (h) **your hotel**

1 _____ You can go back to it. You can check into it. You can be dropped off at it. You can be picked up at it. What is it?

2 _____ You can miss it. You can give it. You can attend it. You can take notes at it. What is it?

3 _____ You can come to it. You can reach it. You can work it out. You can negotiate it. What is it?

4 _____ You can enjoy it. You can change it. You can miss it. You can be booked on to it. What is it?

5 _____ You can fix it. You can cancel it. You can keep it. You can fail to turn up for it. What is it?

6 _____ You can skip it. You can grab it. You can go for it. You can pick up the bill for it. What is it?

7 _____ You can organize it. You can hold it. You can speak at it. You can lead it. What is it?

8 _____ You can phone it. You can e-mail it. You can check with it. You can keep in touch with it. What is it?

Set 3: In a meeting

(a) Decisions   (b) problems   (c) ideas   (d) figures   (e) excuses   (f) views   (g) proposals   (h) your colleagues

1 _____ You can address them. You can deal with them. You can foresee them. You can solve them. What are they?

2 _____ You can develop them. You can share them. You can come up with them. You can brainstorm them. What are they?

3 _____ You can make them. You can consider them. You can put them forward. You can withdraw them. What are they?

4 _____ You can look at them. You can go through them. You can quote them. You can round them up. What are they?

5 _____ You can make them. You can question them. You can reach them. You can put them off. What are they?

6 _____ You can support them. You can attack them. You can back them up. You can chat with them. What are they?

7 _____ You can air them. You can share them. You can express them. You can exchange them. What are they?

8 _____ You can make them. You can look for them. You can invent them. You can refuse to accept them. What are they?

10 TEACHING VOCABULARY

Most teachers take pride in making tall claims about their knowledge and expertise in teaching structure, syntax and grammar. Teaching vocabulary is hardly considered an area of any significant importance. Many teachers encourage the students to consult dictionaries to look up the meanings of the words they come across. They do so without realizing that the learners are likely to develop a habit or mindset of seeing words as hurdles in their learning process because they start seeing words as stumbling stones in their academic growth. Whereas, the case is just the contrary; it's the words that the students / learners need the most to understand even the specific grammatical structure or syntax. But since the students develop a pattern or habit of looking up words in complete "isolation" in the dictionary than seeing them in the context and in association with other words, they develop an attitude of treating words as "distinct" entities or "aliens" which have no business to be there at the first place. Words have a tendency to be different in their meaning, adopt different shades of meaning or even stretch the meaning beyond their apparent or obvious limits such as, idioms, metaphors, expressions, clichés and various other figurative usages. Thus, for an effective and comprehensive acquisition of vocabulary, it is advisable that words be taught in association and context rather in isolation. A learner is much more likely to remember words and their usage in this way than learning or memorizing lists of words in complete isolation. Words have associations and belongings where they seem more apt and appropriate than being found or noticed in random and haphazard settings.

I. Teaching vocabulary by levels

1.1 Low Beginning

Focus on topics which can be seen or experienced first-hand (food, clothing, feelings)

Types of Materials: Picture dictionary highly recommended; items from the real world

1.2 High Beginning

Focus on expanding lists of everyday items and defining relationships among them

Types of Materials: Picture dictionary, classified groups of words (verbs, prepositions)

1.3 Low Intermediate

Focus on abstract and specialized words, word forms, simple idioms and phrasal verbs

Types of Materials: texts on specialized topics which provide rich vocabulary in context

1.4 Intermediate to Upper Intermediate

Focus on terminology for a variety of subjects, more idioms and phrasal verbs

Types of Materials: Texts which provide contextualized technical terms and phrases

1.5 Advanced

Focus on recognizing subtle distinctions in words from a wide variety of topics

Types of Materials: Authentic texts, articles, professional writing and creative writing

II. Why do we fail with vocabulary?

According to William A Nagy there are two main reasons for our failure to learn or teach vocabulary in an effective way. First, we do not focus on the in-depth knowledge of the words. Secondly, we fail to emphasize the importance of reading comprehension, that is to say that if a reader can manage to understand the meaning of a word without pausing and looking up a word in the dictionary, he /she is actually is in the process of building vocabulary skills. One does not need to know every word in a text to understand it. Hence it is not teaching vocabulary but promoting and encouraging more reading to get the students more exposed to reading text. As a matter of fact, research shows that even every sixth word could be replaced with an "unfamiliar" synonym or close synonym to help the reader exercise his/her inferring skills.

Students now a days struggle with even simple vocabulary because they are not exposed to reading much as used to be the case in the past few decades. Thus they complain they don't read because they don't have enough vocabulary (word knowledge) the truth however, is the other way around; they don't have enough vocabulary because they don't read.

Definition Approach: The most common method of understanding the meaning and usage of a word is looking up the definition of the word. However, this traditional method has its negative sides. Most definitions are not too accurate or reliable when it comes to seeing the word in a text. Definitions tell very little as to how the word is to be used.

III. A quick approach to a word

1 Quickly give the <u>meaning</u> by:

(a) Using an L1 translation,

(b) Using a known L2 synonym or a simple definition in the L2,

(c) Showing an object or picture

(d) Giving quick demonstration,

(e) Drawing a simple picture or diagram

(f) Breaking the word into parts and giving the meaning of the parts and the whole word (the word part strategy)

(g) Giving several example sentences with the word in context to show the meaning

(h) Commenting on the underlying meaning of the word and other referents.

2 Draw attention to the <u>form</u> of the word by:

(a) Showing how the spelling of the word is like the spelling of known words,

(b) Giving the stress pattern of the word and its pronunciation,

(c) Showing the prefix, stem and suffix that make up the word,

(d) Getting the learners to repeat the pronunciation of the word,

(e) Writing the word on the board,

(f) Pointing out any spelling irregularity in the word.

3 Draw attention to the _use_ of the word by:

(a) Quickly showing the grammatical pattern the word fits into (countable/ uncountable, Transitive / Intransitive, etc.)

(b) Giving a few similar collocates,

(c) Mentioning any restrictions on the use of the word (formal, colloquial, impolite, only used in the United States, only used with children, old fashioned, technical, infrequent)

(d) Giving a well-known opposite, or a well-known word describing the group or lexical set it fits into

(e) Telling where and how the word may not be used

4. Principles:

1. Keep the teaching simple and clear. Don't give complicated explanations.
2. Relate the present teaching to past knowledge by showing a pattern or analogies.
3. Use both oral and written presentation - write it on the whiteboard and explain.
4. Give most attention to words that are already partly known.
5. Tell the learners if it is a high frequency word that is worth noting for future attention.
6. Don't bring in other unknown or poorly known related words

What is involved in knowing a word? Part of effective vocabulary teaching involves working out what needs to be taught about a word. This is called the **_learning burden of a word_** and differs from word to word according to the ways in which the word relates to first language knowledge and already existing knowledge of the second language and or other known languages.

5. Useful prepared exercises for vocabulary learning

Meaning	Form	Use
1. Word and meaning matching 2. Labeling 3. Sentence completion 4. Crossword puzzles 5. Semantic analysis 6. Completing lexical sets	1. Following spelling rules 2. Recognizing word parts 3. Building word family tables	1. Sentence completion 2. Collocation matching 3. Collocation tables 4. Interpreting dictionary entries

Criteria:

A good vocabulary exercise:

1. Focuses on useful words, preferably high frequency words that have already been met before.

2. Focuses on a useful aspect of learning burden. It has a useful learning goal.

3. Gets learners to meet or use the word in ways that establish new mental connectionsfor the word. It sets up useful learning conditions involving generative use.

4. Involves the learners in actively searching for and evaluating the target words in the exercise.

5. Does not bring related unknown or partly known words together. It avoids interference.

6. Discovering learning difficulties:

Meaning	Form and meaning	Is the word a loan word in the L1?
	Concept and referents Associations	Is there an L1 word with roughly the same meaning?
		Does the word fit into the same sets as an L1 word of similar meaning?
Form	Spoken form Written form Word parts	Can the learners repeat the word accurately if they hear it?
		Can the learners write the word correctly if they hear it?
		Can the learners identify known affixes in the word?
Use	Grammatical functions Collocation Constraints on use	Does the word fit into predictable grammar patterns?
		Does the word have the same collocations as an L1 word of similar meaning?
		Does the word have the same restrictions on its use as an L1 word of similar meaning?

7. Useful but easily prepared vocabulary learning exercises

Word meaning	
Find the core meaning	The learners look at dictionary entries and find the shared meaning in the various senses of the word
Word card testing	The learners work in pairs. Each learner gives their pack of cards to their partner who tests them on their recall of the meaning by saying the word and getting them to give the translation. This can also be done by giving the translation and getting them to give the word form.
Using the dictionary:	When a useful word occurs in a reading text, the teacher trains learners in the strategy of using a dictionary
Guessing from context.	Whenever a guessable word occurs in a reading text the teacher trains the learners in the guessing from context strategy
Word form	
Spelling dictation	The teacher says words or phrases and the learners write them
Pronunciation	The teacher writes words on the board and the learners pronounce them getting feedback from the teacher. Each learner picks what word to say
Word parts	The teacher writes words on the board and the learners cut them into parts and give the meanings of the parts
Word use	
Possible collocates	The learners work together in pairs or small groups to list collocates for a given word
Word detectives	A learner reports on a word he or she has found in their reading. They talk about the meaning, spelling, pronunciation, word parts, etymology, collocates and grammar of the word.
Choosing the words	1. As words come up in class, one learner (the class secretary) has the job of noting them for future attention. 2. The teacher chooses words that have appeared in work in the last week or two. 3. The teacher chooses words that the learners need to know.

8. Useful prepared exercises for vocabulary learning

Meaning	Form	Use
Word and meaning matching Labeling Sentence completion Crossword puzzles Semantic analysis Completing lexical sets	Following spelling rules Recognizing word parts Building word family tables	Sentence completion Collocation matching Collocation tables Interpreting dictionary entries

Criteria: A good vocabulary exercise: -
1 focuses on useful words, preferably high frequency words that have already been met before.
2 focuses on a useful aspect of learning burden. It has a useful learning goal.
3 gets learners to meet or use the word in ways that establish new mental connections for the word. It sets up useful learning conditions involving generative use.
4 involves the learners in actively searching for and evaluating the target words in the exercise.
5 does not bring related unknown or partly known words together. It avoids interference.

9. Context Clues: Types of Context Clues

Definition	Explanation
Synonym	Experience
Antonym	Knowledge of Subject
Examples	

10. Learning new words when reading

The first way to figure out the meaning of a word is from its context. The **context** is the other words and sentences that are around the new word. When you figure out the meaning of a word from context, you are making a guess about what the word means. To do this, you use the hints and clues of the other words and sentences. You won't always be right, but many times you will be. You might not be able to guess the exact meaning of a word, but you may be close enough to get the meaning of the sentence it is in. A basic strategy for unlocking the meaning of an unfamiliar word is to search the context of the sentence in which a new word appears for clues. Sometimes this can be easy to do because the author may have provided a *definition* or a *synonym* right there next to or near a term that you can use to unlock its meaning. A *definition* is a statement giving the meaning of a word. A *synonym* is a word that means almost the same as another.

For example, read the following sentence: "Don't think of words as separate, discrete items, or entities." What is the meaning of the word *entities*? The definition is right there - separate, discrete items. But what is the meaning of *discrete*? The meaning of that word is right there too--separate.

When in doubt about the meaning of an unfamiliar word, look around in the sentence; check to see if there is a definition or synonym clue to help you unlock the meaning.

Another kind of context clue (in addition to definitions and synonyms embedded in sentences) is a word or words of opposite meaning (*antonym*) set somewhere near a word that is unfamiliar. If you find a word or words of opposite meaning and you recognize it or them, you are "home free." You can unlock the meaning of the unfamiliar word.

For example, read the following sentence: "I was not exactly enamored of the travel plans my agent made for me; my lack of enthusiasm was triggered by the eight-hour layover required between flights." What is the meaning of the word *enamored*? You can use the context of the sentence to reason in this way: *Enamored of* means just the opposite of *lacking in enthusiasm for*.

10.1 Strategy:

Step 1: Check for synonyms or definitions embedded right there. If you find a synonym or definition, reread the sentence with the new term keeping that synonym or definition in mind.

Step 2: Check for an antonym clue. If you find one, think about its meaning, actually telling yourself the opposite meaning. Then reread the sentence and rephrase it in your own mind.

11. Context Clues: Substitution

At times, rereading a sentence that contains an unfamiliar term and substituting a word or phrase for it that makes sense can help you to unlock the meaning of the unfamiliar word. To understand the substitution strategy, read the following sentence:

"When we stayed at the military base, each Saturday we went to the commissary to buy the food and supplies we would need for the next week."

Although you may never have visited a commissary, given the use of the word in this sentence, you immediately can substitute the word *store* for the word commissary. You probably can wrestle an even more complete meaning for commissary from the overall context of the sentence: a store for food and supplies that is located on a military base.

11.1 Steps in the substitution strategy are as follows:

Step 1: When you read a sentence that you have trouble understanding because of an unfamiliar word in it, reread the sentence and substitute a word that seems to make sense in the context.

Step 2: Read on. If the word you substituted does not make sense in the context of the rest of the paragraph, try again.

Step 3: If the sentence still does not make sense to you and you do not understand the main point the author is making in the paragraph, look for synonym, definition, and antonym clues. If you are still uncertain, check a dictionary.

12. Context Clues: Multiple Meanings

As you have learned, a basic strategy for unlocking the meaning of an unfamiliar word is to search the context of the sentence in which a new word appears for clues. This is especially important when a word has multiple meanings that you already know and you must decide the particular one that applies. Try using the following strategy:

Step 1: Check the context for clues: definitions and synonyms given "right there" as well as words of opposite meaning - antonyms.

Step 2: Substitute each meaning you know in the context of the sentence until you find one that makes good sense there. (Hennings, p. 48)

References and Acknowledgement:

Pauk, Walter. How to Study in College.Fourth Edition. 1989.

Mohr, C., & Nist, S. Improving Vocabulary Skills. 1997

Hennings, Dorothy. Vocabulary Growth.Strategies for College Word Study. 2001

13. Ways of helping learners remember previously met words:

> **1.** Spend time on a word by dealing with two or three aspects of the word, such as its spelling, its pronunciation, its parts, related derived forms, its meaning, its collocations, its grammar, or restrictions on its use.
>
> **2.** Get learners to do graded reading and listening to stories at the appropriate level.
>
> **3.** Get learners to do speaking and writing activities based on written input that contains the words.
>
> **4.** Get learners to do prepared activities that involve testing and teaching vocabulary, such as *Same or different? Find the difference, Word and picture matching.*
>
> **5.** Set aside a time each week for word by word revision of the vocabulary that occurred previously. List the words on the board and do the following activities.
>
>   a) Go round the class getting each learner to say one of the words.
>   b) Break the words into parts and label the meanings of the parts.
>   c) Suggest collocations for the words.
>   d) Recall the sentence where the word occurred and suggest another context.
>   e) Look at derived forms of the words.

14. Teaching Meanings of words:

The goal of teaching word-meaning can be achieved in many ways. Here are some of the most prominent ones.

14.1 By demonstration or pictures

1. Using an object
2. Using a cut-out figure
3. Using gesture
4. Performing an action
5. Photographs or pictures
6. White board drawings or diagrams
7. Realia – showing real objects / items / things

14.2 By verbal explanation

1. Analytical definition
2. Putting the new words in a defining context
3. Translating the word in native language
4. Using examples
5. Clear descriptions

Un-teaching/ Unlearning

Process of erasing the wrong pronunciation and concept of a word previously learned

E.g. Stoma**ch** – /K/   Head**ache** /K/   **Ch**emistry /k/

---

15. What vocabulary does a language learner need?

The General Service List (West, 1953) The GSL contains 2000 headwords and was developed in the 1940s. The frequency figures for most items are based on a 5,000,000 word written corpus.

16. Vocabulary learning strategies: Four Macro Skills

Importance of vocabulary learning strategies and its application in the classroom setting

1) General vocabulary learning strategies;
2) A taxonomy of vocabulary learning strategies and
3) The most frequently used vocabulary learning strategies
   (Oxford, 1990; Schmitt, 1997; Nation, 2001; Lip, 2009).

17. Taxonomy (classification) of vocabulary learning strategies

Two main types of strategies: Discovery Strategies and Consolidation Strategies

Discovery strategies include determination strategies and social strategies while consolidation strategies encompass social strategies, memory strategies, cognitive strategies and metacognitive strategies.

According to Akbari & Tahririan (2009), "Schmitt's (1997) taxonomy seems to be the most comprehensive and has the advantage of being organized around an established scheme of language learning strategies."

Other well-known taxonomies of vocabulary learning strategies are social, memory, cognitive, and metacognitive strategies, **guessing, dictionary, note-taking, memory and activation strategies.** The most frequently used and most useful vocabulary learning strategies are:

1) Spelling the word in the mind repeatedly
2) Analyzing the word by breaking down the sound segments (units)
3) Remembering words by putting it in particular context
4) Asking classmates for the meaning of the word
5) The use of electronic dictionaries, bilingual dictionaries
6) Guessing from context

Source: Oxford's (1990) **Gu and Johnson's (1996)**

The following table shows the vocabulary learning/teaching strategies

17.1 Method A

1	Using flash card
2	Labeling things
3	Word list
4	Spoken repetition

17.2 Method B

1	Learning new words in sentences
2	Using word card
3	Keeping vocabulary notebooks
4	Memorizing word lists
5	Written repetition
6	Learning new words through extensive reading
7	Classwork
8	Using dictionaries
9	Learning roots, prefixes and suffixes
10	Learning new words by watching movies
11	Keeping vocabulary notebooks
12	Using word card

18. Approaches to Vocabulary Learning:

a. *Direct Approach:*

Exercises, activities , word building exercises , guessing words from the context , learning word lists , word games

b. *Indirect Approach:*

Grasping / understanding the message
Interpreting the message
Guessing the message / items from the context

18.1 The Four Ways from Indirect to Direct Method

1. Material is prepared with vocabulary learning as the main consideration
2. Words are dealt with as they occur
3. Vocabulary is taught in connection with other language activities
4. In-class and out of class- vocabulary activities and skills

18.2 Points a teachers needs to consider in teaching vocabulary (3 vital questions)

1. What vocabulary my learners need to know?
2. How will they learn this vocabulary?
3. How to test the present level of SS Vocabulary and what they need to know?

18.3 How will they learn this vocabulary?

a. Receptive Learning:

Being able to recognize a word and recall its meaning when it is met , words generally understood when heard or read or seen , range from well-known to barely known

b. Productive Learning:

Productive vocabulary, generally refers to words which can be produced within an appropriate context and match the intended meaning of the speaker

Being able to recognize a word and recall its meaning when it is met plus the ability to speak or write the needed vocabulary at the appropriate time.
Productive Vocabulary of 3000 base words

19. Questions for the teacher to consider before teaching Vocabulary:

1. Do you expect learning to occur during or outside the class?
2. Will you focus on receptive or productive learning?
3. Which skills – listening-speaking, reading or writing, will involve most of the vocabulary learning?
4. Is your aim the quality or the quantity of vocabulary?
5. Is your focus - the words or the strategies?
6. Will you teach from the in-context and / or decontextualized learning?
7. Will your teaching be teacher-directed class activities, group work, individual or pair work?

20. What are the reasons for testing?

1. To find the learners present vocabulary level and magnitude
2. To compare vocabulary knowledge before and after the study /lessons
3. To keep a continuing check on progress
4. To encourage learning by setting short term targets
5. To see the effectiveness of your own teaching approaches
6. To investigate, research and discover new methods to learning and teaching

21. Tips for teaching Vocabulary

The Old-Spice Tips

1. Matching synonyms
2. Matching opposites
3. Fill in the blanks

II. Variations on the above

1. Choose all the possible answers

He ate lunch in the _____.

cafeteria / restaurant / snack / snack bar / salad bar / diner

2. Where would you find . . . ?

an MD	_____	a) in the British or Canadian Parliament
a Ph.D.	_____	b) on a ruler
an MP	_____	c) on a machine or an engine
in. / cm	_____	d) in a hospital
hp	_____	e) in a university

3. Compete the phrases

to make an	_____	a) a secret
to achieve	_____	b) appointment
to reveal	_____	b) deadline
to grasp	_____	c) a goal
to meet	_____	d) an idea

4. Correct the mistakes

He felt *exhausted* after a <u>long nap</u>.
Possible corrections: *"refreshed"* for "exhausted" or after <u>running a race</u> for <u>"a long nap"</u>

5. Label a picture

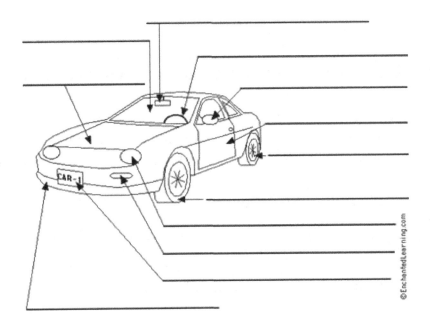

6. Cross out the word that doesn't belong with the others in the group. (Odd one out)

uncle / father / aunt / brother
MD / UNO / PhD / MBA
field / river / farm / park

7. Categories: You give the example; students give the category, or vice versa.

gun, knife club: **weapon**
house: bedroom, door, kitchen

8. Complete the sentences.

I was exhausted after _____

III. Distinguishing shades of meaning & near synonyms

1. Analogies – (good for even lower levels)

easy :	hard	cold : _____	(hot)
skyscraper :	city	tree : _____	(forest)
break :	glass :	dig : _____	(hole)

2. Choose the two possible answers that can complete each sentence:

She longed for . . .

    (a) her freedom.
    (b) her lover who was far away.
    (c) bill at the restaurant
    (d) the pen she dropped on the floor

Correct Grammatical construction

He wondered about . . .

    (a) his future
    (b) that he didn't know what to do
    (c) the meaning of life.
    (d) it was so hot.

3. Word domains (?)

e.g., general category: break, damage

He smashed the	-----	car's bumper / tree branch / old bag
She splintered the	-----	can / board / mirror
He shattered the	-----	mirror / water / curtains
She shredded the	-----	can / tree branch /curtains

4. Which word in each pair is stronger, more forceful, or more intense?

| ___ to amaze | ___ to boil | ___ to throw | ___ to embarrass |
| ___ to shock | ___ to simmer | ___ to toss | ___ to humiliate |

5. Arrange the words on a scale

hot - warm - luke - warm - cool - cold
despise - hate - dislike

6. Which word in each pair is slang?

___ a kid / ___ a child
___ disgusting / ___ gross
___ to fail / ___ to flunk

7. Which word has a more positive connotation?

Or, Which word would be more polite when talking about a person?

___ thin /   ___ skinny
___ fat /   ___ overweight
___ frugal /   ___ miserly

8. Complete the definitions. How are these actions performed?

Shove = to push	_____	(forcefully, hard)
Shatter = to break	_____	(into many pieces)
Tap = to hit	_____	(lightly, softly)

IV. Things to do with the vocabulary in a reading passage:

1. Guessing word meaning from context but make sure it is really possible to guess the meaning from context.
2. Give students the definitions; let them find the words.
   e.g., find a word in paragraph 5 that means "angry"
   This is a good way to deal with a difficult article without simply giving students the vocabulary.
3. Teach students when not to look up a word.

   a) Can you get a general sense of the word? e.g., a person? something good/bad? a movement? a way of speaking?
   b) Take a magic marker and block out all the words you don't know. Then read the passage and answer the comprehension questions.

Follow up/reinforcement

4. **Parts of speech**
   With a corpus of words you've already studied, give sentences that require a different part of speech. (Dictionary use)
5. **Different meanings of familiar vocabulary**
   E.g. **fair**   fair = reasonable, just   fair = beautiful, white skin

V. Teaching students how to guess word meaning from context

Types of context clues:

1. **Cause & effect**: label the sentence C & E, then make a guess.
   Because we **tarried** too long at the restaurant, we **missed** the beginning of the movie.
   The door was **open,** so the dog **got out** of the house.

2. **Opposite/contrast:** underline the two words or phrases in contrast to one another, and then make a guess.
   Even though I **studied hard**, I **failed** the test.
   My last apartment was really **small**, but my new one is quite **spacious.**

3. **Synonyms or paraphrases** (found elsewhere in the sentence or paragraph)
   Samuel was **deaf**, but he didn't let his **handicap** get in the way of his success.

Sally's **flower** garden included dozens of **marigolds,** which she **tended** with great **care.**

4. **Examples in the text**

The **baboon,** like other **apes,** is a very social **animal.**

VII. Miscellaneous

1. Word sheets

For example: Which words have positive/negative connotations? Which words refer to people? Which words are verbs? What's the opposite of X? I'll give you a word; tell me what the opposite is in the list. What's a more polite way of saying X?

2. Looking for words that are similar in meaning or suggest the same or similar idea

Words for go up: soar, rise, raise, increase, elevate
Words for go down: fall, plummet, sink, decrease

Other categories of words that might work: words that describe movement, travel; words related to crime; names of government positions (president, mayor, etc.)

VI. Fun & games

1. Act out/pantomime

Give students cards with instructions like the ones below. Have them perform the actions without speaking. The other students try to guess the word or expression the student is pantomiming.

Open the door fearfully.
Walk across the room cautiously.
Whisper in somebody's ear
Gossip about somebody

2. Crossword Puzzles

Several software programs are available which allow you to make your own puzzles. Clues can be synonyms, opposites, fill-in-the-blank sentences, etc.

3. The Category Game

Divide the class into teams. One person from a team sits in front of the class. The rest of the team members are given a card with a category, for example: Things that are red. The team members take turns giving examples of the category until the person in the "hot seat" guesses or all the team members have given a clue. If the person in front cannot guess, the other team can confer and try to guess.

NOTE: The clues must be examples, not definitions. In the above example, ketchup, blood, and a stop sign are all acceptable clues. Color is not.

e.g., things that are yellow/expensive/fragile/made of glass/found on a farm

American authors/state capitals/things in a woman's purse/warm clothing

4. Password

Divide the class into two teams. One person from each team sits in a chair in front of the class. Those two people receive a card with a vocabulary word. The first person gives a one-word clue to his/her team. If no one from the team can guess, the second person gives a clue to his/her team. This alternates back and forth until someone from one of the teams guesses the word, or until a specified number of clues have been given.

5. Drawing pictures

This works well if you have an empty classroom nearby. Divide the class into two groups. Give each one a list of vocabulary words (idiomatic expressions also work well for this). The students draw pictures - but no words - on the board so that the students in the other group can guess the words or expressions they're trying to represent. This is a fun way to review some vocabulary and break up the class routine.

VIII. Miscellaneous Activities

1. **Matching pictures** with words (this is different from labeling a picture)
2. **Cloze test:**
   A cloze test is an exercise, test, or assessment consisting of a portion of text with certain words removed (cloze text), where the participant is asked to replace the missing words. Cloze tests require the ability to understand context and vocabulary in order to identify the correct words or type of words that belong in the deleted passages of a text. Sometimes every fifth, seventh or tenth word may be left out. It really depends on the preference of the teacher.
3. **Writing words for definitions:** Sometimes the first letter of the word (answer) may be given
4. **Completing sentences** with the similar sounding words, e.g., homonyms or homographs, as Fair or fare, tail or tale
5. **Completing crossword**
6. Joining beginnings/ endings of words with the other part of a words e.g. mort +gage
7. **Completing passages** with words from the box. Sometimes there could be more words than the required number.
8. **Unscrambling word** / Rearranging jumbled letters to make words, e.g., idray = diary
9. Leaving words out from ***phrasal words*** to complete sentences. Students may be made to guess the missing word or the missing words may be given in a box to choose from.
10. **Numbers for letters:** Assign a number for each letter in the alphabet and then write the numbers in groups and ask students to find the letter for each number to make the words. Of course the numbers you write in groups must correspond to letters in such a way that they indeed make some words. This means you must first prepare the word and number game to get the right combinations. E.g. if C = 2 , A=3 and B = 1 then , 231 will make the word CAB (taxi)
11. **Words with missing spellings:** In this activity you must be careful in selecting the intended missing letters so that when the students are doing the activity, they find a logical sequence of the missing letters particular with regards to the (phonemes) sounds. Unless, the objective of this activity is to make it harder for the students to guess the letters. If you choose to remove the consonants the activity will be easier than removing the vowels. E.g. Missing consonants - brea_fas_ , Missing vowels - br-akf-st. However, this may not always be the case, as it really depends on the words.

12. **Who is the leader/ head?** You may give four or five words of the same category and ask the students to write the main word or the principal word covering all those words. E.g. hand , wind, strap, time = watch or clock ; wing, tail, fly, pilot = airplane

13. Filling in with the missing prefixes or suffixes. E.g. (suffix) depend + *able* or *ence*

    (prefix) *dis* + ability , *in* + consistent

14. Choosing the correct alternative: E.g., I visit my parents only once a month now. ***Previously*** I could visit them twice a a month.
    (a)   Former   (b) Previously   (c) Prior

15. **Collocation:** Match the words in column A that go best with the words in columns B

A	B	Answers
1. have	a. **an anniversary**	1 - c
2. celebrate	b. **a club**	2 – a
3. join	c. **a party**	3 - b
4. win	d. **an excuse**	4 – e
5. make	e. **a prize**	5 – d

Collocation activities can also work in the reverse mode. You may give more than one correct collocations for a word or the head word, except <u>**one**</u> in the group and ask the students to spot the one that <u>**does not**</u> collocate with the main word or the head word

E.g., Can you find the verb which does not collocate with the noun in bold?

1. ____ acknowledge, feel, express, make, hide, overcome, admit	a. **shame**
2. ____ apply for, catch, create, get, hold, hunt for, lose, take up	b. **job**
3. ____ acquire, brush up, enrich, learn, pick up, tell, use	c. **language**
4. ____ assess, cause, mend, repair, suffer, sustain, take	d. **damage**
5. ____ beg, answer, kneel in, offer, say, utter	e. **prayer**
6. ____ brush, cap, drill, fill, gnash, grit, wash	f. **teeth**
7. ____ derive, enhance, find, give, pursue, reach, savor,	g. **pleasure**
8. ____ disturb, interrupt, maintain, observe, pierce, reduce to, suffer	h. **silence**

Answers:

1. make 2. catch 3. tell 4. take 5. beg 6. wash 7. reach 8. suffer (only with suffer in silence)

Collocation Activity

Match words in column A with the words they collocate in column B (more than one collocations are possible)

No.	A Words		B Collocations	No.	A Words	B collocations	
1	look	A	ill	32	sandy	expectations	A
2	take	B	proposal	33	book a	confidence	B
3	high	C	white	34	turn a	dream/nightmare	C
4	hot	D	strike	35	build	success	D
5	fall	E	benefit	36	lose	room, seat	E
6	make	F	alike	37	have a	law/rules	F
7	black and	G	mistake	38	achieve	business	G
8	go on	H	temperature	39	prepare a	tears	H
9	ups and	I	fancy to sb.	40	make an	apology	I
10	deliver	J	view	41	offer an	promise	J
11	match and	K	area	42	give a	favor	K
12	give	L	downs	43	face a	advantage	L
13	attend	M	message	44	find a	contribution	M
14	causal	N	contrast	45	take	hurt	N
15	keep in	O	attendant	46	pay a	solution	O
16	stay in	P	dress	47	take	compliment	P
17	fair	Q	contact	48	call in	disappointed	Q
18	slim	R	complexion	49	run a	holiday / break	R
19	play a	S	touch	50	make a	divorce	S
20	jet-black	T	election	51	do a	problem	T
21	lose	U	joke on sb	52	bitterly	meeting	U
22	no-go	V	hair	54	deeply	position / job	V
23	spectacular	W	lecture	55	shed	excuse	W
24	fasten	X	temperament	56	abide by	beaches	X
25	flight	Y	news	57	keep	question	Y
26	take a	Z	seat-belt	58	live up to	corner	Z
27	board a	#	discount	58	take a	faith	#
28	earn a	%	flight	59	get/give	try	%
29	contest	&	figure	60	arrange a	dish	&
30	cast	*	livelihood	61	spend	chance	*
31	get	+	plane	62	apply for a	Time, money	+

16. Word-Train

Call a student to the whiteboard and ask him/her to write a (any) word on the board, then ask this student to choose another student to come up to the white board and continue writing another word that begins with the last letter of the previous word. Let this go until all the students (depending) get to write a word. This will make a long train of so many words. Then ask the students to search how many words they can spot by identifying spelling patterns. This activity may be done in teams as, girls vs. boys or the right section of the class vs. the left section of the class etc.

E.g., Balloon (continue with the letter "n" as in **new** , continue with the letter "w" as **wet** again go on with "t" and, just keep going.

You may like to restrict the choice of words as only nouns or verbs or adjectives etc. This will make the activity a little harder but more challenging and more interesting. Try it! It is fun.

17. Group the words: Write ten or twenty words 'randomly' on the white board and then draw big boxes, circles or columns with ample space to write in. Each box, circle or column must have a topic or area written as a title. Now ask the students to toss in (write) the words in the box, circle or column they best fit in or belong to. The words that may appear to have been written randomly actually must be carefully selected so that they indeed can go in one of the box, circle or column drawn on the board.

(Of course, this activity can also be prepared on a paper / handout / worksheet)

18. Homonyms: Choose the correct word: Students may be given a pair of similar sounding words to choose from. These words may have the same sound but different spellings but have the tendency to confuse the students.

E.g., Mr. Dan Hein is the ***principle / principal*** of LOGOS International School.

The ***weather / whether*** in Phnom Penh changes several times in day.

Note:

Homophones can be two-way (two-form) three-way or even four-way. See the chart below:

Two Way Homophones

First Variation	Second Variation	Notes
Ad	Add	This really counts as *ad* is an abbreviation for advertisement.

Aid (help)	Aide (assistance)	
Ail (trouble, pain)	Ale (drink (n) , wine)	
Altar (place of sacrifice) table in a place of worship	Alter (to change)	
Arc (curve, bend)	Ark (big ship)	
Assistance	Assistants	
Ate	Eight	
Attendance	Attendants	
Bare (simple, naked)	Bear (an animal)	
Be	Bee	
Beat (to hit)	Beet (a plant, vegetable)	
Berth (bench, long seat)	Birth (to be born)	

Three Way Homophones

First Variation	Second Variation	Third Variation	Notes
Accent	*Ascent*	*Assent*	
Are	Hour	Our	"Are" and "Our" - words confused on a sign in a shop window read "Try *are* (our) delicious cakes".
Aye (also ay)	Eye	I	
Buy	By	Bye	
Cite	Sight	Site	
Ewe (female sheep)	You	Yew	
For	Fore	Four	

Four Way Homo Phones

First Variation	Second Variation	Third Variation	Forth Variation	Notes
Right	Write	Wright	Rite	Not completely sure that the wright is a word. It's in dictionary. com though as a noun.

TESTING VOCABULARY

One of the most important tasks in teaching vocabulary is gauging or measuring the progress in learning vocabulary. How do we know the level of progress a learner has scaled or achieved? In this unit we will look at some of the procedures and measure that can be applied to achieve this rather difficult goal.

1. Reasons for testing

1. Determining the level of progress
2. Encouraging students
3. Finding out about learning difficulties
4. Finding out about achievement
5. Placing students
6. Selecting students
7. Finding out about proficiency

A good knowledge of English vocabulary is important for anyone who wants to use the language, so knowledge of vocabulary is often tested. It is important that the test maker be aware of his / her aims and objectives in testing vocabulary.

2. Types of Vocabulary Knowledge

A fair knowledge of vocabulary can be divided into four types.

1. The first is **active speaking vocabulary**, that is, words that the speaker is able to use in speaking.
2. The second is **passive listening vocabulary**, which is, words that the listener recognizes but cannot necessarily produce when speaking.
3. The third type is **passive reading vocabulary**, which refers to words that a reader recognizes but would not necessarily be able to produce.

4. Finally, there is **active writing vocabulary,** which is, words that a writer is able to employ (use) in writing. This typology can be expressed in the following chart:

	Oral	**Graphic**
Active	active spoken	active written
Passive	passive listening	passive reading

A teacher may focus on all of the four areas in preparing a test. If not, he/she should be well aware of the procedure, objective and the outcome of the testing activity. The Most traditional vocabulary tests only test passive reading vocabulary, since they are paper and pencil /pen tests and rely on reading. Method of testing vocabulary must change with the aim of testing any particular area from the types given above. If the type of learning the students have been exposed to emphasized reading, then it is appropriate to give passive reading vocabulary the most attention.

3. Multiple Choice Tasks

Research indicates that the best distracters for vocabulary items are either:

1) Words that have a similar meaning to the correct word but which are inappropriate in context, or
2) Words that appear to be related but which do not fit in the context.

When choosing the four or five alternatives, care should be taken to choose words that are of a similar level of difficulty. If the correct alternative is much more difficult than any of the other alternatives, the student might choose it, not because he/she knows that it is correct but because all of the others can be eliminated.

Alternatives should be the same part of speech as the word in the stem. If one is a different part of speech, that can easily be eliminated as a possible answer.

4. Synonym/Definition Items

The simplest multiple choice item has a single word in the stem, with four or five alternatives. Students choose from among the alternatives the word or the definition that is the closest in meaning to the word in the stem. Alternatively, the definition might be the stem, and the students choose from four or five words that one which fits the definition. Obviously the definition needs to be simply and clearly written.

5. Picture Items

The stem in the previous type of item can be replaced with a picture. The students choose which of the four or five alternatives matches the picture. Obviously it should be clear what is being depicted in the picture, so that the test is of the meaning of the word, not the student's ability to interpret the picture. This type of test is appropriate for elementary students.

6. Sentence Items

Another option is to test the vocabulary item by putting it in a sentence and having the students choose the alternative that has the same meaning as a word in the sentence that is underlined, in italics, in bold type, etc. This is a preferred type of multiple choice vocabulary item, since the problem item appears in context and the context helps give the vocabulary word a specific meaning. However, in this case, the students should not be able to surmise the meaning of the word from the context, unless the intention of the item is to test that skill.

7. Context Items

Another type of multiple choice item is one that has a sentence with a blank in it, and the students choose which of the alternatives fit in the sentence. These items are difficult to write, because it is difficult to provide the right amount of context. If enough context is not provided, the question becomes difficult to answer.

a). Sometimes such questions involve a grammatical component. For example,

Would you please _____ the proposal.
a. consider b. think c. make d. give

In this case, "think" (about) is similar to the correct answer, but it does not fit grammatically. While a few of these types of items might be acceptable, **too many of them will put too much emphasis on grammar rather than vocabulary.**

b). Sometimes vocabulary items test collocations. For example,

I _____ my watch to see what time it was.
a. looked at b. saw c. watched d. gazed at

In this case, what is being tested is the knowledge of the collocation "look at my watch." Again, knowing collocations is part of knowing vocabulary, but the test should not be dominated by such items.

c). Set Items

Another type of item is one where students are presented with a set of words. In the case of a recognition type of item, the students decide which word in the set does not fit with the others; in the case of production type items, the students indicates what topic ties all of the words together.

For example,

d). Circle the word that does not fit

Dollar   reil   pound   money   (answer = money)

e). Write down the subject that each group of words is related to.

Bedroom   living room kitchen   dining room   (subject = house)

f). Matching Items

Another type of item is one in which the students is presented with a short passage or several unconnected sentences with blanks. The students chooses from among a list of words that are given (usually more words than blanks) the word which fits in each blank. In these items, it is preferable to have all the words in a set the same part of speech, the same tense in the case of verbs, etc., so that students need to choose what fits in the blank based on meaning, not grammar. The purpose of having extra words is that the students cannot answer the last item by having eliminated all other possibilities. On the other hand, the more items there are, the more likely that two items could possibly fit in the same blank.

A variation of this type of items is one in which the student is given a reading passage and a list of words and is instructed to find synonyms in the passage for each word in the list.

g). Completion Items

Completion items are similar to those described above, except that students are not given words from which to choose. They must provide the words for the blanks. The problem with this type of item is that it is very difficult to write items for which there is one and only one answer.

h). Word Formation Items

Another type of item tests not the students' knowledge of the meaning of words but their knowledge of word forms. In this case, students are given a sentence or paragraph, and they are instructed to fill in blanks with the correct forms of the words that they are given. (A variation on this is to write multiple choice items, in which the stem is a sentence with a blank, and students choose from among four forms of the same word.) For example,

i). Write the correct form of the word in capital letters in the blank.

HONEST
Darren says he didn't cheat, but I _____ don't know what to think. (answer: honestly)

j). Guessing Meaning from Context

Another vocabulary-related skill to test is the ability to guess the meaning of an unknown word from context. In testing this skill, students are usually presented with a word that they would be unlikely to know and are asked to figure out what it means. Among the clues from the context are:

Pollution from that factory is **contaminating** the local farmers' fields

Testing this skill can be done as a multiple choice item or by requiring the students to supply a definition. The problem with the latter type of item is that it is very difficult to evaluate the answers, because some are likely to be almost correct but not exactly. It is necessary that the meaning of the target word be very clear from the context, and for this type of item, pretesting is particularly important for that reason.

k). Multiple choices

This is a question which consists of a so called *stem (the main word)* and four options from which only one is correct. The examinee has to choose the right answer (Ur 38). The form of the multiple choice can also vary, here are three possible forms:

He accused me of ...... lies.

    a. speaking
    b. saying
    c. telling
    d. talking

Everything we wanted was **to be.**

    a. under control
    b. within reach
    c. well cared for
    d. being prepared

According to the writer, what did Tom immediately do?

    a. He ran home.
    b. He met Bob.
    c. He began to shout.
    d. He phoned the police

l). Cloze Test

Cloze test is test based on a text with gaps which are put there regularly after every seventh, eighth or ninth word. The examinee has to complete the gaps with appropriate words. Mostly more than one option is possible. The first three or more lines of the text are without gaps (Scrivener 261).

Example of a cloze test / C Test:

Seventy years ago no one _____ ever heard the word 'robot'. It _____ first used by a Czechoslovakian writer, Karel Capek _____ the 1920's. He wrote a play about a scientist _____ invents machines which he _____ robots, from the Czech word robota, meaning 'slave-like work'… (O'Connell 193).

The advantage of cloze tests is that it is quite easy to create them. The teacher just needs to find a suitable text and delete words from it. Nevertheless, Hughes does not consider cloze tests much reliable because we do not know what ability (speaking, writing, reading etc.) of the examinee it shows. Moreover, the regular interval of every ninth word does not work very well because some deleted words are very difficult to

determine (Hughes 62-67). This is a kind of cloze test but with initial letters of words that are omitted.

Example of a C-Test:

There are usually five men in the crew of a fire engine. One o_____ them dri_____ the eng_____. The lea_____ sits bes_____ the dri_____. The ot_____ firemen s_____ inside t_____ cab o_____ the f_____ engine.T_____ leader h_____ usually be_____ in t_____ Fire Ser_____ for ma_____ years... (Hughes 71).

This test is more advantageous for the examinee as the texts are shorter and less difficult. On the other hand, the gaps are so close to one another that the learner can not get lost in the text (Hughes 71).

Dictation

The examiner dictates a text and students write it down. Here we examine mainly spelling or pronunciation and also listening. Dictation is an easy way of testing for the teacher because the preparation is minimal (Ur 40). However, it is demanding to assess such tests, Hughes recommends that we should consider the dictation correct as long as there is the right order of words and that misspelled words should be accepted because phonologically it is correct (Hughes 71-72).

m). Paused dictation - a text with missing words, students fill in the missing words while the teacher dictates (Berka, Váňová 36-37).

Example:

The police are _____ for a three-day-old baby-girl _____ yesterday from the _____ ward of a London hospital. The baby was removed from her _____ early yesterday morning. Police are anxious to find a _____ seen _____ round the hospital _____ that night ...

(Berka, Váňová 39).

n). True / False

o). Teacher may give a meaning of a word that may sound true or could be false. This could be in:

1. Questions and answers
2. Gap-filling
4. Transformation
5. Rewriting
6. Matching
7. Error correction
8. Translation
9. Rearranging words
10. Information transfer

Acknowledgment

Bc. Ivana PavlůMASARYK UNIVERSITY BRNO, FACULTY OF EDUCATION

Department of English Language and Literature

From: Bc. Ivana PavlůMASARYK UNIVERSITY BRNO, FACULTY OF EDUCATION

Adapted from: S. Kathleen Kitao work on teaching vocabulary

12 INTERESTING LANGUAGE FACTS

1. There are more than 2,700 major languages spoken throughout the world.

2. There are over 583 different languages and dialects spoken in Indonesia alone, including English and Dutch.

3. More than 2,000 languages are spoken in the entire continent of Africa.

4. The language spoken by the people most is Mandarin, a type of Chinese. Second is English.

5. The most difficult language to speak is Basque. It is not related to any language in the world. It is spoken in north-western Spain and south-western France.

6. The Berbers of Northern Africa have no written form of their language.

7. Somalia is the only country in the world where every citizen speaks one language, Somali.

8. The only country where Latin is the official language is Vatican City.

9. The Cambodian alphabet is the world's largest alphabet, with 74 letters.

10. The world's shortest alphabet, used in the Solomon Islands, has only 11.

11. English, the second most spoken language in the world, has more words than any other language. But English speakers generally use only about 1% of the language. About one third of the more than one million English words are technical terms.

12. The language of Taki, spoken in parts of French Guinea, consists of only 340 words.

MIND YOUR WORDS ▬▬▬

13. The Irish language has three dialects, the Connact Irish, Munster Irish, and Ulster Irish.

14. The language Malayalam, spoken in parts of India, is the only language whose name is a palindrome.(can be read from both sides)

15. Tigrinya, spoken by half of Eritrea's population, is a Semitic language based on Ge'ez, the ancient liturgical (and now extinct vernacular) language of the Ethiopian Orthodox Church.

16. Modern Japanese employs four writing systems: kanji (adapted from the Chinese hanji), hiragana, katakana, and romaji.

17. Today, 58 countries in the world and the United Nations include English as an official language, followed by French with 32 countries and the United Nations, and Arabic at 25 countries and the United Nations.

18. There are more than 7,000 dialects in the world.

19. Sign language for the deaf was first systematized in France during the 18th century by Abbot Charles-Michel l'Epée.

20. French Sign Language (FSL) was brought to the United States in 1816 by Thomas Gallaudet, founder of the American School for the Deaf in Hartford, Connecticut, whom developed American Sign Language (ASL).

21. By the time a child is 5 years old, he/she will on average have spent 9,100 hours learning its native language.

22. What is known as standard Italian today dates back to last century, when the great Italian novelist Alessandro Manzoni (1785-1873) gave Italy a national language by resolving that it should be Tuscan Italian.

23. German is commonly divided into two forms, Low German (Plattdeutsch) and High German (Hochdeutsch).

24. There are 33 letters in the Cyrillic alphabet.

25. The country Nigeria itself has more than 250 different languages, making the production of newspapers and television shows a challenge. Major languages include, French, Arabic, Hausa, Djerma, and Songhai.

26. Many linguists estimate that of the 6,800 languages currently spoken, only about 3,000 will remain viable by the end of the century.

27. Some 95% of the world's population living today learn one of about 100 languages as a first language, leaving the remaining 6,700 languages spoken by 5% of the population.

28. Two areas of the world have the largest number of languages (some 300 to 400 total) that are currently becoming extinct: Australia and North America (Aboriginals and Native American languages).

29. About 140 languages are thought to be dead and dying in Australia and some 80 to 90 in North America.

30. Votic, a Finno-Ugric tongue of the Uralic language family in the Kingisepp district on the Leningrad region of Russia, has less than a hundred remaining speakers.

31. According to the 2000 Census, of the nearly 47 million Americans at least 5 years old who spoke a language other than English, about 60% of them spoke Spanish.

32. Esperanto was an artifical language devised by a Polish eye doctor, L. L. Zamenhof, introduced in 1887. The name comes from his pen name, Dr. Esperanto, which in the language means one who hopes." Based on Indo-European roots with a simple grammar, it was intended to be an international second language that people from different countries could learn easily and use to communicate. Thousands of books have been published in Esperanto, and there are 100,000 or more Esperanto speakers in the world according to some estimates.

33. Mandarin Chinese is a tonal language. It uses 4 different tones to convey different meanings: flat, rising, falling then rising, or falling.

34. The language with the largest number of consonantal sounds was that of the Ubykns in the Caucasus, with 82. The last fully competent speaker, Tevtik Esenc, died in Istanbul in October 1992.

35. The language with the most vowels is **Sedang**, a central Vietnamese language, with 55 distinguishable vowel sounds.

ENGLISH LANGUAGE FACTS

English is currently one of the most widely spoken and written languages worldwide, with some 380 million native speakers. English is spoken by one out of every six people in the world. It is the primary language of the United States, the U.K., Australia, New Zealand and, partly, Canada.

ENGLISH LANGUAGE HISTORY

English is an Anglo-Frisian language brought to Britain in the 5th Century AD by Germanic settlers from various parts of northwest Germany. The original Old English language was subsequently influenced by two successive waves of invasion. The first was by speakers of languages in the Scandinavian branch of the Germanic family, who colonized parts of Britain in the 8th and 9th centuries.

ENGLISH LANGUAGE STATISTICS

English is currently one of the most widely spoken and written languages worldwide, with some 380 million native speakers.

Through the global influence of native English speakers in cinema, music, broadcasting, science, and the Internet in recent decades, English is now the most widely learned second language in the world.

Because a working knowledge of English is required in many fields and occupations, education ministries around the world mandate the teaching of English to at least a basic level.

Here are some other facts about English you might be interested in knowing.

    a. English is the most widespread language in the world and is more widely spoken and written than any other language.

    b. Over 400 million people use the English vocabulary as a mother tongue, only surpassed in numbers, but not in distribution by speakers of the many varieties of Chinese.

    c. Over 700 million people, speak English, as a foreign language.

    d. Did you know that of all the world's languages (over 2,700) English is arguably the richest in vocabulary; and that the Oxford English Dictionary lists about 500,000 words, and there are a half-million technical and scientific terms still not recorded in dictionaries?

e. Three-quarters of the world's mail, telexes and cables are in English.

f. More than half of the world's technical and scientific periodicals are in English

g. English is the medium for 80% of the information stored in the world's computers

h. English is the language of navigation, aviation and of Christianity; it is the ecumenical language of the World Council of Churches

i. Five of the largest broadcasting companies in the world (CBS, NBC, ABC, BBC and CBC) transmit in English, reaching millions of people all over the world.The main language used throughout the world on the internet is English. The media that make up the Internet are overwhelmingly American in origin, so it is no wonder that the mother tongue of the Web is English.

Four factors determine the degree to which a given language finds use on the Internet:

1. The number of users of the language
2. The extent of its use as an official language
3. The economic power of the language
4. The volume of information spread in that language

Today, English dominates in all four respects. It is studied as a foreign language throughout the world and employed by a majority of Internet users. Of the 163 member nations of the U.N., more use English as their official language than any other. The easiest way to calculate the economic influence of a language may be to add up the gross domestic products (GDP) of all the nations where it is spoken. People who count English as their mother tongue make up less than 10% of the world's population, but possess over 30% of the world's economic power. Therefore, in terms of the quantity of transmitted information, English is the leader by far. After English, 26 nations in the U.N. cite French as their official tongue, 21 Spanish and 17 Arabic. Each of these three languages forms a substantial linguistic community on the Internet.

PART II
VOCABULARY BANK

1 GENERAL SERVICE WORD LIST

able	air	ask	between	by
about	all	associate	beyond	call
above	allow	at	big	can
accept	almost	attack	bill	capital
accord	alone	attempt	bird	captain
account	along	average	black	car
accountable	already	away	blood	care
across	also	back	blow	carry
act	although	bad	blue	case
active	always	ball	board	castle
active	among	bank	boat	catch
actor	amount	bar	body	cause
actress	ancient	base	book	centre / center
actual	and	battle	both	certain
add	animal	be	box	chance
address	another	bear	boy	change
admit	answer	beauty	branch	character
adopt	any	because	bread	charge
advance	appear	become	break	chief
advantage	apply	bed	bridge	child
adventure	appoint	before	bright	choose
affair	arise	begin	bring	church
after	arm	behind	broad	circle
again	army	believe	brother	city
against	around	belong	build	claim
age	arrive	below	burn	class
agent	art	beneath	business	clear
ago	article	beside	but	close
agree	as	best	buy	cloud

coal	date	distance	every	fine
coast	door	distinguish	example	finish
coin	doubt	district	except	fire
cold	down	divide	exchange	first
college	draw	do	exercise	fish
colony	dream	doctor	exist	fit
Color / colour	dress	dog	expect	five
come	drink	dollar	expense	fix
command	drive	each	experience	floor
committee	drop	ear	experiment	flow
common	dry	early	explain	flower
company	due	earth	express	fly
complete	duty	east	extend	follow
concern	daughter	easy	eye	food
condition	day	eat	face	for
consider	dead	effect	fact	force
contain	deal	efficient	factory	foreign
content	dear	effort	fail	forest
continue	decide	egg	fair	forget
control	declare	eight	faith	form
corn	deep	either	fall	former
cost	defeat	elect	familiar	forth
cotton	degree	eleven	family	fortune
could	demand	else	famous	four
council	department	empire	far	free
count	depend	employ	farm	fresh
country	describe	end	fast	friday
course	desert	enemy	father	friend
court	desire	english	favour	from
cover	destroy	enjoy	fear	front
cross	detail	enough	feel	full
crowd	determine	enter	fellow	furnish
crown	develop	equal	few	future
cry	die	escape	field	gain
current	difference	even	fight	game
cut	difficult	evening	figure	garden
danger	direct	event	fill	gas
dark	discover	ever	find	gate

gather	home	kill	little	mind
general	honour / honor	kind	live	miner
gentle	hope	king	local	minister
get	horse	know	long	minute
gift	hot	lack	look	miss
girl	hour	lady	lord	mister
give	house	lake	lose	modern
glad	how	land	loss	moment
glass	however	language	love	Monday
go	human	large	low	money
god	hundred	last	machine	month
gold	husband	late	main	moon
good	idea	latter	make	moral
great	if	laugh	man	more
green	ill	laughter	manner	moreover
ground	important	law	manufacture	morning
group	in	lay	many	most
grow	inch	lead	mark	mother
half	include	learn	market	motor
hand	increase	leave	marry	mountain
happen	indeed	left	mass	mouth
happy	independent	length	master	move
hard	industry	less	material	Mrs.
hardly	influence	let	matter	much
have	instead	letter	maybe	music
he	interest	level	mean	must
head	into	library	measure	name
hear	introduce	lie	meet	nation
heart	iron	life	member	native
heat	it	lift	memory	nature
heaven	join	light	mention	near
heavy	joint	like	mere	necessary
help	jointed	likely	metal	necessity
here	joy	limit	middle	need
high	judge	line	might	neighbor
hill	just	lip	mile	neither
history	justice	listen	milk	never
hold	keep	literature	million	new

news	order	position	question	rich
newspaper	ordinary	possess	quite	ride
next	organize	possible	race	right
night	other	post	raise	ring
nine	otherwise	pound	rank	rise
no	ought	poverty	rate	river
noble	out	power	rather	road
none	over	prepare	reach	rock
nor	owe	present	read	roll
north	own	president	ready	room
not	page	press	real	rough
note	paint	pressure	realize	round
notice	paper	pretty	really	royal
now	part	prevent	reason	rule
number	particular	price	receipt	run
numerical	party	private	receive	safe
numerous	pass	problem	recent	sail
object	past	produce	recognize	sale
observe	pay	product	record	salt
occasion	peace	profit	red	same
of	people	progress	reduce	saturday
off	per	promise	refuse	save
offer	perhaps	proof	regard	say
office	permit	proper	relation	scarce
official	person	property	relative	scene
often	picture	propose	religion	school
oh	piece	protect	remain	science
oil	place	prove	remark	sea
old	plain	provide	remember	season
on	plan	provision	reply	seat
once	plant	public	report	second
one	play	pull	represent	secret
only	please	purpose	republic	secretary
open	point	put	reserve	see
operate	political	quality	respect	seem
opinion	poor	quantity	rest	sell
opportunity	popular	quarter	result	send
or	population	queen	return	sense

sensitive	sky	still	teach	train
separate	sleep	stock	tear	travel
serious	small	stone	tell	tree
serve	smile	stop	temple	trouble
service	snow	store	ten	true
set	so	story	term	trust
settle	social	strange	test	try
seven	society	stream	than	Tuesday
several	soft	street	the	turn
shadow	soldier	strength	then	twelve
shake	some	strike	there	twenty
shall	son	strong	therefore	two
shape	soon	struggle	they	type
share	sort	student	thing	under
she	soul	study	think	understand
shine	sound	subject	thirteen	union
ship	south	substance	thirty	unite
shoot	space	succeed	this	university
shore	speak	such	though	unless
short	special	suffer	thousand	until
should	speed	suggest	three	up
shoulder	spend	summer	through	upon
show	spirit	sun	throw	use
side	spite	Sunday	Thursday	usual
sight	spot	supply	thus	valley
sign	spread	support	till	value
silence	spring	suppose	time	variety
silver	square	sure	to	various
simple	stage	surface	today	very
since	stand	surprise	together	vessel
sing	standard	surround	ton	victory
single	star	sweet	too	view
sir	start	sword	top	village
sister	state	system	total	virtue
sit	station	table	touch	visit
situation	stay	take	toward	voice
six	steel	talk	town	vote
size	step	tax	trade	wage

wait	Wednesday	white	wise	would
walk	week	who	wish	wound
wall	welcome	whole	with	write
want	well	why	within	wrong
war	west	wide	without	year
watch	western	wife	woman	yes
water	what	wild	wonder	yesterday
wave	when	will	wood	yet
way	where	win	word	yield
we	whether	wind	work	you
wealth	which	window	world	young
wear	while	winter	worth	youth

To see **Headwords of the Academic Word List,** visit: http://www.victoria.ac.nz/lals/
resources/academicwordlist/awl-headwords

2 ACADEMIC WORD LIST

Academic Word List Coxhead (2000). The most frequent word in each family is in italics. There are 570 headwords and about 3000 words altogether. For more information see The Academic Word List. For more practice see: Schmitt & Schmitt (2005), or the Compleat Lexical Tutor.

No	Headwords	Other words in the family.	Definition
1	**abandon**	abandoned, abandoning, abandonment, abandons	**abandon**
2	**abstract**	abstraction, abstractions, abstractly, abstracts	**abstract**
3	**academy**	academia, *academic*, academically, academics, academies	**academy**
4	**access**	accessed, accesses, accessibility, accessible, accessing, inaccessible	**access**
5	**accommodate**	accommodated, accommodates, accommodating, *accommodation*	**accommodate**
6	**accompany**	*accompanied*, accompanies, accompaniment, accompanying, unaccompanied	**accompany**
7	**accumulate**	accumulated, accumulating, *accumulation*, accumulates	**accumulate**
8	**accurate**	accuracy, accurately, inaccuracy, inaccuracies, inaccurate	**accurate**
9	**achieve**	achievable, achieved, achievement, achievements, achieves, achieving	**achieve**
10	**acknowledge**	*acknowledged*, acknowledges, acknowledging, acknowledgement, acknowledgements	**acknowledge**

11	acquire	acquired, acquires, acquiring, *acquisition*, acquisitions	acquire
12	adapt	adaptability, adaptable, *adaptation*, adaptations, adapted, adapting, adaptive, adapts	adapt
13	adequate	adequacy, adequately, inadequacies, inadequacy, inadequate, inadequately	adequate
14	adjacent		adjacent
15	adjust	adjusted, adjusting, *adjustment*, adjustments, adjusts, readjust, readjusted, readjusting, readjustment, readjustments, readjusts	adjust
16	administrate	administrates, *administration*, administrations, administrative, administratively, administrator, administrators	administrate
17	adult	adulthood, *adults*	adult
18	advocate	advocacy, advocated, advocates, advocating	advocate
19	Affect	affected, affecting, affective, affectively, affects, unaffected	affect
20	aggregate	aggregated, aggregates, aggregating, aggregation	aggregate
21	aid	aided, aiding, aids, unaided	aid
22	albeit		albeit
23	allocate	allocated, allocates, allocating, *allocation*, allocations	allocate
24	alter	alterable, alteration, alterations, altered, altering, alternate, alternating, alters, unalterable, unaltered	alter
25	alternative	alternatively, alternatives	alternative
26	ambiguous	ambiguities, ambiguity, unambiguous, unambiguously	ambiguous
27	amend	amended, amending, *amendment*, amendments, amends	amend
28	analogy	analogies, *analogous*	analogy

29	**analyze**	analyzed, analyzer, analyzers, analyses, analyzing, *analysis*, analyst, analysts, analytic, analytical, analytically	**analyze**
30	**annual**	annually	**annual**
31	**anticipate**	*anticipated,* anticipates, anticipating, anticipation, unanticipated	**anticipate**
32	**apparent**	apparently	**apparent**
33	**append**	*appendix*, appended, appends, appending, appendices, appendixes	**append**
34	**appreciate**	appreciable, appreciably, appreciated, appreciates, appreciating, *appreciation,* unappreciated	**appreciate**
35	**approach**	approachable, approached, approaches, approaching, unapproachable	**approach**
36	**appropriate**	appropriacy, appropriately, appropriateness, inappropriacy, inappropriate, inappropriately	**appropriate**
36	**approximate**	*approximated*, approximately, approximates, approximating, approximation, approximations	**approximate**
37	**arbitrary**	arbitrariness, arbitrarily	**arbitrary**
38	**area**	areas	**area**
39	**aspect**	*aspects*	**aspect**
40	**assemble**	assembled, assembles, assemblies, assembling, *assembly*	**assemble**
41	**assess**	assessable, assessed, assesses, assessing, *assessment*, assessments, reassess, reassessed, reassessing, reassessment, unassessed	**assess**
42	**assign**	*assigned,* assigning, assignment, assignments, assigns, reassign, reassigned, reassigning, reassigns, unassigned	**assign**
43	**assist**	*assistance,* assistant, assistants, assisted, assisting, assists, unassisted	**assist**
44	**assume**	assumed, assumes, assuming, assumption, assumptions	**assume**

45	assure	*assurance*, assurances, assured, assuredly, assures, assuring	assure
46	attach	*attached,* attaches, attaching, attachment, attachments, unattached	attach
47	attain	attainable, *attained,* attaining, attainment, attainments, attains, unattainable	attain
48	attitude	*attitudes*	attitude
49	attribute	attributable, *attributed,* attributes, attributing, attribution	attribute
50	author	authored, authoring, authors, authorship	author
51	authority	authoritative, authorities	authority
52	automate	automatic, automated, automates, automating, *automatically,* automation	automate
53	available	availability, unavailable	available
54	aware	awareness, unaware	aware
55	behalf		behalf
56	benefit	beneficial, beneficiary, beneficiaries, benefited, benefiting, benefits	benefit
57	bias	biased, biases, biasing, unbiased	bias
58	bond	bonded, bonding, bonds	bond
59	brief	brevity, briefed, briefing, briefly, briefs	brief
60	bulk	bulky	bulk
61	capable	capabilities, capability, incapable	capable
61	capacity	capacities, incapacitate, incapacitated	capacity
62	category	*categories*, categorization, categorize, categorized, categorizes, categorizing, categorizing	category
63	cease	ceased, ceaseless, *ceases*, ceasing	cease
64	challenge	challenged, challenger, challengers, challenges, challenging	challenge
65	channel	channeled, channeling, channels	channel
66	chapter	chapters	chapter
67	chart	charted, charting, charts, uncharted	chart
68	chemical	chemically, chemicals	chemical
69	circumstance	*circumstances*	circumstance

70	cite	citation, citations, *cited,* citing, cites	cite
71	civil		civil
72	clarify	clarification, clarified, clarifies, clarifying, *clarity*	clarify
73	classic	*classical,* classics	classic
74	clause	clauses	clause
75	code	coded, codes, coding	code
76	coherent	*coherence,* coherently, incoherent, incoherently	coherent
77	coincide	coincided, coincides, coinciding, coincidence, coincidences, coincident, coincidental	coincide
78	collapse	collapsed, collapses, collapsible, collapsing	collapse
79	colleague	*colleagues*	colleague
80	commence	*commenced,* commences, commencement, commencing, recommences, recommenced, recommencing	commence
81	comment	commentaries, commentary, commentator, commentators, commented, commenting, *comments*	comment
82	commission	commissioned, commissioner, commissioners, commissioning, commissions	commission
83	commit	*commitment,* commitments, commits, committed, committing	commit
84	commodity	commodities	commodity
85	communicate	communicable, communicated, communicates, communicating, *communication,* communications, communicative, communicatively, uncommunicative	communicate
86	community	communities	community
87	compatible	compatibility, incompatibility, *incompatible*	compatible
88	compensate	compensated, compensates, compensating, *compensation,* compensations, compensatory	compensate

89	compile	compilation, compilations, *compiled*, compiles, compiling	compile
90	complement	complementary, complemented, complementing, complements	complement
91	complex	complexities, complexity	complex
92	component	componentry, *components*	component
93	compound	compounded, compounding, *compounds*	compound
94	comprehensive	comprehensively	comprehensive
95	comprise	comprised, comprises, comprising	comprise
96	compute	computation, computational, computations, computable, *computer*, computed, computerized, computers, computing	compute
97	conceive	conceivable, conceivably, *conceived*, conceives, conceiving, inconceivable, inconceivably	conceive
98	concentrate	concentrated, concentrates, concentrating, *concentration*	concentrate
99	concept	conception, concepts, conceptual, conceptualization, conceptualize, conceptualized, conceptualizes, conceptualizing, conceptually	concept
100	conclude	concluded, concludes, concluding, *conclusion*, conclusions, conclusive, conclusively, inconclusive, inconclusively	conclude
101	concurrent	concurrently	concurrent
102	conduct	conducted, conducting, conducts	conduct
103	confer	*conference,* conferences, conferred, conferring, confers	confer
104	confine	*confined*, confines, confining, unconfined	confine
105	confirm	confirmation, *confirmed*, confirming, confirms	confirm
106	conflict	conflicted, conflicting, conflicts	conflict

107	conform	conformable, conformability, conformance, conformation, conformed, conforming, conformist, conformists, *conformity*, conforms, nonconformist, nonconformists, nonconformity, non-conformist, non-conformists, non-conformity	conform
108	consent	consensus, consented, consenting, consents	consent
109	consequent	consequence, *consequences*, consequently	consequent
110	considerable	considerably	considerable
111	consist	consisted, consistency, *consistent*, consistently, consisting, consists, inconsistencies, inconsistency, inconsistent	consist
112	constant	constancy, constantly, constants, inconstancy, inconstantly	constant
113	constitute	constituencies, constituency, constituent, constituents, constituted, constitutes, constituting, constitution, constitutions, *constitutional*, constitutionally, constitutive, unconstitutional	constitute
114	constrain	constrained, constraining, constrains, constraint, *constraints*, unconstrained	constrain
115	construct	constructed, constructing, *construction*, constructions, constructive, constructs, reconstruct, reconstructed, reconstructing, reconstruction, reconstructs	construct
116	consult	consultancy, consultant, consultants, *consultation,* consultations, consultative, consulted, consults, consulting	consult
117	consume	consumed, *consumer,* consumers, consumes, consuming, consumption	consume
118	contact	contactable, contacted, contacting, contacts	contact
119	contemporary	contemporaries	contemporary

120	**context**	contexts, contextual, contextualize, contextualized, contextualizing, uncontextualized	**context**
121	**contract**	contracted, contracting, contractor, contractors, contracts	**contract**
122	**contradict**	contradicted, contradicting, *contradiction*, contradictions, contradictory, contradicts	**contradict**
123	**contrary**	contrarily	**contrary**
124	**contrast**	contrasted, contrasting, contrastive, contrasts	**contrast**
125	**contribute**	contributed, contributes, contributing, *contribution*, contributions, contributor, contributors	**contribute**
126	**controversy**	controversies, controversial, controversially, uncontroversial	**controversy**
127	**convene**	*convention*, convenes, convened, convening, conventional, conventionally, conventions, unconventional	**convene**
128	**converse**	*conversely*	**converse**
129	**convert**	conversion, conversions, *converted*, convertible, converting, converts	**convert**
130	**convince**	*convinced*, convinces, convincing, convincingly, unconvinced	**convince**
131	**cooperate**	cooperated, cooperates, cooperating, cooperation, *cooperative*, cooperatively, co-operate, co-operated, co-operates, co-operation, co-operative, co-operatively	**cooperate**
132	**coordinate**	coordinated, coordinates, coordinating, *coordination*, coordinator, coordinators, co-ordinate, co-ordinated, co-ordinates, co-coordinating, co-ordination, co-coordinator, co-coordinators	**coordinate**
133	**core**	cores, coring, cored	**core**
134	**corporate**	corporates, corporation, corporations	**corporate**

135	**correspond**	corresponded, correspondence, *corresponding*, correspondingly, corresponds	**correspond**
136	**couple**	coupled, coupling, couples	**couple**
137	**create**	created, creates, creating, creation, creations, creative, creatively, creativity, creator, creators, recreate, recreated, recreates, recreating	**create**
138	**credit**	credited, crediting, creditor, creditors, credits	**credit**
139	**criteria**	criterion	**criteria**
140	**crucial**	crucially	**crucial**
141	**culture**	*cultural,* culturally, cultured, cultures, uncultured	**culture**
142	**currency**	currencies	**currency**
143	**cycle**	cycled, cycles, cyclic, cyclical, cycling	**cycle**
144	**data**		**data**
145	**debate**	debatable, debated, debates, debating	**debate**
146	**decade**	*decades*	**decade**
147	**decline**	declined, declines, declining	**decline**
148	**deduce**	deduced, deduces, deducing, *deduction*, deductions	**deduce**
149	**define**	definable, defined, defines, defining, *definition*, definitions, redefine, redefined, redefines, redefining, undefined	**define**
150	**definite**	definitely, definitive, indefinite, indefinitely	**definite**
151	**demonstrate**	demonstrable, demonstrably, demonstrated, demonstrates, demonstrating, demonstration, demonstrations, demonstrative, demonstratively, demonstrator, demonstrators	**demonstrate**
152	**denote**	denotation, denotations, denoted, denotes, denoting	**denote**
152	**deny**	deniable, denial, denials, denied, denies, denying, undeniable	**deny**

153	depress	depressed, depresses, depressing, *depression*	depress
154	derive	derivation, derivations, derivative, derivatives, *derived*, derives, deriving	derive
155	design	designed, designer, designers, designing, designs	design
156	despite		despite
157	detect	detectable, *detected*, detecting, detection, detective, detectives, detector, detectors, detects	detect
158	deviate	deviated, deviates, deviating, *deviation*, deviations	deviate
159	device	devices	device
160	devote	*devoted*, devotedly, devotes, devoting, devotion, devotions	devote
161	differentiate	differentiated, differentiates, differentiating, *differentiation*	differentiate
162	dimension	dimensional, *dimensions*, multidimensional	dimension
163	diminish	*diminished*, diminishes, diminishing, diminution, undiminished	diminish
164	discrete	discretely, *discretion*, discretionary, indiscrete, indiscretion	discrete
165	discriminate	discriminated, discriminates, discriminating, *discrimination*	discriminate
166	displace	displaced, *displacement*, displaces, displacing	displace
167	display	displayed, displaying, displays	display
168	dispose	disposable, *disposal,* disposed, disposes, disposing	dispose
169	distinct	*distinction*, distinctions, distinctive, distinctively, distinctly, indistinct, indistinctly	distinct
170	distort	*distorted*, distorting, distortion, distortions, distorts	distort

171	distribute	distributed, distributing, *distribution,* distributional, distributions, distributive, distributor, distributors, redistribute, redistributed, redistributes, redistributing, redistribution	distribute
172	diverse	diversely, diversification, diversified, diversifies, diversify, diversifying, *diversity*	diverse
173	document	documentation, documented, documenting, documents	document
174	domain	domains	domain
175	domestic	domestically, domesticate, domesticated, domesticating, domestics	domestic
176	dominate	dominance, *dominant,* dominated, dominates, dominating, domination	dominate
177	draft	drafted, drafting, drafts, redraft, redrafted, redrafting, redrafts	draft
178	drama	dramas, *dramatic,* dramatically, dramatize, dramatized, dramatizing, dramatizes, dramatization, dramatizations, dramatist, dramatists, dramatization, dramatizations, dramatizing	drama
179	duration		duration
180	dynamic	dynamically, dynamics	dynamic
181	economy	*economic,* economical, economically, economics, economies, economist, economists, uneconomical	economy
182	edit	edited, editing, *edition,* editions, editor, editorial, editorials, editors, edits	edit
183	element	*elements*	element
184	eliminate	eliminated, eliminates, eliminating, elimination	eliminate
185	emerge	*emerged,* emergence, emergent, emerges, emerging	emerge
186	emphasis	emphasize, emphasized, emphasizing, emphatic, emphatically	emphasis

187	**empirical**	empirically, empiricism	**empirical**
188	**enable**	enabled, enables, enabling	**enable**
189	**encounter**	*encountered,* encountering, encounters	**encounter**
190	**energy**	energetic, energetically, energies	**energy**
191	**enforce**	enforced, *enforcement,* enforces, enforcing	**enforce**
192	**enhance**	*enhanced,* enhancement, enhances, enhancing	**enhance**
193	**enormous**	enormity, enormously	**enormous**
194	**ensure**	ensured, ensures, ensuring	**ensure**
195	**entity**	*entities*	**entity**
196	**environment**	environmental, environmentalist, environmentalists, environmentally, environments	**environment**
197	**equate**	equated, equates, equating, *equation,* equations	**equate**
198	**equip**	*equipment,* equipped, equipping, equips	**equip**
199	**equivalent**	equivalence	**equivalent**
200	**erode**	eroded, erodes, eroding, *erosion*	**erode**
201	**error**	erroneous, erroneously, errors	**error**
201	**establish**	disestablish, disestablished, disestablishes, disestablishing, disestablishment, *established,* establishes, establishing, establishment, establishments	**establish**
202	**estate**	estates	**estate**
203	**estimate**	estimated, estimates, estimating, estimation, estimations, over-estimate, overestimate, overestimated, overestimates, overestimating, underestimate, underestimated, underestimates, underestimating	**estimate**
204	**ethic**	*ethical,* ethically, ethics, unethical	**ethic**
205	**ethnic**	ethnicity	**ethnic**

206	**evaluate**	evaluated, evaluates, evaluating, *evaluation*, evaluations, evaluative, re-evaluate, re-evaluated, re-evaluates, re-evaluating, re-evaluation	**evaluate**
207	**eventual**	eventuality, *eventually*	**eventual**
208	**evident**	evidenced, *evidence*, evidential, evidently	**evident**
209	**evolve**	*evolution*, evolved, evolving, evolves, evolutionary, evolutionist, evolutionists	**evolve**
210	**exceed**	exceeded, exceeding, exceeds	**exceed**
211	**exclude**	*excluded*, excludes, excluding, exclusion, exclusionary, exclusionist, exclusions, exclusive, exclusively	**exclude**
212	**exhibit**	exhibited, exhibiting, exhibition, exhibitions, exhibits	**exhibit**
213	**expand**	expanded, expanding, expands, *expansion*, expansionism, expansive	**expand**
214	**expert**	expertise, expertly, experts	**expert**
215	**explicit**	explicitly	**explicit**
216	**exploit**	*exploitation*, exploited, exploiting, exploits	**exploit**
217	**export**	exported, exporter, exporters, exporting, exports	**export**
218	**expose**	exposed, exposes, exposing, *exposure*, exposures	**expose**
219	**external**	externalization, externalize, externalized, externalizes, externalizing, externality	**external**
220	**extract**	extracted, extracting, extraction, extracts	**extract**
221	**facilitate**	facilitated, facilitates, facilities, facilitating, facilitation, facilitator, facilitators, facility	**facilitate**
222	**factor**	factored, factoring, *factors*	**factor**
223	**feature**	featured, *features,* featuring	**feature**
224	**federal**	federation, federations	**federal**
225	**fee**	*fees*	**fee**

226	file	filed, files, filing	file
227	final	finalize, finalized, finalizes, finalizing, finality, finally, finals	final
228	finance	financed, finances, *financial*, financially, financier, financiers, financing	finance
229	finite	infinite, infinitely	finite
230	flexible	*flexibility,* inflexible, inflexibility	flexible
231	fluctuate	fluctuated, fluctuates, fluctuating, fluctuation, *fluctuations*	fluctuate
235	focus	focused, focuses, focusing, refocus, refocused, refocuses, refocusing	focus
236	format	formatted, formatting, formats	format
237	formula	formulae, formulas, formulate, formulated, formulating, formulation, formulations, reformulate, reformulated, reformulating, reformulation, reformulations	formula
238	forthcoming		forthcoming
239	found	*founded,* founder, founders, founding, unfounded	found
240	foundation	foundations	foundation
241	framework	frameworks	framework
242	function	functional, functionally, functioned, functioning, functions	function
243	fund	funded, funder, funders, funding, *funds*	fund
245	fundamental	fundamentally	fundamental
246	furthermore		furthermore
247	gender	genders	gender
248	generate	*generated,* generates, generating	generate
249	generation	generations	generation
250	globe	*global*, globally, globalization, globalization	globe
251	goal	*goals*	goal
252	grade	graded, grades, grading	grade
253	grant	*granted,* granting, grants	grant
253	guarantee	guaranteed, guaranteeing, guarantees	guarantee
254	guideline	*guidelines*	guideline

256	hence		hence
256	hierarchy	*hierarchical*, hierarchies	hierarchy
257	highlight	*highlighted*, highlighting, highlights	highlight
258	hypothesis	hypotheses, hypothesize, hypothesized, hypothesizes, hypothesizing, hypothetical, hypothetically	hypothesis
259	identical	identically	identical
260	identify	identifiable, identification, *identified*, identifies, identifying, identities, identity, unidentifiable	identify
261	ideology	ideological, ideologically, ideologies	ideology
262	ignorant	ignorance, ignore, *ignored*, ignores, ignoring	ignorant
263	illustrate	*illustrated*, illustrates, illustrating, illustration, illustrations, illustrative	illustrate
264	image	imagery, images	image
265	immigrate	immigrant, immigrants, immigrated, immigrates, immigrating, *immigration*	immigrate
266	impact	impacted, impacting, impacts	impact
267	implement	*implementation*, implemented, implementing, implements	implement
268	implicate	implicated, implicates, implicating, implication, *implications*	implicate
269	implicit	implicitly	implicit
270	imply	implied, *implies*, implying	imply
271	impose	*imposed*, imposes, imposing, imposition	impose
272	incentive	incentives	incentive
273	incidence	incident, incidentally, incidents	incidence
274	incline	*inclination*, inclinations, inclined, inclines, inclining	incline
275	income	incomes	income
276	incorporate	*incorporated*, incorporates, incorporating, incorporation	incorporate
277	index	indexed, indexes, indexing	index

278	**indicate**	indicated, indicates, indicating, indication, indications, indicative, indicator, indicators	**indicate**
279	**individual**	individualized, individuality, individualism, individualist, individualists, individualistic, individually, individuals	**individual**
280	**induce**	*induced*, induces, inducing, induction	**induce**
281	**inevitable**	inevitability, *inevitably*	**inevitable**
282	**infer**	inference, inferences, *inferred*, inferring, infers	**infer**
283	**infrastructure**	infrastructures	**infrastructure**
284	**inherent**	inherently	**inherent**
285	**inhibit**	inhibited, inhibiting, *inhibition*, inhibitions, inhibits	**inhibit**
286	**initial**	initially	**initial**
286	**initiate**	initiated, initiates, initiating, initiation, initiations, initiative, *initiatives*, initiator, initiators	**initiate**
287	**injure**	injured, injures, injuries, injuring, *injury*, uninjured	**injure**
288	**innovate**	*innovation*, innovated, innovates, innovating, innovations, innovative, innovator, innovators	**innovate**
289	**input**	inputs	**input**
290	**insert**	inserted, inserting, insertion, inserts	**insert**
291	**insight**	insightful, *insights*	**insight**
292	**inspect**	inspected, inspecting, *inspection*, inspections, inspector, inspectors, inspects	**inspect**
293	**instance**	instances	**instance**
294	**institute**	instituted, institutes, instituting, institution, institutional, institutionalize, institutionalized, institutionalizes, institutionalizing, institutionally, institutions	**institute**
295	**instruct**	instruction, instructed, instructing, *instructions,* instructive, instructor, instructors, instructs	**instruct**

296	integral		integral
297	integrate	integrated, integrates, integrating, *integration*	integrate
298	integrity		integrity
299	intelligent	*intelligence*, intelligently, unintelligent	intelligent
300	intense	intensely, intenseness, intensification, intensified, intensifies, intensify, intensifying, intension, *intensity*, intensive, intensively	intense
301	interact	interacted, interacting, *interaction*, interactions, interactive, interactively, interacts	interact
302	intermediate		intermediate
303	internal	internalize, internalized, internalizes, internalizing, internally	internal
304	interpret	*interpretation*, interpretations, interpretative, interpreted, interpreting, interpretive, interprets, misinterpret, misinterpretation, misinterpretations, misinterpreted, misinterpreting, misinterprets, reinterpret, reinterpreted, reinterprets, reinterpreting, reinterpretation, reinterpretations	interpret
305	interval	intervals	interval
306	intervene	intervened, intervenes, intervening, *intervention,* interventions	intervene
307	intrinsic	intrinsically	intrinsic
308	invest	invested, investing, *investment*, investments, investor, investors, invests, reinvest, reinvested, reinvesting, reinvestment, reinvests	invest
309	investigate	investigated, investigates, investigating, *investigation*, investigations, investigative, investigator, investigators	investigate
310	invoke	*invoked*, invokes, invoking	invoke
311	involve	*involved*, involvement, involves, involving, uninvolved	involve

312	isolate	*isolated,* isolates, isolating, isolation, isolationism	isolate
313	issue	issued, *issues,* issuing	issue
314	item	itemization, itemize, itemized, itemizes, itemizing, *items*	item
315	job	jobs	job
316	journal	journals	journal
317	justify	justifiable, justifiably, *justification,* justifications, justified, justifies, justifying, unjustified	justify
318	label	labeled, labeling, labels	label
319	labour	labored, laboring, labors	labour
320	layer	layered, layering, layers	layer
321	lecture	lectured, lecturer, lecturers, lectures, lecturing	lecture
322	legal	illegal, illegality, illegally, legality, legally	legal
323	legislate	legislated, legislates, legislating, *legislation,* legislative, legislator, legislators, legislature	legislate
324	levy	levies	levy
325	liberal	liberalize, liberalism, liberalization, liberalized, liberalizes, liberalizing, liberalization, liberate, liberated, liberates, liberation, liberations, liberating, liberator, liberators, liberally, liberals	liberal
326	license	licenses, license, licensed, licensing, licenses, unlicensed	license
327	likewise		likewise
328	link	linkage, linkages, linked, linking, links	link
329	locate	located, locating, *location,* locations, relocate, relocated, relocates, relocating, relocation	locate
330	logic	illogical, illogically, logical, logically, logician, logicians	logic
331	maintain	maintained, maintaining, maintains, *maintenance*	maintain

332	major	majorities, majority	major
333	manipulate	manipulated, manipulates, manipulating, *manipulation,* manipulations, manipulative	**manipulate**
334	manual	manually, manuals	**manual**
335	margin	*marginal,* marginally, margins	**margin**
336	mature	immature, immaturity, maturation, maturational, matured, matures, maturing, maturity	**mature**
337	maximize	max, maximized, maximizes, maximizing, maximization, *maximum*	**maximize**
338	mechanism	mechanisms	**mechanism**
339	media		media
340	mediate	mediated, mediates, mediating, *mediation*	mediate
341	medical	medically	**medical**
342	medium		**medium**
343	mental	mentality, mentally	mental
344	method	methodical, methodological, methodologies, methodology, methods	method
345	migrate	migrant, migrants, migrated, migrates, migrating, *migration,* migrations, migratory	**migrate**
346	military		military
347	minimal	mineralization, minimalize, minimalizes, minimalized, minimalizing, minimalist, minimalists, minimalistic, minimally	minimal
348	minimize	*minimized,* minimizes, minimizing	**minimize**
349	minimum		**minimum**
350	ministry	ministered, ministering, ministerial, ministries	**ministry**
351	minor	*minorities,* minority, minors	**minor**
352	mode	modes	**mode**
353	modify	modification, modifications, *modified,* modifies, modifying, unmodified	**modify**

354	monitor	monitored, *monitoring,* monitors, unmonitored	monitor
355	motive	motivate, motivated, motivates, motivating, *motivation,* motivations, motives, unmotivated	motive
356	mutual	mutually	mutual
357	negate	*negative,* negated, negates, negating, negatively, negatives	negate
358	network	networked, networking, networks	network
359	neutral	neutralization, neutralize, neutralized, neutralizes, neutralizing, neutrality	neutral
360	nevertheless		nevertheless
361	nonetheless		nonetheless
362	norm	*norms*	norm
363	normal	abnormal, abnormally, normalization, normalize, normalized, normalizes, normalizing, normality, normally	normal
364	notion	notions	notion
365	notwithstanding		notwithstanding
366	nuclear		nuclear
367	objective	objectively, objectivity	objective
368	obtain	obtainable, *obtained,* obtaining, obtains, unobtainable	obtain
369	obvious	obviously	obvious
370	occupy	occupancy, occupant, occupants, occupation, *occupational,* occupations, occupied, occupier, occupiers, occupies, occupying	occupy
371	occur	occurred, occurrence, occurrences, occurring, occurs, reoccur, reoccurred, reoccurring, reoccurs	occur
372	odd	odds	odd
373	offset	offsets, offsetting	offset
374	ongoing		ongoing
375	option	optional, options	option
376	orient	orientate, orientated, orientates, *orientation,* orientating, oriented, orienting, orients, reorient, reorientation	orient

377	outcome	*outcomes*	outcome
378	output	outputs	output
379	overall		overall
380	overlap	overlapped, overlapping, overlaps	overlap
381	overseas		overseas
382	panel	paneled, paneling, panels	panel
383	paradigm	paradigms	paradigm
384	paragraph	paragraphing, paragraphs	paragraph
385	parallel	paralleled, parallels, unparalleled	parallel
386	parameter	*parameters*	parameter
387	participate	participant, participants, participated, participates, participating, *participation*, participatory	participate
388	partner	partners, *partnership*, partnerships	partner
389	passive	passively, passivity	passive
390	perceive	*perceived,* perceives, perceiving, perception, perceptions	perceive
391	percent	percentage, percentages	percent
392	period	periodic, periodical, periodically, periodicals, periods	period
393	persist	persisted, persistence, *persistent,* persistently, persisting, persists	persist
394	perspective	perspectives	perspective
395	phase	phased, phases, phasing	phase
396	phenomenon	phenomena, phenomenal	phenomenon
397	philosophy	philosopher, philosophers, philosophical, philosophically, philosophies, philosophize, philosophized, philosophizes, philosophizing	philosophy
398	physical	physically	physical
399	plus	pluses	plus
400	policy	policies	policy
401	portion	portions	portion
402	pose	*posed,* poses, posing	pose
403	positive	positively	positive
404	potential	potentially	potential
405	practitioner	*practitioners*	practitioner

406	precede	preceded, precedence, precedent, precedes, *preceding,* unprecedented	**precede**
407	precise	imprecise, precisely, precision	**precise**
408	predict	predictability, predictable, predictably, *predicted,* predicting, prediction, predictions, predicts, unpredictability, unpredictable	**predict**
409	predominant	predominance, *predominantly,* predominate, predominated, predominates, predominating	**predominant**
410	preliminary	preliminaries	**preliminary**
411	presume	presumably, presumed, presumes, presuming, *presumption,* presumptions, presumptuous	**presume**
412	previous	previously	**previous**
413	primary	primarily	**primary**
414	prime	primacy	**prime**
415	principal	principally	**principal**
416	principle	principled, principles, unprincipled	**principle**
417	prior		**prior**
418	priority	priorities, prioritization, prioritize, prioritized, prioritizes, prioritizing	**priority**
419	proceed	procedural, *procedure,* procedures, proceeded, proceeding, proceedings, proceeds	**proceed**
420	process	processed, processes, processing	**process**
421	professional	professionally, professionals, professionalism	**professional**
422	prohibit	*prohibited,* prohibiting, prohibition, prohibitions, prohibitive, prohibits	**prohibit**
423	project	projected, projecting, projection, projections, projects	**project**
424	promote	promoted, promoter, promoters, promotes, promoting, promotion, promotions	**promote**
425	proportion	disproportion, disproportionate, disproportionately, proportional, proportionally, proportionate, proportionately, proportions	**proportion**

426	**prospect**	prospective, prospects	**prospect**
427	**protocol**	protocols	**protocol**
428	**psychology**	psychological, psychologically, psychologist, psychologists	**psychology**
429	**publication**	publications	**publication**
430	**publish**	*published,* publisher, publishers, publishes, publishing, unpublished	**publish**
431	**purchase**	purchased, purchaser, purchasers, purchases, purchasing	**purchase**
432	**pursue**	pursued, pursues, pursuing, pursuit, pursuits	**pursue**
433	**qualitative**	qualitatively	**qualitative**
434	**quote**	*quotation,* quotations, quoted, quotes, quoting	**quote**
435	**radical**	radically, radicals	**radical**
436	**random**	randomly, randomness	**random**
437	**range**	ranged, ranges, ranging	**range**
437	**ratio**	ratios	**ratio**
438	**rational**	irrational, rationalization, rationalizations, rationalize, rationalized, rationalizes, rationalizing, rationalism, rationality, rationally	**rational**
439	**react**	reacted, reacts, reacting, *reaction,* reactionaries, reactionary, reactions, reactive, reactivate, reactivation, reactor, reactors	**react**
440	**recover**	recoverable, recovered, recovering, recovers, *recovery*	**recover**
441	**refine**	refined, refinement, refinements, refines, refining	**refine**
442	**regime**	regimes	**regime**
443	**region**	regional, regionally, regions	**region**
444	**register**	deregister, deregistered, deregistering, deregisters, deregistration, *registered,* registering, registers, registration	**register**

445	regulate	deregulated, deregulates, deregulating, deregulation, regulated, regulates, regulating, regulation,regulations, regulator, regulators, regulatory, unregulated	regulate
446	reinforce	*reinforced*, reinforcement, reinforcements, reinforces, reinforcing	reinforce
447	reject	*rejected,* rejecting, rejection, rejects, rejections	reject
448	relax	relaxation, *relaxed*, relaxes, relaxing	relax
449	release	released, releases, releasing	release
450	relevant	irrelevance, irrelevant, relevance	relevant
451	reluctance	*reluctant*, reluctantly	reluctance
452	rely	reliability, reliable, reliably, *reliance*, reliant, relied, relies, relying, unreliable	rely
453	remove	removable, removal, removals, *removed*, removes, removing	remove
454	require	*required*, requirement, requirements, requires, requiring	require
455	research	researched, researcher, researchers, researches, researching	research
456	reside	resided, residence, *resident*, residential, residents, resides, residing	reside
457	resolve	*resolution,* resolved, resolves, resolving, unresolved	resolve
458	resource	resourced, resourceful, *resources*, resourcing, unresourceful, under-resourced	resource
459	respond	responded, respondent, respondents, responding, responds, *response*, responses, responsive, responsiveness, unresponsive	respond
460	restore	restoration, restored, restores, restoring	restore
461	restrain	restrained, restraining, restrains, restraint, *restraints*, unrestrained	restrain

462	restrict	*restricted,* restricting, restriction, restrictions, restrictive, restrictively, restricts, unrestricted, unrestrictive	restrict
463	retain	*retained,* retaining, retainer, retainers, retains, retention, retentive	retain
464	reveal	*revealed,* revealing, reveals, revelation, revelations	reveal
465	revenue	revenues	revenue
466	reverse	reversal, reversed, reverses, reversible, reversing, reversals, irreversible	reverse
467	revise	revised, revises, revising, *revision,* revisions	revise
468	revolution	revolutionary, revolutionaries, revolutionize, revolutionized, revolutionizes, revolutionizing, revolutionist, revolutionists, revolutions	revolution
469	rigid	rigidities, rigidity, rigidly	rigid
470	role	roles	role
471	route	routed, routes, routing	route
472	scenario	scenarios	scenario
473	schedule	reschedule, rescheduled, reschedules, rescheduling, scheduled, schedules, scheduling, unscheduled	schedule
474	scheme	schematic, schematically, schemed, schemes, scheming	scheme
475	scope		scope
476	section	sectioned, sectioning, sections	section
477	sector	sectors	sector
478	secure	insecure, insecurities, insecurity, secured, securely, secures, securing, securities, *security*	secure
479	seek	seeking, seeks, *sought*	seek
480	select	selected, selecting, selection, selections, selective, selectively, selector, selectors, selects	select
481	sequence	sequenced, sequences, sequencing, sequential, sequentially	sequence

482	series		series
483	sex	sexes, sexism, sexual, sexuality, sexually	sex
484	shift	shifted, shifting, shifts	shift
485	significant	insignificant, insignificantly, significance, significantly, signified, signifies, signify, signifying	significant
486	similar	dissimilar, similarities, similarity, similarly	similar
487	simulate	simulated, simulates, simulating, *simulation*	simulate
488	site	sites	site
489	so-called		so-called
490	sole	*solely*	sole
491	somewhat		somewhat
492	source	sourced, sources, sourcing	source
493	specific	specifically, specification, specifications, specificity, specifics	specific
494	specify	specifiable, *specified,* specifies, specifying, unspecified	specify
495	sphere	spheres, spherical, spherically	sphere
496	stable	instability, stabilization, stabilize, stabilized, stabilizes, stabilizing, *stability,* unstable	stable
497	statistic	statistician, statisticians, statistical, statistically, *statistics*	statistic
498	status		status
499	straightforward		straightforward
500	strategy	strategic, *strategies,* strategically, strategist, strategists	strategy
501	stress	stressed, stresses, stressful, stressing, unstressed	stress
502	structure	restructure, restructured, restructures, restructuring, structural, structurally, structured, structures, structuring, unstructured	structure
503	style	styled, *styles,* styling, stylish, stylize, stylized, stylizes, stylizing	style

504	submit	submission, submissions, submits, *submitted*, submitting	submit
505	subordinate	subordinates, subordination	subordinate
506	subsequent	subsequently	subsequent
507	subsidy	*subsidiary*, subsidies, subsidize, subsidized, subsidizes, subsidizing	subsidy
508	substitute	substituted, substitutes, substituting, *substitution*	substitute
509	successor	succession, successions, *successive*, successively, successors	successor
510	sufficient	sufficiency, insufficient, insufficiently, sufficiently	sufficient
511	sum	summation, summed, summing, sums	sum
512	summary	summaries, summarize, summarized, summarizes, summarizing, summarization, summarizations	summary
513	supplement	*supplementary*, supplemented, supplementing, supplements	supplement
514	survey	surveyed, surveying, surveys	survey
515	survive	survival, survived, survives, surviving, survivor, survivors	survive
516	suspend	*suspended*, suspending, suspends, suspension	suspend
517	sustain	*sustainable*, sustainability, sustained, sustaining, sustains, sustenance, unsustainable	sustain
518	symbol	***symbolic,*** symbolically, symbolize, symbolizes, symbolized, symbolizing, symbolism, symbols	symbol
519	tape	taped, *tapes*, taping	tape
520	target	targeted, targeting, targets	target
521	task	tasks	task
522	team	teamed, teaming, teams	team
523	technical	technically	technical
524	technique	*techniques*	technique
525	technology	technological, technologically	technology
526	temporary	temporarily	temporary

527	tense	*tension*, tensely, tenser, tensest, tensions	tense
528	terminate	terminal, terminals, terminated, terminates, terminating, *termination*, terminations	terminate
529	text	texts, textual	text
530	theme	themes, thematic, thematically	theme
531	theory	theoretical, theoretically, theories, theorist, theorists	theory
532	thereby		thereby
533	thesis	theses	thesis
534	topic	topical, topics	topic
535	trace	traceable, traced, traces, tracing	trace
536	tradition	non-traditional, *traditional*, traditionalist, traditionally, traditions	tradition
537	transfer	transferable, transference, transferred, transferring, transfers	transfer
538	transform	*transformation*, transformations, transformed, transforming, transforms	transform
539	transit	transited, transiting, *transition*, transitional, transitions, transitory, transits	transit
540	transmit	*transmission*, transmissions, transmitted, transmitting, transmits	transmit
541	transport	transportation, transported, transporter, transporters, transporting, transports	transport
542	trend	trends	trend
543	trigger	triggered, triggering, triggers	trigger
544	ultimate	*ultimately*	ultimate
545	undergo	undergoes, undergoing, undergone, underwent	undergo
546	underlie	underlay, underlies, *underlying*	underlie
547	undertake	*undertaken,* undertakes, undertaking, undertook	undertake
548	uniform	uniformity, uniformly	uniform
549	unify	unification, *unified*, unifies, unifying	unify
550	unique	uniquely, uniqueness	unique

551	utilize	utilization, utilized, utilizes, utilizing, utilizer, utilizers, *utility*, utilities	utilize
552	valid	invalidate, invalidity, validate, validated, validating, validation, *validity*, validly	valid
553	vary	invariable, invariably, variability, variable, *variables,* variably, variance, variant, variants, variation, variations, varied, varies, varying	vary
554	vehicle	vehicles	vehicle
555	version	versions	version
556	via		via
557	vein		
558	violate	violated, violates, violating, *violation*, violations	violate
559	virtual	*virtually*	virtual
560	visible	visibility, visibly, invisible, invisibility	visible
561	vision	visions	vision
562	visual	visualize, visualized, visualized, visualizing, visualization, visually	visual
563	volume	volumes, vol.	volume
564	voluntary	voluntarily, volunteer, volunteering, volunteered, volunteers	voluntary
565	Vertical		
566	Velocity		
567	welfare		welfare
568	whereas		whereas
569	whereby		whereby
570	widespread		widespread
571	Withdraw		
572	Ex-ray		

3 UNIVERSITY WORD LIST

The University Word List (UWL) is a list of vocabulary items common in academic texts. It is composed of 808 words, divided into 11 levels. This list is designed to be a list of specialized vocabulary for students who know about 2,000 generally common words and plan to study in an English-language college or university. Think of it as the most common 800 words in academic texts excluding the 2,000 words of the General Service List (GSL) (West, 1953). This list is linked to the GSL. If students study the GSL, followed by the UWL, there should be no repetition.

The list is divided into 11 levels. Level 1 has the greatest frequency and range, level 2 next, etc. The occurrences of the words of the first three levels is about half of the total occurrences of the entire list. Nation (1990 p.19) estimates that the words on this list account for 8% of the words in a typical academic text.

This list was first published in 1984 (Xue and Nation). A new version has been published and is called the Academic Word List (AWL).

University Word List

Level 1

No	Word	Meaning / synonym	No	Word	Meaning / synonym
1	Alternative	other, substitute	8	compensate	recompense, pay
2	analyze	study, evaluate	9	complex	complicated, intricate
3	approach	confront, reach out	10	comply	obey, submit
4	arbitrary	random, casual	11	component	piece, element
5	assess	consider, evaluate	12	concept	idea, thought
6	assign	give, ascribe	13	conclude	settle, close
7	assume	guess,	14	consist	comprise, involve

No	Word	Meaning / synonym	No	Word	Meaning / synonym
15	constant	continuous, endless	49	magnitude	size, extent
16	construct	build, create	50	method	manner, technique
17	consult	refer, check	51	minimum	least, smallest
18	contact	communicate, talk	52	modify	change, adjust
19	context	setting, situation	53	negative	bad, undesirable
20	criterion	measure, standard	54	obvious	clear, apparent
21	data	information, facts	55	potential	conceivable, possible
22	define	describe, explain	56	presume	imagine, assume
23	definite	certain, fixed	57	prime	key, major
24	denote	indicate, represent	58	proceed	continue, progress
25	derive	originate, arise	59	publish	issue, distribute
26	devise	develop, plan	60	pursue	follow, chase
27	dimension	measurement	61	random	accidental, chance
28	distinct	different, individual	62	range	compass, collection
29	element	part, component	63	region	area, section
30	environment	setting, atmosphere	64	require	need, entail
31	equate	associate, compare	65	restrict	limit, control
32	equivalent	same, corresponding	66	reverse	opposite, contrary
33	establish	start, form	67	role	character, job
34	evaluate	analyze, assess	68	similar	alike, related
35	evident	obvious, apparent	69	specify	state, identify
36	formulate	communicate, convey	70	status	position, standing
37	guarantee	promise, pledge	71	subsequent	following, ensuing
38	hypothesis	theory, guess	72	suffice	serve, adequate
39	identify	classify, recognize	73	sum	amount, quantity
40	ignore	disregard, overlook	74	summary	concise, abridgment
41	illustrate	demonstrate, show	75	technique	method, procedure
42	impact	influence, effect	76	tense	nervous, anxious
43	implicit	implied, unspoken	77	ultimate	final, last
44	imply	suggest, indicate	78	usage	practice, tradition
45	indicate	suggest, point to	79	valid	useable, effective
46	initial	first, original	80	vary	differ, fluctuate
47	interpret	understand, deduce	81	vertical	upright
48	involve	contain, include			

Level 2

No	Word	Meaning / synonym	No	Word	Meaning / synonym
1	Accelerate	hurry, quicken	36	focus	emphasis, center
2	achieve	accomplish, attain	37	function	purpose, role
3	adjacent	together, neighboring	38	generate	make, create
4	affect	move, influence	39	individual	separate, distinct
5	approximate	estimate, guess	40	infer	assume, conclude
6	assert	proclaim, emphasize	41	inhibit	hinder, prevent
7	authorize	allow, approve	42	innovation	advancement
8	automatic	involuntary, reflex	43	intense	strong, powerful
9	aware	conscious, mindful	44	intuitive	instinctive
10	chapter	section, part	45	isolate	separate, detach
11	complicate	confuse, thwart	46	magnetic	attractive, compelling
12	comprehend	understand, follow	47	major	main, chief
13	conceive	consider, imagine	48	manipulate	use, control
14	concentrate	think, ponder	49	mathematics	math
15	consequent	resulting, following	50	mature	develop, grow
16	contrast	difference, distinction	51	notion	idea, belief
17	contribute	pay, add	52	obtain	get, acquire
18	convert	change, alter	53	occur	happen, ensue
19	create	make, generate	54	passive	inactive, inert
20	crucial	vital, critical	55	period	era, age
21	decade	period, era	56	perspective	viewpoint, outlook
22	demonstrate	show, prove	57	pertinent	relevant, appropriate
23	design	strategy, plan	58	phase	stage, segment
24	devote	dedicate, give	59	phenomena	marvel, spectacle
25	distort	misrepresent, twist	60	portion	percentage, share
26	emphasize	accentuate, highlight	61	precede	lead, come before
27	empirical	observed, realistic	62	precise	detailed, accurate
28	ensure	guarantee, warrant	63	principle	standard, norm
29	entity	being, individual	64	react	respond, answer
30	equilibrium	balance, stability	65	respective	corresponding
31	expand	enlarge, increase	66	section	segment, piece
32	expose	show, uncover	67	segment	section, part
33	external	outer, exterior	68	select	choose, pick
34	feasible	possible, viable	69	sequence	order, arrangement
35	fluctuate	vary, change	70	series	successions

No	Word	Meaning / synonym	No	Word	Meaning / synonym
71	shift	change, move	79	technology	equipment
72	signify	indicate, show	80	theory	idea, hypothesis
73	simultaneous	concurrent	81	trace	hint, suggestion
74	sophisticated	refined, urbane	82	tradition	ritual, practice
75	species	class, type	83	transmit	spread, convey
76	stable	steady, constant	84	undergo	experience, feel
77	statistic	measurement, figure	85	verbal	spoken, vocal
78	structure	building	86	verify	confirm, prove

Level 3

No	Word	Meaning / synonym	No	Word	Meaning / synonym
1	Abandon	leave, isolate	25	discrete	isolated, distinct
2	accomplish	achieve, complete	26	disperse	scatter, disband
3	adapt	adjust, familiarize	27	dispose	arrange, classify
4	adequate	sufficient, acceptable	28	drama	play, performance
5	adjust	modify, amend	29	dynamic	lively, energetic
6	appreciate	esteem, value	30	economy	wealth, management
7	appropriate	proper, suitable	31	estimate	guess, approximation
8	area	part, region	32	exclude	ignore, dismiss
9	attitude	outlook, approach	33	exert	apply, utilize
10	chemical	substance	34	explicit	clear, obvious
11	circumstance	condition, situation	35	exploit	deed, adventure
12	classic	model, standard	36	factor	aspect, cause
13	commune	collective	37	feature	article, piece
14	conduct	behavior, manner	38	final	last, concluding
15	conflict	struggle, battle	39	geography	layout, characteristics
16	consume	eat, devour	40	image	picture, appearance
17	convene	assemble, organize	41	intellect	intelligence
18	coordinate	organize, manage	42	intelligent	clever, bright
19	correspond	agree, relate	43	issue	problem, concern
20	credible	trustworthy, reliable	44	labor	work, toil
21	critic	judge	45	maintain	uphold, preserve
22	dedicate	commit, give	46	manifest	obvious, apparent
23	deficient	incomplete, lacking	47	maximum	full, supreme
24	deviate	diverge, stray	48	motive	reason, cause

No	Word	Meaning / synonym	No	Word	Meaning / synonym
49	network	system, set-up	63	relevance	significance
50	norm	custom, model	64	rely	trust, depend
51	notate	write, construct	65	reveal	disclose, expose
52	occupy	inhabit, reside	66	rotate	alternate, revolve
53	orientate	position, place	67	satellite	separate, unrelated
54	physical	bodily, corporeal	68	scheme	plan, arrangement
55	plot	plan, scheme	69	seek	pursue, find
56	pole	stick	70	source	basis, foundation
57	positive	optimistic, confident	71	superficial	shallow, artificial
58	preposition		72	task	job, chore
59	prestige	respect, status	73	transition	change, shift
60	previous	preceding, former	74	underlie	motivate, cause
61	proprietor	owner, manager	75	visual	graphic, pictoral
62	rational	balanced, normal			

Level 4

No	Word	Meaning / synonym	No	Word	Meaning / synonym
1	Acquire	obtain, get	19	constitute	establish, create
2	administer	manage, control	20	contaminate	pollute, infect
3	aesthetic	visual, appealing	21	contradict	deny, oppose
4	allege	claim, assert	22	culture	philosophy, nation
5	allocate	allot, assign	23	dedicate	devote, give
6	alter	change, modify	24	denominator	
7	analogy	similarity, correlation	25	dense	thick, solid
8	appraise	assess, evaluate	26	diagram	drawing, illustration
9	assemble	collect, accumulate	27	discourse	speech, dialogue
10	assure	promise, guarantee	28	distribute	allocate, dispense
11	atmosphere	air, sky	29	diverse	varied, assorted
12	atom	particle, bit	30	dominate	control, govern
13	attribute	trait, characteristic	31	elaborate	extravagant
14	avail	gain, benefit	32	eliminate	remove, exclude
15	axis	alliance, partnership	33	embody	exemplify, symbolize
16	bomb	mine, explosive	34	emotion	feeling, sentiment
17	capable	adept, skillful	35	energy	vigor, liveliness
18	cease	stop, finish	36	eventual	ultimate, final

No	Word	Meaning / synonym	No	Word	Meaning / synonym
37	forgo	relinquish, omit	59	predict	foresee, prophesy
38	fragment	piece, portion	60	project	plan, scheme
39	goal	aim, objective	61	proportion	amount, quantity
40	here	now	62	psychology	mindset, thinking
41	dirty	unclean, murky	63	reject	discard, scrap
42	impress	amaze, astonish	64	release	statement, publication
43	incident	event, occurrence	65	research	examination, study
44	incompatible	mismatched, unsuited	66	reservoir	pool, lake
45	induce	persuade, convince	67	revolt	rebellion, mutiny
46	integrate	mix, assimilate	68	speculate	guess, infer
47	internal	interior, center	69	sphere	range, scope
48	intervene	mediate, intercede	70	spontaneous	unplanned, impulsive
49	investigate	inspect, study	71	stipulate	require, specify
50	judicial	legal	72	subside	diminish, lessen
51	justify	validate, vindicate	73	subsidize	fund, support
52	litigate	sue, prosecute	74	superimpose	cover, overlay
53	logic	reason, sense	75	symbol	sign, representation
54	military	martial, army	76	tentative	uncertain, cautious
55	mobile	movable, portable	77	text	writing, manuscript
56	perpendicular	upright	78	theorem	formula, statement
57	persist	persevere, continue	79	upsurge	increase, rise
58	philosophy	viewpoint, idea			

Level 5

No	Word	Meaning / synonym	No	Word	Meaning / synonym
1	Absorb	attract, soak in	11	confront	face, tackle
2	abstract	intangible, theoretical	12	contract	agreement, bond
3	accurate	precise, exact	13	contrary	opposing, different
4	advocate	supporter, promoter	14	crisis	disaster, catastrophe
5	aid	help, assist	15	deny	reject, refute
6	biology	natural science	16	dictate	speak, state
7	category	group, class	17	diffuse	disperse, spread
8	client	customer, client	18	dispute	argument, conflict
9	code	rules, system	19	duration	length, extent
10	compound	mix, composite	20	edit	revise, correct

No	Word	Meaning / synonym	No	Word	Meaning / synonym
21	electron		46	perpetrate	commit, do
22	enlighten	inform, explain	47	preliminary	beginning, prelude
23	err	mistake, wrong	48	radius	
24	execute	perform, implement	49	respond	react, answer
25	expel	banish, eject	50	restore	return, repair
26	fraud	deception, scam	51	retain	hold, maintain
27	grant	donation, award	52	retard	slow, delay
28	graph	chart, diagram	53	rudimentary	basic, elementary
29	gravity	magnitube, severity	54	secure	safe, protected
30	homogeneous	uniform, consistent	55	stimulate	arouse, inspire
31	implement	apply, execute	56	stress	pressure, anxiety
32	impose	compel, force	57	style	mathod, manner
33	incorporate	include, integrate	58	subtle	slight, faint
34	insist	persist, maintain	59	superior	greater, advanced
35	institute	organization	60	supplement	complement, increase
36	instruct	teach, train	61	suppress	restrain, curb
37	intersect	cross, overlap	62	symptom	indication, sign
38	interval	gap, break	63	synthetic	artificial, fake
39	job	work, occupation	64	tiny	minute, small
40	kindred	relatives, family	65	trait	mannerism, feature
41	label	tag, mark	66	transfer	move, shift
42	legitimate	lawful, legal	67	transform	change, alter
43	objective	aim, purpose	68	trivial	small, unimportant
44	overlap	cross, intersect	69	vast	huge, enormous
45	parenthesis	addition, afterthought	70	version	account, description

Level 6

No	Word	Meaning / synonym	No	Word	Meaning / synonym
1	Abnormal	unusual, strange	8	arouse	stimulate, provoke
2	academic	educational, studious	9	aspect	feature, characteristic
3	accompany	attend, escort	10	assist	help, aid
4	adjective		11	attain	reach, achieve
5	adult	mature, grown	12	awe	fear, amazement
6	agitate	disturb, trouble	13	benefit	advantage, profit
7	appeal	plea, request	14	civic	public, local

No	Word	Meaning / synonym	No	Word	Meaning / synonym
15	clarify	explain, simplify	47	medium	average, intermediate
16	collide	crash, bump	48	metabolism	
17	comment	remark, observation	49	microscope	
18	commit	entrust, assign	50	minor	small, trivial
19	compute	calculate	51	nerve	courage, bravery
20	conform	accept, follow	52	niche	slot, position
21	conjunction	combination	53	oblige	compel, require
22	console	comfort, calm	54	participate	join, contribute
23	contemplate	consider, think	55	planet	earth, world
24	contend	compete, challenge	56	propagate	spread, broadcast
25	contingent	dependent, reliant	57	propensity	tendency, inclination
26	controversy	argument, conflict	58	prosper	thrive, flourish
27	converse	talk, communicate	59	protest	complain, dispute
28	cooperate	help, assist	60	radical	drastic, thorough
29	cycle	series, sequence	61	reign	control
30	decline	refuse, reject	62	reinforce	strengthen, support
31	degenerate	deteriorate, worsen	63	revise	amend, modify
32	doctrine	policy, principle	64	sanction	authorize, permit
33	extract	remove, extort	65	scalar	
34	fertile	lush, productive	66	strata	
35	found	establish, originate	67	subjective	personal, biased
36	hemisphere		68	sustain	maintain, uphold
37	hierarchy	order	69	tangent	departure
38	identical	equal, alike	70	terminology	language, jargon
39	incline	slant	71	tone	pitch, quality
40	income	wage, profit	72	topic	theme, subject
41	instinct	intuition, impulse	73	uniform	consistent, identical
42	interact	cooperate, relate	74	urban	metropolitan
43	interlock	join, intertwine	75	virtual	practical, effective
44	interlude	interval, break	76	volume	quantity, amount
45	legal	lawful, official	77	voluntary	unpaid, charitable
46	locate	place, position			

Level 7

No	Word	Meaning / synonym	No	Word	Meaning / synonym
1	Adolescent	youth, juvenile	36	incentive	reason, motivation
2	affiliate	associate, partner	37	incessant	non-stop, continual
3	affluence	wealth, prosperity	38	intermediate	halfway, middle
4	alcohol		39	invade	attack, assault
5	aristocrat	noble	40	inverse	opposite, contrary
6	astronomy		41	invoke	summon, appeal
7	cell	unit, compartment	42	migrate	travel, journey
8	collapse	fall, disintegrate	43	morphology	
9	colloquial	informal, spoken	44	muscle	force, strength
10	commodity	product, service	45	navy	fleet, armada
11	competence	capabitlity, aptitude	46	neutral	unbiased, impartial
12	concentric	circular	47	nutrient	
13	confer	talk, discuss	48	obsolete	outdated, archaic
14	configuration	pattern, design	49	odor	smell
15	congress	assembly	50	parliament	assembly, congress
16	conserve	preserve, save	51	peasant	
17	continent		52	plead	beg, implore
18	corporate	commercial, shared	53	policy	rule, strategy
19	creditor		54	pragmatic	practical, realistic
20	crystal	precious stone	55	precipitate	hurry, quicken
21	cumbersome	heavy, burdensome	56	prevail	triumph, succeed
22	defer	postpone, delay	57	prudence	caution, discretion
23	degrade	humiliate, shame	58	rectangle	four-sided
24	democracy		59	reform	modify, change
25	depress	sadden, demoralize	60	refute	disprove, counter
26	dissolve	melt, liquefy	61	repudiate	reject, deny
27	divine	heavenly, godly	62	revive	restore, renew
28	domestic	family, household	63	rhythm	beat, pace
29	ethics	principles, morals	64	saint	
30	finance	money, business	65	schedule	plan, agenda
31	fraction	part, portion	66	score	achieve, attain
32	friction	resistance, roughness	67	sibling	
33	fuse	combine, blend	68	sketch	draw, outline
34	geometry		69	sociology	
35	horror	dread, revulsion	70	spectrum	

No	Word	Meaning / synonym	No	Word	Meaning / synonym
71	stereotype	model	75	tissue	handkerchief
72	terror	fear, horror	76	transact	perform, conduct
73	texture	feel, surface	77	x-ray	
74	thermal				

Level 8

No	Word	Meaning / synonym	No	Word	Meaning / synonym
1	Adhere	follow, obey	29	launch	inauguration, start
2	aggregate	collective, total	39	legislate	enact, establish
3	aggression	violence, hostility	30	lens	viewpoint
4	align	arrange	31	liable	responsible
5	allude	indicate, mention	32	linguistic	verbal
6	ally	friend, partner	33	locomotion	movement, kinesis
7	bore	drag	34	magic	mystic, enchanted
8	bureaucracy	government	35	metaphor	symbol, imagery
9	cater	provide, supply	36	monarch	ruler, king
10	circulate	mingle, socialize	37	nuclear	atomic, fissionable
11	coincide	concur, overlap	38	oscillate	waver, hesitate
12	consent	agreement, accord	39	oxygen	
13	correlate	relate, associate	40	partisan	biased, opinionated
14	currency	money, cash	41	pendulum	swing
15	deprive	remove, deny	42	pervade	permeate, infiltrate
16	detect	notice, perceive	43	postulate	assume, guess
17	detriment	harm, loss	44	premise	evidence, principle
18	discern	recognize, separate	45	proclaim	announce, declare
19	dissipate	disperse, scatter	46	provoke	incite, aggravate
20	drug	medicine, remedy	47	rebel	insurgent
21	evolve	change, advance	48	reluctance	hesitancy
22	fallacy	mistake, delusion	49	reproduce	copy, duplicate
23	finite	limited, restricted	50	rigid	unbending, inelastic
24	fraternal	brotherly, friendly	51	secrete	conceal, hide
25	frustrate	aggravate, upset	52	sex	gender
26	imperial	grand, majestic	53	solar	planetary, lunar
27	index	directory, catalogue	54	spatial	
28	invest	finance, endow	55	subordinate	minor, inferior

No	Word	Meaning / synonym	No	Word	Meaning / synonym
56	supreme	highest, ultimate	59	trend	fashion, style
57	territory	land, area	60	utilize	use, employ
58	treaty	agreement, truce	61	utter	complete, absolute

Level 9

No	Word	Meaning / synonym	No	Word	Meaning / synonym
1	Acid	critical, harsh	24	indigenous	native, original
2	amorphous	formless, shapeless	25	innate	inborn, instinctive
3	ambiguity	doubt, uncertainty	26	integer	number, digit
4	asset	advantage, benefit	27	intrinsic	basic, essential
5	averse	opposed, hostile	28	liberate	free, unshackle
6	carbon		29	margin	boundary, border
7	complement	supplement, pair	30	material	physical, substantial
8	condense	abbreviate, shorten	31	matrix	environment
9	confine	restrain, limit	32	molecule	particle, bit
10	construe	interpret, understand	33	momentum	energy, motion
11	displace	move, shift	34	odd	strange, abnormal
12	diverge	deviate, wander	35	orbit	path, trajectory
13	drastic	radical, severe	36	residue	remainder
14	efficient	effective, capable	37	reverberate	echo, resound
15	enumerate	number, count	38	rural	countryside
16	evaporate	vanish, fade	39	stationary	still, inactive
17	evoke	remind, conjure	40	subdivide	split, partition
18	exhaust	drain, finish	41	suspend	postpone, delay
19	faction	group, side	42	unduly	improperly
20	federal	central, national	43	velocity	speed, rate
21	frontier	border, boundary	44	vibrate	shake, tremble
22	fund	trust, deposit	45	violate	disrupt, disturb
23	illuminate	light, brighten	46	vocabulary	language

Level 10

No	Word	Meaning / synonym	No	Word	Meaning / synonym
1	Access	admittance, entrance	35	fossil	remains, relic
2	angular	bony, thin	36	inconsistent	varying, unreliable
3	anomaly	abnormality, oddity	37	inflation	rise, increase
4	anonymous	nameless, unknown	38	ingenious	clever, inventive
5	anthropology		39	inherent	innate, natural
6	append	add, join	40	interrelate	connect, correlate
7	appendix	addition, supplement	41	interview	meeting, discussion
8	ascribe	assign, accredit	42	intimacy	closeness, confidence
9	aspiration	ambition, goal	43	maternal	motherly
10	assent	approval, acceptance	44	myth	legend, parable
11	assimilate	integrate, adapt	45	null	worthless, useless
12	auspices	support, patronage	46	option	choice, selection
13	clinic	hospital	47	outcome	consequence, result
14	coefficient	number	48	perpetual	continuous, lasting
15	cogent	forceful, persuasive	49	priority	precedence, urgency
16	comprise	include, encompass	50	procure	obtain, acquire
17	compulsion	urge, obligation	51	prohibit	forbid, ban
18	converge	join, unite	52	province	region, area
19	deflect	repel, rebound	53	purport	relevance, importance
20	deliberate	thoughtful, war	54	quote	costing, figure
21	dispense	distribute, allot	55	recur	persist, reappear
22	elevate	raise, lift	56	remove	eliminate, eradicate
23	elicit	prompt, stimulate	57	render	reduce, condense
24	eloquent	articulate, fluent	58	repress	curb, limit
25	emancipate	liberate, free	59	resident	inhabitant, local
26	embrace	hold, hug	60	rigor	precision, accuracy
27	emerge	arise, appear	61	saturate	soak, drench
28	enhance	improve, increase	62	skeleton	frame, carcass
29	enrich	improve, develop	63	surplus	access, additional
30	episode	incident, event	64	tangible	touchable, concrete
31	equidistant	central, middle	65	tolerate	accept, endure
32	exponent	supporter, promoter	66	triangle	trio
33	facilitate	enable, assist	67	vague	unclear, ambiguous
34	fluent	smooth, effortless			

Level 11

No	Word	Meaning / synonym	No	Word	Meaning / synonym
1	Accumulate	collect, amass	36	fulfill	achieve, accomplish
2	annual	yearly	37	fundamental	important, essential
3	apparatus	device, gadget	38	genuine	authentic, real
4	arithmetic	math	39	germ	origin, beginning
5	attach	join, fasten	40	harbor	port, dock
6	battery	series, set	41	hero	champion, star
7	breed	type, kind	42	hostile	aggressive
8	bubble	fizz, simmer	43	huge	large, massive
9	bulk	majority	44	import	significance
10	calendar		45	impulse	urge, whim
11	cancel	stop, withdraw	46	inferior	lower, substandard
12	capture	seize, arrest	47	injure	hurt, wound
13	career	job, occupation	48	inspect	examine, check
14	catalogue	list, index	49	instance	example, occasion
15	challenge	contest, defy	50	irrigate	water, dampen
16	channel	canal, passage	51	item	piece, article
17	circuit	route, track	52	journal	magazine, paper
18	column	pillar, post	53	laboratory	workshop
19	communicate	talk, converse	54	layer	cover, coating
20	compel	force, require	55	lecture	talk, address
21	cylinder	tube, pipe	56	leisure	freedom, relaxation
22	debate	discussion, argument	57	luxury	extravagance
23	decimal	number, unit	58	mental	psychological
24	defect	flaw, fault	59	moist	damp, wet
25	diameter	span, distance	60	novel	new, original
26	digest	summary	61	pest	annoyance, bother
27	drain	trench, ditch	62	pollution	contamination, fog
28	enable	allow, empower	63	port	harbor, haven
29	equipment	gear, tools	64	process	method, procedure
30	expert	professional, adept	65	ratio	proportion, percentage
31	export	spread, transfer	66	resource	supply, store
32	fare	tariff, charge	67	revolve	rotate, orbit
33	fate	destiny, fortune	68	route	direction, path
34	fluid	liquid, watery	69	shrink	contract, shrivel
35	fuel	energy	70	site	place, location

No	Word	Meaning / synonym	No	Word	Meaning / synonym
71	starve	famish	81	traffic	transportation
72	survey	study, review	82	transparent	clear, translucent
73	switch	change, shift	83	transport	conveyance
74	tape	adhesive	84	tropical	hot, humid
75	team	squad, crew	85	undertake	assume, start
76	telescope	minimize, reduce	86	vein	channel, pathway
77	temporary	brief, momentary	87	vital	energetic, vibrant
78	theft	robbery, burglary	88	volt	
79	tire	exhaust, fatigue	89	withdraw	remove, extract
80	tractor				

4 WORD FAMILIES

Introduction

Word families are groups of words that are closely (enough) related to each other to form a 'family'.

Word families can be created by grouping words in two main ways. This can be accomplished when:

a) they are similar in form: word - wordy - word (verb) - wording - word-list
   family - familiar - unfamiliar - familiarity – familiarize
b) their meanings are related: big – little: size ; dog – puppy: kennel

Why bother about word families?

Form-based families are important because sometimes they reveal hidden patterns of spelling as *ceive* (in receive, deceive, conceive), always corresponds to *ception* in the corresponding noun (re**ceive** - reception, de**ceive** - deception, con**ceive** – conception, per**ceive** - perception)

Meaning-based families are important because they reveal links and patterns of meaning in different words

An understanding of word families also allows either the form or the meaning of unfamiliar words to be guessed by identifying some relationship in their structure and patterns. Take for example the word, *skate-board*, we can guess that someone using a skate-board is a *skate-boarder* engaged in *skate-boarding*, and if we see the word untouchability we can guess from knowledge of other word families that it means 'state (**-ity**) of (**un-**) not being able to, **be** (-abil-) touched (touch).Thus, the state or condition of not being able to touch.

Form-based families

In the form-based word family in "teach" – "teacher", similarity of form is most easily explained by recognizing two morphemes in teach**er**: a root word which is also found in **teach**; and a **derivational suffix** (**er**) which is also found in other words such as lectur**er,** driv**er,** and learn**er.**

The family link can be shown through definitions: one word provides material out of which the other's definition is built (a teacher is a 'a person who teaches'). Similarly, a duckling is 'a small duck'; replaying is 'playing again', and so on.

Meaning-based families

Some words are closely related in meaning but not in form. For example, a female lion is a lioness, but a female dog is a bitch, while a male sheep is a ram and a female sheep is a ewe. The word families dog – bitch and sheep – ram – ewe are based solely on meaning, without the additional help provided by similarity of form as in lion – lioness.

Links that are based on meaning are far richer and more extensive than those based on form. Even the most straightforward-looking word, such as book, has a multitude of meaning-based links to other words:

BOOK: booklet, page, volume, journal, publication, author, publisher, title, edition, paper, cover, index, chapter, contents, novel, textbook, literature, literacy, bookseller, bookshop, bookshelf, library, read, write, consult, collect, bookworm (both meanings), bibliophile,…

As can be seen from this list, similarity of form supports a few of these links, namely those in which the related word also contains the root word **book**: textbook, bookseller, bookshop, bookshelf, and bookworm. The remaining links are no less clear or accessible for having no counterpart in form.

Meaning-based links are important for vocabulary growth, not just as an aid when guessing the meanings of new words, but also when strengthening existing vocabulary.

Noun-Based Word families:

Noun	Verb	Adjective	Adverb	Related Words
BEAUTY	beautify	beautiful	beautifully	beauteous
CRITIC	criticize	critical	critically	Criticism
DECOR	decorate	decorated / decorative	decoratively	Decorator, decoration
DRAMA	dramatize	dramatic	dramatically	Dramatist/ dramatization
GLORY	glorify	glorious	gloriously	Glorification, inglorious
HORROR	horrify	horrible	horribly , horrifying	Horrendous(ness)
LENGTH	lengthen	long / lengthy	Lengthily/ lengthwise	Lengthiness
COURAGE	encourage	Courageous	courageously	Encouragement / discourage
SYMPATHY	sympathize	sympathetic	sympathetically	Unsympathetic
DANGER	endanger	Dangerous	dangerously	Endangerment

Verb-Based Word families:

Verb	Noun	Adjective	Adverb	Related Words
ADD	addition	additional	additionally	addable, additive
ADMIRE	admiration	admirable	admirably	admirer
CHEER	cheerfulness	cheerful	cheerfully	cheerless , cheerleader
CREATE	creation	creative	creatively	creativity
DECIDE	decision	decisive	decisively	decisiveness, indecisive
INFORM	information	informative	informatively	uninformed
MOVE	movement	moveable, moving	movingly	motion
PLEASE	pleasure	pleasant, pleasing	pleasantly	displeasure, unpleasant
OBEY	obedience	obedient	obediently	disobedience
SATISFY	satisfaction	satisfactory	satisfactorily	unsatisfactory

Adjective-Based Word families:

Adjective	Noun	Verb	Adverb	Related Words
ABLE	ability	enable	ably	disability
ACTIVE	activity	activate	actively	activation
CLEAN	cleanliness	clean	cleanly	cleanse
DEEP	depth	deepen	deeply	deepening
FULL	fullness	fill	fully	filling. refill, fulfillment
HOT	heat	heat	hotly	heater
HIGH	height	heighten	highly	highness
PURE	purity	purify	purely	purification
SAFE	safety	save	safely	savior
SIMPLE	simplicity	simplify	simply	simplification

Word Families (by form)

   1. ab: cab dab gab jab tab crab drab
   2. ack: back hack Jack lack pack quack rack sack tack black clack crack knack shack slack smack snack stack track whack
   3. ad: bad tad glad fad clad dad brad had lad mad pad sad
   4. ag: bag gag hag jag lag nag sag tag rag wag brag drag snag flag
   5. ail: bail fail frail Gail hail jail mail nail quail rail sail snail tail trail wail
   6. ain: brain chain drain gain grain lain main pain plain rain Spain sprain stain strain train vain
   7. ake: bake brake cake drake fake flake Jake lake make rake shake nake stake take wake
   8. ale: bale Dale female gale inhale male pale sale scale stale tale whale
   9. all: ball call fall gall hall mall small stall tall wall
   10. am: am ham jam Pam Sam yam
   11. ame: became blame came dame fame flame frame game lame name nickname same shame tame
   12. an: ban bran can clan Dan fan flan Fran man pan plan tan than van
   13. and: and band bland brand grand hand land sand
   14. ank: bank blank clank crank dank drank flank Frank Hank lank prank plank rank sank shrank spank tank thank yank
   15. ap: apple cap chap clap flap gap happy lap map nap pap rap sap slap scrap snap strap trap wrap tap yap

16. **ar:**   are bar car far jar star

17. **ash:**   ash bash cash clash crash dash eyelash flash gash hash mash rash smash splash trash

18. **at:**   acrobat at bat brat cat chat doormat fat flat hat mat pat rat sat splat that

19. **ate:**   crate date gate grate hate Kate late locate Nate plate rate skate slate state

20. **aw:**   awful claw crawl draw drawing flaw gnaw jaw law paw raw saw straw strawberry

21. **ay:**   bay clay day gray hay pay play say spray stay stray sway today tray way

22. **eat:**   beat cheat eating heat heater meat meatball neat repeat seat treat wheat

23. **ed:**   bed Ed fed Fred led Ned red shed sled Ted wed

24. **ell:**   bell cell fell seashell sell shell smell spell tell well yell yellow

25. **en:**   Ben den hen Jen men pen ten then when yen

26. **est:**   best chest contest crest forest jest nest pest rest test vest west

27. **et:**   bet get jet let met net pet set wet yet

28. **ice:**   dice ice mice nice price rice slice spice twice

29. **ick:**   brick chick click kick lick pick sick slick stick trick

30. **ide:**   bride glide hide pride ride side slide stride tide wide

31. **ig:**   big dig fig gig jig pig rig twig wig

32. **ight:**   bright fight flight fright knight might night light right sight tight tonight

33. **ill:**   bill chill dill drill fill grill hill Jill mill pill quill shrill sill spill still thrill will

34. **in:**   bin chin fin grin in into kin pin shin skin spin thin tin twin

35. **ine:**   dine fine line mine nine pine vine shine spine whine

35. **ing:**   bing bring cling ding king ping ring sing spring sting swing thing wing zing

36. **ink:**   blink drink ink kink link rink sink stink think wink

37. **ip:**   chip clip dip drip flip grip hip lip nip rip ship sip skip snip strip tip trip whip zip

38. **it:**   bit fit hit it kit knit lit pit quit sit slit

39. **ock:**   block clock dock flock hock knock lock mock rock shock sock smock stock

40. **oke:**   broke Coke joke poke smoke spoke stroke woke yoke

41. **og:**   bog clog dog fog frog hog jog log smog

42. **old:**   bold cold fold gold hold mold sold told

43. **op:**   chop crop drop flop gumdrop hop mop pop shop stop top

44.ore: bore chore core lore more pore score shore snore tore wore
45. ot: cot dot got hot knot lot not pot shot spot
46. uck: buck Chuck cluck duck luck pluck stuck struck truck
47. ug: bug chug dug hug mug rug slug snug tug
48. um: chum drum glum gum hum plum strum sum swum yum
49. ump: bump clump dump grump jump lump mump pump stump thump
50. unk: bunk chunk dunk junk skunk stunk sunk trunk

5 GENERAL ROOTS AND PREFIXES

	Root or Prefix	Meaning	Examples
1	a, an	not, without	atheist, anarchy, anonymous apathy, aphasia, anemia, atypical, anesthesia
2	ab	away, down, from, off	absent, abduction, aberrant, abstemious, abnormal, abstract, absorb
3	acro	high, tip, top	acrobat, acrophobia, acronym, acromegaly, acropolis
4	act	do, move	action, react, transaction, proactive, activity, activation, deactivate
5	ad	to, toward	admit, addition, advertisement, adherent, admonish, address, adhesive, adept, adjust
6	alt	high	altitude, altimeter, alto, contralto, altocumulus, exalt
7	ambul	to walk	ambulatory, amble, ambulance, somnambulist, perambulate, preamble
8	anima	soul, life	animation, inanimate, animal, anime, equanimity, animism, animus
9	ante	before	anteroom, antebellum, antedate antecedent, antediluvian
10	anti, ant	against, opposite	antisocial, antiseptic, antithesis, antibody, antichrist, antinomies, antifreeze, antipathy, antigen, antibiotic, antidote, antifungal, antidepressant
11	arm	weapon	army, armament, disarm, rearm, armistice, armor, armory, arms
12	audi	to hear	audience, auditory, audible, auditorium, audiovisual, audition, audiobook
13	auto	self	automobile, automatic, autograph, autonomous, autoimmune, autopilot, autobiography

14	be	thoroughly	bedecked, besmirch, besprinkled, begrudge, begrime, belie, bemoan
15	bell	war	belligerent, antebellum, bellicose, rebel
16	bene	good, well	benefactor, beneficial, benevolent, benediction, beneficiary, benefit
17	bi	two	bicycle, bifocals, biceps, billion, binary, bivalve, bimonthly, bigamy, bimetal, biathlete, bicarbonate
18	bio	life, living	biology, biography, biodiversity, bioavailability, bioflavonoid, biofuel, biohazard, biomass, biorhythm
19	cede, ceed, cess	to go, to yield	succeed, proceed, precede, recede, secession, exceed, succession, excess
20	chron	time	chronology, chronic, chronicle, chronometer, anachronism
21	cide, cis	to kill, to cut	fratricide, suicide, incision, excision, circumcision, precise, concise, precision, homicide, genocide, regicide
22	circum	around	circumnavigate, circumflex, circumstance, circumcision, circumference, circumorbital, circumlocution, circumvent, circumscribe, circulatory
23	clud, clus claus	to close	include, exclude, clause, claustrophobia, enclose, exclusive, reclusive, conclude, preclude
24	con, com	with, together	convene, compress, contemporary, converge, compact, confluence, concatenate, conjoin, combine, convert, compatible, consequence, contract
25	contra, counter	against, opposite	contradict, counteract, contravene, contrary, counterspy, contrapuntal, contraband, contraception, contrast, controversy, counterfeit, counterclaim, counterargument, counterclaim, counterpoint, counterrevolution
26	cred	to believe	credo, credible, credence, credit, credential, credulity, incredulous, creed, incredible
27	commun	to share	commune, community, communism, communicable, communication, commonality, incommunicado
28	cycl	circle, wheel	bicycle, cyclical, cycle, encliclical, motorcycle, tricycle, cyclone

29	de	from, down, away	detach, deploy, derange, deodorize, devoid, 30deflate, degenerate, deice, descend, derail, depress, depart, decompose, destruction
30	dei, div	God, god	divinity, divine, deity, divination, deify, deism
31	demo	people	democracy, demagogue, epidemic, demographic, endemic
32	dia	through, across, between	diameter, diagonal, dialogue, dialect, dialectic, diagnosis, diachronic, diagram, diaphragm, dialysis, diarrhea
33	dict	speak	predict, verdict, malediction, dictionary, dictate, dictum, diction, indict, contradict
34	dis, dys, dif	away, not, negative	dismiss, differ, disallow, disperse, dissuade, disconnect, dysfunction, disproportion, disrespect, distemper, distaste, disarray, dyslexia
35	duc, duct	to lead, pull	produce, abduct, product, transducer, viaduct, aqueduct, induct, deduct, reduce, induce
36	dyn, dyna	power	dynamic, dynamometer, heterodyne, dynamite, dynamo, dynasty
37	ecto	outside, external	ectomorph, ectoderm, ectoplasm, ectopic, ectothermal
38	endo	inside, within	endotoxin, endoscope, endogenous
39	equi	equal	equidistant, equilateral, equilibrium, equinox, equitable, equation, equator
40	e, ex	out, away, from	emit, expulsion, exhale, exit, express, exclusive, enervate, exceed, explosion, eject, exude
41	eu	good, pleasant	euphoria, euphemism, eustress, euphonic, eukaryote
42	exter, extra	outside of	external, extrinsic, exterior, extraordinary, extrabiblical, extracurricular, extrapolate, extraneous, exterminator, extract, extradite, extraterrestrial, extrasensory, extravagant, extreme
43	flu, flux	flow	effluence, influence, effluvium, fluctuate, confluence, reflux, influx
44	flect, flex	to bend	flexible, reflection, deflect, circumflex, inflection, reflex
45	graph, gram	to write	polygraph, grammar, biography, graphite, telegram, autograph, lithograph, historiography, graphic, electrocardiogram, monogram

46	hetero	other	heterodox, heterogeneous, heterosexual, heterodyne
47	homo	same	homogenized, homosexual, homonym, homophone
48	hyper	over, above	hyperactive, hypertensive, hyperbolic, hypersensitive, hyperventilate, hyperkinetic, hyperlink, hypertext, hypersonic, hypertrophy
49	hypo	below, less than	hypotension, hypodermic, hypoglycemia, hypoallergenic, hypothermia, hypothesis
50	in, im	not	inviolate, innocuous, intractable, innocent, impregnable, impossible, incapable, incoherent, impassible, impotent
51	infra	beneath	infrared, infrastructure, infrasonic
52	inter, intro	between	international, intercept, intermission, interoffice, internal, intermittent, introvert, introduce
53	intra	within, into	intranet, intracranial, intravenous, intramural, intramuscular, intraocular
54	jac, ject	to throw	reject, eject, project, trajectory, interject, dejected, inject, ejaculate
55	log, logo, loc, loq	word, speech, speak	monologue, dialogue, locution, colloquial, elocution, soliloquy, ventriloquist, apology, doxology, epilogue, logic, eulogy, loquacious
56	mal	bad, badly	malformation, maladjusted, dismal, malady, malcontent, malfeasance, maleficent, malevolent, malice, malaria, malfunction, malignant
57	mega	great, million	megaphone, megalomaniac, megabyte, megalopolis, acromegaly
58	meso	middle	mesomorph, mesoamerica, mesosphere
59	meta	beyond, change	metaphor, metamorphosis, metabolism, metahistorical, metainformation, metacognitive, metaphysics
60	meter	measure	perimeter, micrometer, ammeter, multimeter, altimeter, geometry, kilometer
61	micro	small	microscope, microprocessor, microfiche, micrometer, micrograph
62	mis	bad, badly	misinform, misinterpret, mispronounce, misnomer, mistake, misogynist, mistrial, misadventure, misanthrope, misread

63	mit, miss	to send	transmit, permit, missile, missionary, remit, admit, missive, mission
64	morph	shape	polymorphic, morpheme, amorphous, metamorphosis, morphology, morphing
65	multi	many	multitude, multipartite, multiply, multipurpose, multicolored, multimedia, multinational
66	neo	new	neologism, neonate, neoclassic, neophyte
67	non	not	nonferrous, nonabrasive, nondescript, nonfat, nonfiction, nonprofit, nonsense, nonentity
68	omni	all	omnipotent, omnivorous, omniscient, omnibus, omnirange, omnipresent
69	pan	all, whole, general, completely	pantheism, pandemic, panacea, panoply, pan-American, panchromatic, pandemonium, panorama
70	para	beside	paraprofessional, paramedic, paraphrase, parachute, paralegal, parallel, comparison
71	per	through, intensive	permit, perspire, perforate, persuade, perceive, perfect, permit, perform, pervasive
72	peri	around	periscope, perimeter, perigee, periodontal, pericope
73	phon	sound	telephone, phonics, phonograph, phonetic, homophone, microphone
74	phot	light	photograph, photosynthesis, photon
75	poly	many	polytheist, polygon, polygamy, polymorphous
76	port	to carry	porter, portable, report, transportation, deport, import, export
77	re	back, again	report, realign, retract, revise, regain, reflect, rename, restate, recombine, recalculate, redo
78	retro	backwards	retrorocket, retrospect, retrogression, retroactive
79	sanct	holy	sanctify, sanctuary, sanction, sanctimonious, sacrosanct
80	scrib, script	to write	inscription, prescribe, proscribe, manuscript, conscript, scribble, scribe, postscript, transcript
81	sect, sec	cut	intersect, transect, dissect, secant, section
82	semi	half	semifinal, semiconscious, semiannual, semimonthly, semicircle
83	spect	to look	inspect, spectator, circumspect, retrospect, prospect, spectacle

84	sub	under, below	submerge, submarine, substandard, subnormal, subvert, subdivision, submersible, submit
85	super, supra	above	superior, suprarenal, superscript, supernatural, supercede, superficial, superhero, superimpose
86	syn	together	synthesis, synchronous, syndicate, synergy, snyopsis, syncretism
87	tele	distance, from afar	television, telephone, telegraph, telemetry, telepathy, teleconference
88	theo, the	God	theology, theist, polytheist, pantheism, 89atheist, monotheist, theophany
89	therm, thermo	heat	thermal, thermometer, thermocouple, thermodynamic, thermoelectric
90	tract	to drag, draw	attract, tractor, traction, extract, retract, protract, detract, subtract, contract, intractable
91	trans	across	transoceanic, transmit, transport, transducer, transit, intransitive
92	un	not	uncooked, unharmed, unintended, unhappy, unenlightened, unremarkable
93	veh, vect, vey	to carry	vector, vehicle, convection, vehement, convey, conveyance, conveyor
94	vert, vers	to turn	convert, revert, advertise, versatile, vertigo, invert, reversion, extravert, introvert
94	ven, vent	to come	convention, prevent, intervention, convent, Advent, invent, inventory
95	verm	worm	vermin, vermicelli, vermiculite, vermicide, vermiform, vermilion
96	vita	life	vital, vitality, vitamins, revitalize
97	vol	to will	benevolent, volition, voluntary, malevolent

"ous" at the end of a word often means "full of".

E.g. famous: full of fame.

glorious; full of glory, gracious, ridiculous, furious, dangerous.

"al" at the end of a word often means "to do with".

E.g. **musical:** to do with music, **criminal**: to do with crime, **historical:** to do with history.

More Word Roots to the Root Words

No.	Root or Prefix	Meaning	Example Words
1	agon	to struggle	agony, protagonist, antagonist, agony, agonize,
2	alg	pain	neuralgia, analgesic, nostalgic,
3	alter	other	alternative, alternator, alteration, altercation, alternate,
4	am	friend	amiable, amorous, amity, enamored, paramour, amicable
5	ambi	both	ambidextrous, ambivalent, ambiguous, ambient
6	anim	alive	animated, animal, inanimate, animator, anime, animation, reanimate
7	anthrop	mankind	anthropology, anthropomorphic, philanthrophy, misanthranthropology, anthropomorphic, philanthrophy, misanthropy
8	eu	good, well	euphoria, eulogy, euphemism, eugenics, eucalyptus, eukaryote, eurythmics, euthanasia
9	fore	before, front	forecast, forefather, foretaste, forehead, foreman, foreboding, forecastle, forearm, forebear, foreclose, foredoom, forego, forefoot, foreground, forehand, foreknowledge, foremost, foreordain, forerunner, foresee, foreshoren, foretell
10	ortho	straight	orthodontics, orthodox, orthopedic, orthoscopic, orthostatic
11	post	after	postscript, postconsumer, postdoctoral, posterior, postimpact, postfeminism, postgraduate, posthumous, postimpressionism, postlude, postmodernism, postpone, postproduction

12	pre	before, in front of	prefix, predict, prelude, predetermined, preamplifier, predestination, prebiotic, preclude, predate, predisposed, preempt, preference, prefigure, prefrontal, preheat, prehistory, presell, presumptuous, prevent, previous, pretext, pretentious, pretend
13	pro	forward	propel, proceed, produce, promote, project, proclaim, procession, profess, proffer, professor, proficient, profile, profound, profuse, progenitor, progress, prolapse, prolegomenon, prolific, prologue, prolong, pronation, pronounce, propellant, prophesy, prophecy, proponent, prorate, proscribe, prosecute, prospect, protect, protest, provide, provoke
14	proto	first, earliest	prototype, protoplasm, protohistory, protocol, protogalaxy, proton, prototypical, protozoa
15	quasi	approximately, resembling, to some degree	quasiperiodical, quasiparticle, quasi-governmental, quasi-scientific, quasi-judicial, quasi-stellar, quasi-public
16	ultra	beyond, extremely	ultraviolet, ultrasonic, ultramarine, ultrafine, ultrasensitive, ultrawide, ultrapure, ultraquiet
17	under	beneath, below, too little	undercoat, underwear, underestimate, underbid, underexpose, undercut, underclassmen, undernourished, underground, undersized, underhand, underlay, undermine, underneath, underpass, underpowered, underline, understand, undertake, undertone, undertow, undervalue, underwrite

6 MOST COMMON

Latin and Greek Word Roots

No.	Roots	Latin (L) / Greek (G)	Meaning	Example
1	Ast (er)	(G)	star	asteroid, astronomy
2	audi	(L)	hear	audible, audience
3	auto	(G)	self	automatic, autopsy
4	bene	(L)	good	benefit, benign
5	bio	(G)	life	biography, biology
6	chrono	(G)	time	chronic, synchronize
7	dict	(L)	say	dictate, diction
8	duc	(L)	lead, make	deduce, produce
9	gen	(L)	give birth	gene, generate
10	geo	(G)	earth	geography, geology
11	graph	(G)	write	autograph, graph
12	jur, jus	(L)	law	jury, justice
13	log, logue	(L)	thought	logic, obloquy
14	Luc	(L)	light	lucid, translucent
15	man(u)	(L)	hand	manual, manure, manuscript – hand written
16	Mand, mend	(L)	order	demand, recommend
17	Mis , mit	(L)	send	missile, transmit, transmission
18	omni	(L)	all	omnivorous
19	path	(G)	feel	empathy, pathetic
20	phil	(G)	love	philosophy, bibliophile
21	Phon	(G)	sound	phonics, telephone
22	photo	(G)	light	photograph, photon
23	port	(L)	carry	export, portable

24	qui(t)	(L)	quiet, rest	acquit, tranquil
25	Scrib, script	(L)	write	ascribe, script
26	Sens, sent	(L)	feel	resent, sensitive
27	tele	(G)	far off	telecast, telephone
28	terr	(L)	earth	terrain, territory
29	vac	(L)	empty	evacuate, vacate
30	vid,vis	(L)	see	visible, video

7 AFFIXES: SUFFIXES AND PREFIXES

7.1 Most Commonly used Suffixes

No.	Suffix	Meaning	Examples
1	able, ible	able to be, capable of being	pourable, drinkable, readable, washable, curable, visible, flexible, collectible
2	ance, ence, ancy	state of, process of	performance, reliance, defiance, radiance, acceptance, ascendancy, discrepancy, infancy
3	ator	one who does [the verb]	terminator, culminator, agitator, instigator, generator, incubator, accelerator, invigorator, elevator
4			
5	dom	condition, office, state	kingdom, freedom, wisdom, sheikdom, fiefdom, sheikdom
6	ee	one who receives	payee, mortgagee, employee, appointee, abductee, examinee, referee, refugee
7	er, or	one who does [the verb]	driver, hiker, reader, manager, polisher, speaker, counselor, author, creator, director, sculptor
8	ful	filled with	frightful, delightful, wonderful, cupful, 9wakeful, bashful, bountiful, beautiful, cheerful, colorful, dreadful, fateful
10	ify	to make into	purify, deify, simplify, clarify, petrify, reify, exemplify, pacify
11	ification	process of making into	purification, deification, simplifiction, clarification, petrification
12	ish	the nature of, resembling	Cornish, Irish, bookish, freakish, foolish, boorish, selfish, sluggish, priggish

13	ism	doctrine, system, characteristic quality	capitalism, heroism, optimism, skepticism, realism, patriotism, communism, idealism, conservatism
14	ist	one who performs; an adherent of an ism	tympanist, cellist, idealist, communist, realist, moralist, pharamacist, pragmatist
15	ize	to make into	rationalize, normalize, realize, capitalize, sterilize, dramatize, utilize, colorize
16	ization	the process of making into	rationalization, normalization, realization, capitalization, dramatization
17	less	without, lacking	loveless, fearless, worthless, nameless, baseless, bottomless, effortless, friendless, noiseless, harmless

7.2 Number Prefixes

No.	Prefix	Meaning	Examples
1	mono, uni	one	monopoly, monotype, monologue, mononucleosis, monorail, monotheist, unilateral, universal, unity, unanimous, uniform
2	bi, di	two	divide, diverge, diglycerides, bifurcate, biweekly, bivalve, biannual, billion
3	tri	three	triangle, trinity, trilateral, triumvirate, tribune, trilogy, tricycle, trillion
4	quat, quad	four	quadrangle, quadruplets, quaternary, quarter, quadrillion
5	quint, penta	five	quintet, quintuplets, pentagon, pentane, pentameter, quintillion
6	hex, ses, sex	six	hexagon, hexameter, sestet, sextuplets, sextillion
7	sept	seven	septet, septennial, septillion, September
8	oct	eight	octopus, octagon, octogenarian, octave, octillion, October
9	non	nine	nonagon, nonagenarian, nonillion
10	dec	ten	decimal, decade, decalogue, decimate, decillion, December
11	cent	hundred	centennial, century, centipede, centillion

12	mill, kilo	thousand (10^3)	millennium, kilobyte, kiloton
13	mega	million (10^6)	megabyte, megaton, megaflop, megawatt
14	giga	billion (10^9)	gigabyte, gigaflop, gigahertz, gigawatt
15	tera	trillion (10^12)	terabyte, teraflop, terawatt
16	peta	quadrillion (10^15)	petabyte
17	exa	quintillion (10^18)	exabyte
18	zetta	sextillion (10^21)	zettabyte
19	yotta	septilion (10^24)	yottabyte
20	milli	thousandth (10^-3)	millisecond, milligram, millivolt, milliwatt, millimeter, millipede
21	micro	millionth (10^-6)	microgram, microvolt, microwave, microsecond
22	nano	billionth (10^-9)	nanosecond, nanobucks, nanofarad, nanometer, nanomachine, nanotube, nanotechnology, nanogram, nanoscale
23	pico	trillionth (10^-12)	picofarad, picocurie, picogram, picomole, picosecond
24	femto	quadrillionth (10^-15)	femtosecond
25	atto	quintillionth (10^-18)	attosecond, attometer
26	zepto	sextillionth (10^-21)	zeptosecond
27	yocto	septillionth (10^-24)	yoctosecond

7.3 Math & Science Affixes and Roots

No.	Root or Affix	Example
1	aqua (water)	aquarium
2	hydro (water)	hydroplane
3	hemi (half)	hemisphere
4	semi (half)	semicircle
5	equi (equal)	equivalent
6	tele (far off)	telescope
7	micro (small)	microfilm
8	onomy (science of)	astronomy
9	ology (study of)	geology

10	uni (one)	universe
11	bi (two)	bicycle
12	tri (three)	triangle
13	octa (eight)	octagon
14	dec (ten)	decade
15	centi (hundred)	centimeter
16	milli (thousand)	millimeter
17	bio (life)	biology
18	astro (star)	astronaut
19	thermo (heat)	thermodynamic
20	meter (measure)	diameter
21	ped (foot)	pedestrian
22	pod (foot)	tripod

Prefixes that mean "no" or "negative": a- de- dis-, in- non- un-, contra

Examples: disqualify, nondescript, unscrupulous, contradict, inadvertent

No.	Prefix	Meaning	Examples
1	a-, an-	without, not	asexual, atypical, amoral, anarchy
2	de-	reverse action, away	defrost, demystify, desensitize, deduct
3	dis-, dif-, di-	not, apart	dissatisfied, disorganized, different, divert
4	in-, il-, it-, im-	not	inappropriate, invisible, illegal, impossible
5	non-	not	nonproductive, nonessential, nonsense
6	un-	not	unlikely, unnoticeable, unreliable
7	contra-, counter-	against	contrary, contradict, counterproductive

Prefixes that indicate: *"when," "where,"* or *"more"*

pre-, post-, ante-, inter-, infra-, traps-, sub-, circum-, ultra

Examples: premature, postscript, anteroom, intervene, transformation

No.	Prefix	Meaning	Examples
1	pre-, pro-	before	pre-dinner, preliminary, previous, prologue

2	post-	after	postwar, postoperative, postpone
3	ante-	before	antecedent, antechamber
4	inter-	between, among	interstate, intercept, interfere
5	intra-	within	intramural, intrastate, intravenous
6	trans-	across	transcontinental, transparent, transaction
7	sub-	under	submarine, submerge, subjugate
8	circum-	around	circumnavigate, circumference
9	ultra-	beyond, on the far side of, excessive	ultrasonic, ultraviolet, ultraconservative

8 NINETY-ONE MOST COMMON PREFIXES & SUFFIXES

No.	Terms	Definitions	Example
1	able, ible	able to be	lovable , visible
2	ade	action or process	blockade, lemonade
3	age	action, state or process	bondage
4	al, -ial	of; like; relating to	formal , colloquial
5	ance	act, process; quality; state of being	attendance
6	ant	one who	applicant
7	ary	**of,** like; relating to	Aviary (of , about birds) Avi-bird
8	ate	characteristic of	compassionate
9	cle, -icle	small	particle
10	cy	fact or state of being	fallacy (sth. being false)
11	dom	state or quality of	kingdom
12	ence , ance	act or state of being	credence , attendance
13	ent, ant	doing, having, showing	attendant, repentant
14	er	one who, that which	teacher
15	ery, ary	place for; act	bravery, gallery, mortuary, aviary
16	esque	like	picturesque
17	ess	female	actress
18	ful	full of	houseful
19	ic	relating to	academic
20	ify	to make	Glorify, magnify
21	ion	condition, result of action;	vision
22	ish	of or belonging to, like	childish , bookish
23	ism	act, practice	tourism , capitalism
24	ity	condition	obscurity
25	ive	of, relating to	archive

26	ize	make, cause to be	modernize
27	less	without	jobless
28	let	small	piglet (small pig)
29	like	like	childlike
30	logy	study or theory of	biology
31	ly	(1) every	individually
32	ly	(2) like	beautifully, likely
33	ment	(1) action or process	improvement, advancement
34	ment	(2) state or quality	firmament , enjoyment
35	ment	(3) product or thing	achievement , basement
36	ness	state or quality of being	calmness
37	or	one who	actor
38	ous	having, characterized by	courageous
39	ship	state or quality	friendship
40	some	like, tending to be	quarrelsome
41	tude	state or quality of being	magnitude, solitude (being alone)
42	y	characterized by	fussy
43	ab	away from	abnormal
44	ad	to motion toward	advance (to move forward)
45	aero	air	aeroplane
46	amphi	both, around	amphitheater
47	an	not	anemia - *emia* word element ,condition of the blood
48	ante	before	ante-war, antemeridian
49	anti	against	antiseptic , antiterrorism
50	ap	nearness to	apperception
51	auto	self	autograph , autos-start
52	bene	good	beneficent
53	bi	two	bicycle (two cycles, wheels)
54	circum	around	circumference
55	co, con	together, cooperate,	cooperate, congruent
56	contra	against	Contradict: *contra* –against , *dict* -speak
57	de	opposite of	.defame, devalue, decompose
58	dis	opposite	discourage

59	ex	out, beyond	exit, expose, external
60	extra	outside, beyond	extraordinary , extrajudicial
61	for	not, miss	forgo
62	fore	before	forehand , foretell
63	hyper	more than normal	hyperactive
64	il	not	illegal
65	im	(1) into	impersonate
66	im	(2) not	impossible
67	in	not, go into	incorrect, infuse
68	inter	among, between	intercity
69	intra	within	intrapersonal
70	ir	not	irregular
71	mal	malfunction	wrong, bad
72	mis	wrong, bad, no, not	misuse
73	neo	(Greek, from neos)new	neoclassic, neocolonialism,
74	non	not, opposite of	nonprofit
75	ob	against	obdurate, obscure
76	per	through, one	Peradventure, pervade
77	post	after	postwar
78	pre	before	preview
79	pro	(1) before, for, in support of	prodemocracy
80	pro	(2) forward	proactive
81	re	back, again	redo , recall
82	retro	backward	retrospect
83	se	apart	secessions , separate, segregate: to separate
84	self	of the self	self-serving
85	semi	half, partly	semicircle
86	sub	under, beneath	sub-inspector, subdivision, subway subjective, subjugate
87	super	over	supersonic, supernatural
88	sur	over, above	surreal, surface (over or on the face, on the top layer, from top)
89	trans	across, over	transatlantic , transform
90	ultra	extremely	ultraliberal, ultraviolet
91	un	not, lack of, opposite	unlucky, unfair

9 OGDEN'S LIST OF 850 WORDS

This list can actually be applied to learning any language to get around with simple everyday communication in that particular language

Ogden's Word lists

9.1 OPERATIONS - 100 words

No	Word	No	Word	No	Word	No	Word
1	come	20	across	39	as	58	he
2	get	21	after	40	for	59	you
3	give	22	against	41	of	60	who
4	go	23	among	42	till	61	and
5	keep	24	at	43	than	62	because
6	let	25	before	44	a	63	but
7	make	26	between	45	the	64	or
8	put	27	by	46	all	65	if
9	seem	28	down	47	any	66	though
10	take	29	from	48	every	67	while
11	be	30	in	49	little	68	how
12	do	31	off	50	much	69	when
13	have	32	on	51	no	70	where
14	say	33	over	52	other	71	why
15	see	34	through	53	some	72	again
16	send	35	to	54	such	73	ever
17	may	36	under	55	that	74	far
18	will	37	up	56	this	75	forward
19	about	38	with	57	I	76	here

No	Word	No	Word	No	Word	No	Word
77	near	83	together	89	only	95	north
78	now	84	well	90	quite	96	south
79	out	85	almost	91	so	97	east
80	still	86	enough	92	very	98	west
81	then	87	even	93	tomorrow	99	please
82	there	88	not	94	yesterday	100	yes

9.2 THINGS - 400 General words

No	Word	No	Word	No	Word	No	Word
1	account	26	birth	51	committee	76	day
2	act	27	bit	52	company	77	death
3	addition	28	bite	53	comparison	78	debt
4	adjustment	29	blood	54	competition	79	decision
5	advertisement	30	blow	55	condition	80	degree
6	agreement	31	body	56	connection	81	design
7	air	32	brass	57	control	82	desire
8	amount	33	bread	58	cook	83	destruction
9	amusement	34	breath	59	copper	84	detail
10	animal	35	brother	60	copy	85	development
11	answer	36	building	61	cork	86	digestion
12	apparatus	37	burn	62	cotton	87	direction
13	approval	38	burst	63	cough	88	discovery
14	argument	39	business	64	country	89	discussion
15	art	40	butter	65	cover	90	disease
16	attack	41	canvas	66	crack	91	disgust
17	attempt	42	care	67	credit	92	distance
18	attention	43	cause	68	crime	93	distribution
19	attraction	44	chalk	69	crush	94	division
20	authority	45	chance	70	cry	95	doubt
21	back	46	change	71	current	96	drink
22	balance	47	cloth	72	curve	97	driving
23	base	48	coal	73	damage	98	dust
24	behavior	49	color	74	danger	99	earth
25	belief	50	comfort	75	daughter	100	edge

No	Word	No	Word	No	Word	No	Word
101	education	138	group	175	law	212	motion
102	effect	139	growth	176	lead	213	mountain
103	end	140	guide	177	learning	214	move
104	error	141	harbor	178	leather	215	music
105	event	142	harmony	179	letter	216	name
106	example	143	hate	180	level	217	nation
107	exchange	144	hearing	181	lift	218	need
108	existence	145	heat	182	light	219	news
109	expansion	146	help	183	limit	220	night
110	experience	147	history	184	linen	221	noise
111	expert	148	hole	185	liquid	222	note
112	fact	149	hope	186	list	223	number
113	fall	150	hour	187	look	224	observation
114	family	151	humor	188	loss	225	offer
115	father	152	ice	189	love	226	oil
116	fear	153	idea	190	machine	227	operation
117	feeling	154	impulse	191	man	228	opinion
118	fiction	155	increase	192	manager	229	order
119	field	156	industry	193	mark	230	organization
120	fight	157	ink	194	market	231	ornament
121	fire	158	insect	195	mass	232	owner
122	flame	159	instrument	196	meal	233	page
123	flight	160	insurance	197	measure	234	pain
124	flower	161	interest	198	meat	235	paint
125	fold	162	invention	199	meeting	236	paper
126	food	163	iron	200	memory	237	part
127	force	164	jelly	201	metal	238	paste
128	form	165	join	202	middle	239	payment
129	friend	166	journey	203	milk	240	peace
130	front	167	judge	204	mind	241	person
131	fruit	168	jump	205	mine	242	place
132	glass	169	kick	206	minute	243	plant
133	gold	170	kiss	207	mist	244	play
134	government	171	knowledge	208	money	245	pleasure
135	grain	172	land	209	month	246	point
136	grass	173	language	210	morning	247	poison
137	grip	174	laugh	211	mother	248	polish

No	Word	No	Word	No	Word	No	Word
249	porter	287	roll	325	society	363	tin
250	position	288	room	326	son	364	top
251	powder	289	rub	327	song	365	touch
252	power	290	rule	328	sort	366	trade
253	price	291	run	329	sound	367	transport
254	print	292	salt	330	soup	368	trick
255	process	293	sand	331	space	369	trouble
256	produce	294	scale	332	stage	370	turn
257	profit	295	science	333	start	371	twist
258	property	296	sea	334	statement	372	unit
259	prose	297	seat	335	steam	373	use
260	protest	298	secretary	336	steel	374	value
261	pull	299	selection	337	step	375	verse
262	punishment	300	self	338	stitch	376	vessel
263	purpose	301	sense	339	stone	377	view
264	push	302	servant	340	stop	378	voice
265	quality	303	sex	341	story	379	walk
266	question	304	shade	342	stretch	380	war
267	rain	305	shake	343	structure	381	wash
268	range	306	shame	344	substance	382	waste
269	rate	307	shock	345	sugar	383	water
270	ray	308	side	346	suggestion	384	wave
271	reaction	309	sign	347	summer	385	wax
272	reading	310	silk	348	support	386	way
273	reason	311	silver	349	surprise	387	weather
274	record	312	sister	350	swim	388	week
275	regret	313	size	351	system	389	weight
276	relation	314	sky	352	talk	390	wind
277	religion	315	sleep	353	taste	391	wine
278	representative	316	slip	354	tax	392	winter
279	request	317	slope	355	teaching	393	woman
280	respect	318	smash	356	tendency	394	wood
281	rest	319	smell	357	test	395	wool
282	reward	320	smile	358	theory	396	word
283	rhythm	321	smoke	359	thing	397	work
284	rice	322	sneeze	360	thought	398	wound
285	river	323	snow	361	thunder	399	writing
286	road	324	soap	362	time	400	year

9.3 THINGS - 200 Pictorial words

No	Word	No	Word	No	Word	No	Word
1	angle	36	button	71	feather	106	library
2	ant	37	cake	72	finger	107	line
3	apple	38	camera	73	fish	108	lip
4	arch	39	card	74	flag	109	lock
5	arm	40	cart	75	floor	110	map
6	army	41	carriage	76	fly	111	match
7	baby	42	cat	77	foot	112	monkey
8	bag	43	chain	78	fork	113	moon
9	ball	44	cheese	79	fowl	114	mouth
10	band	45	chest	80	frame	115	muscle
11	basin	46	chin	81	garden	116	nail
12	basket	47	church	82	girl	117	neck
13	bath	48	circle	83	glove	118	needle
14	bed	49	clock	84	goat	119	nerve
15	bee	50	cloud	85	gun	120	net
16	bell	51	coat	86	hair	121	nose
17	berry	52	collar	87	hammer	122	nut
18	bird	53	comb	88	hand	123	office
19	blade	54	cord	89	hat	124	orange
20	board	55	cow	90	head	125	oven
21	boat	56	cup	91	heart	126	parcel
22	bone	57	curtain	92	hook	127	pen
23	book	58	cushion	93	horn	128	pencil
24	boot	59	dog	94	horse	129	picture
25	bottle	60	door	95	hospital	130	pig
26	box	61	drain	96	house	131	pin
27	boy	62	drawer	97	island	132	pipe
28	brain	63	dress	98	jewel	133	plane
29	brake	64	drop	99	kettle	134	plate
30	branch	65	ear	100	key	135	plough/plow
31	brick	66	egg	101	knee	136	pocket
32	bridge	67	engine	102	knife	137	pot
33	brush	68	eye	103	knot	138	potato
34	bucket	69	face	104	leaf	139	prison
35	bulb	70	farm	105	leg	140	pump

No	Word	No	Word	No	Word	No	Word
141	rail	156	shirt	171	stick	186	town
142	rat	157	shoe	172	stocking	187	train
143	receipt	158	skin	173	stomach	188	tray
144	ring	159	skirt	174	store	189	tree
145	rod	160	snake	175	street	190	trousers
146	roof	161	sock	176	sun	191	umbrella
147	root	162	spade	177	table	192	wall
148	sail	163	sponge	178	tail	193	watch
149	school	164	spoon	179	thread	194	wheel
150	scissors	165	spring	180	throat	195	whip
151	screw	166	square	181	thumb	196	whistle
152	seed	167	stamp	182	ticket	197	window
153	sheep	168	star	183	toe	198	wing
154	shelf	169	station	184	tongue	199	wire
155	ship	170	stem	185	tooth	200	worm

9.4 QUALITIES - 100 General

No	Word	No	Word	No	Word	No	Word
1	able	19	cut	37	grey/gray	55	necessary
2	acid	20	deep	38	hanging	56	new
3	angry	21	dependent	39	happy	57	normal
4	automatic	22	early	40	hard	58	open
5	beautiful	23	elastic	41	healthy	59	parallel
6	black	24	electric	42	high	60	past
7	boiling	25	equal	43	hollow	61	physical
8	bright	26	fat	44	important	62	political
9	broken	27	fertile	45	kind	63	poor
10	brown	28	first	46	like	64	possible
11	cheap	29	fixed	47	living	65	present
12	chemical	30	flat	48	long	66	private
13	chief	31	free	49	male	67	probable
14	clean	32	frequent	50	married	68	quick
15	clear	33	full	51	material	69	quiet
16	common	34	general	52	medical	70	ready
17	complex	35	good	53	military	71	red
18	conscious	36	great	54	natural	72	regular

No	Word	No	Word	No	Word	No	Word
73	responsible	80	sharp	87	sweet	94	waiting
74	right	81	smooth	88	tall	95	warm
75	round	82	sticky	89	thick	96	wet
76	same	83	stiff	90	tight	97	wide
77	second	84	straight	91	tired	98	wise
78	separate	85	strong	92	true	99	yellow
79	serious	86	sudden	93	violent	100	young

9.5 QUALITIES - 50 Opposites

No	Word						
1	awake	13	delicate	26	left	39	short
2	bad	14	different	27	loose	40	shut
3	bent	15	dirty	28	loud	41	simple
4	bitter	16	dry	29	low	42	slow
5	blue	17	false	30	mixed	43	small
6	certain	18	feeble	31	narrow	44	soft
7	cold	19	female	32	old	45	solid
8	complete	20	foolish	33	opposite	46	special
9	cruel	21	future	34	public	47	strange
10	dark	22	green	35	rough	48	thin
11	dead	23	ill	36	sad	49	white
12	dear	24	last	37	safe	50	wrong
		25	late	38	secret		

10 OGDEN'S BASIC ENGLISH 850 WORD LIST (ALPHABETIC)

A

a , able , about , account , acid , across , act , addition , adjustment , advertisement , after , again , against , agreement , air , all , almost , among , amount , amusement , and , angle , angry , animal , answer , ant , any , apparatus , apple , approval , arch , argument , arm , army , art , as , at , attack , attempt , attention , attraction , authority , automatic , awake .

B

baby , back , bad , bag , balance , ball , band , base , basin , basket , bath , be , beautiful , because , bed , bee , before , behavior , belief , bell , bent , berry , between , bird , birth , bit , bite , bitter , black , blade , blood , blow , blue , board , boat , body , boiling , bone , book , boot , bottle , box , boy , brain , brake , branch , brass , bread , breath , brick , bridge , bright , broken , brother , brown , brush , bucket , building , bulb , burn , burst , business , but , butter , button , by .

C

cake , camera , canvas , card , care , carriage , cart , cat , cause , certain , chain , chalk , chance , change , cheap , cheese , chemical , chest , chief , chin , church , circle , clean , clear , clock , cloth , cloud , coal , coat , cold , collar , color , comb , come , comfort , committee , common , company , comparison , complete , competition , complex , condition , connection , conscious , control , cook , copper , copy , cord , cork , cotton , cough , country , cover , cow , crack , credit , crime , cruel , crush , cry , cup , current , curtain , curve , cushion , cut .

D

damage , danger , dark , daughter , day , dead , dear , death , debt , decision , deep , degree , delicate , dependent , design , desire , destruction , detail , development

219

, different , digestion , direction , dirty , discovery , discussion , disease , disgust , distance , distribution , division , do , dog , door , doubt , down , drain , drawer , dress , drink , driving , drop , dry , dust .

E

ear , early , earth , east , edge , education , effect , egg , elastic , electric , end , engine , enough , equal , error , even , event , ever , every , example , exchange , existence , expansion , experience , expert , eye .

F

face , fact , fall , false , family , far , farm , fat , father , fear , feather , feeble , feeling , female , fertile , fiction , field , fight , finger , fire , first , fish , fixed , flag , flame , flat , flight , floor , flower , fly , fold , food , foolish , foot , for , force , fork , form , forward , fowl , frame , free , frequent , friend , from , front , fruit , full , future .

G

garden , general , get , girl , give , glass , glove , go , goat , gold , good , government , grain , grass , great , green , grey/gray , grip , group , growth , guide , gun .

H

hair , hammer , hand , hanging , happy , harbor , hard , harmony , hat , hate , have , he , head , healthy , hearing , heart , heat , help , here , high , history , hole , hollow , hook , hope , horn , horse , hospital , hour , house , how , humor .

I

I , ice , idea , if , ill , important , impulse , in , increase , industry , ink , insect , instrument , insurance , interest , invention , iron , island .

J

jelly , jewel , join , journey , judge , jump .

K

keep , kettle , key , kick , kind , kiss , knee , knife , knot , knowledge .

L

land , language , last , late , laugh , law , lead , leaf , learning , leather, left , leg , let , letter , level , library , lift , light , like , limit , line , linen , lip , liquid , list , little (less ,least) , living , lock , long , loose , loss , loud , love , low .

M

machine , make , male , man , manager , map , mark , market , married , match , material , mass , may , meal , measure , meat , medical , meeting , memory , metal , middle , military , milk , mind , mine , minute , mist , mixed , money , monkey , month , moon , morning , mother , motion , mountain , mouth , move , much (more, most) , muscle , music .

N

nail , name , narrow , nation , natural , near , necessary , neck , need , needle , nerve , net , new , news , night , no , noise , normal , north , nose , not , note , now , number , nut .

O

observation , of , off , offer , office , oil , old , on , only , open , operation , opinion , opposite , or , orange , order , organization , ornament , other , out , oven , over , owner.

P

page , pain , paint , paper , parallel , parcel , part , past , paste , payment , peace , pen , pencil , person , physical , picture , pig , pin , pipe , place , plane , plant , plate , play , please , pleasure , plough/plow , pocket , point , poison , polish , political , poor , porter , position , possible , pot , potato , powder , power , present , price , print , prison , private , probable , process , produce , profit , property , prose , protest , public , pull , pump , punishment , purpose , push , put .

Q

quality , question , quick , quiet , quite .

R

rail , rain , range , rat , rate , ray , reaction , red , reading , ready , reason , receipt , record , regret , regular , relation , religion , representative , request , respect , responsible , rest , reward , rhythm , rice , right , ring , river , road , rod , roll , roof , room , root , rough , round , rub , rule , run .

S

sad , safe , sail , salt , same , sand , say , scale , school , science , scissors , screw , sea , seat , second , secret , secretary , see , seed , selection , self , send , seem , sense , separate , serious , servant , sex , shade , shake , shame , sharp , sheep , shelf , ship , shirt , shock , shoe , short , shut , side , sign , silk , silver , simple , sister , size , skin , skirt , sky , sleep , slip , slope , slow , small , smash , smell , smile , smoke , smooth , snake , sneeze , snow , so , soap , society , sock , soft , solid , some , son , song , sort , sound , south , soup , space , spade , special , sponge , spoon , spring , square , stamp , stage , star , start , statement , station , steam , stem , steel , step , stick , sticky , still , stitch , stocking , stomach , stone , stop , store , story , strange , street , stretch , stiff , straight , strong , structure , substance , sugar , suggestion , summer , support , surprise , such , sudden , sun , sweet , swim , system .

T

table , tail , take , talk , tall , taste , tax , teaching , tendency , test , than , that , the , then , theory , there , thick , thin , thing , this , though , thought , thread , throat , through , thumb , thunder , ticket , tight , till , time , tin , tired , to , toe , together , tomorrow , tongue , tooth , top , touch , town , trade , train , transport , tray , tree , trick , trouble , trousers , true , turn , twist .

U

umbrella , under , unit , up , use .

V

value , verse , very , vessel , view , violent , voice .

W

waiting , walk , wall , war , warm , wash , waste , watch , water , wave , wax , way , weather , week , weight , well , west , wet , wheel , when , where , while , whip , whistle , white , who , why , wide , will , wind , window , wine , wing , winter , wire , wise , with , woman , wood , wool , word , work , worm , wound , writing , wrong .

X , Y , Z

year , yellow , yes , yesterday , you , young .

 # OGDEN'S BASIC ENGLISH "INTERNATIONAL WORD LIST"

in alphabetical order
"International Words" are similar in western languages, and are names in Diplomacy or Institutions, or in international standards, with a presumption that they are understood and need not be specially taught.

A: alcohol , Algebra , aluminum/aluminium , ammonia , anesthetic , April , Arithmetic , asbestos , August , autobus , automobile .

B: ballet , Bang , bank , bar , beef , beer , Biology , bomb .

C: cafe , calendar , catarrh , centi , champagne , chauffeur , chemist , Chemistry , check , chocolate , chorus cigarette , circus , citron , club , cocktail , coffee , cognac , College , colony .

D: dance , December , deci , degree , Dominion , dynamite .

E: eight , electricity , eleven , Embassy , Empire , encyclopedia , engineer .

F: February , fifteen , fifth , fifty , five , four , fourteen , fourth , forty , Friday .

G: gas , Geography , Geology , Geometry , gram , glycerin .

H: half , Hiss , hotel , hundred , hyena , hygiene , hysteria .

I: Imperial , inferno , influenza , international .

J: January , jazz , July , June .

K: kilo, King .

L: latitude , lava , liter/litre , liqueur , longitude .

M: macaroni , madam , magnetic , malaria , mania , March , Mathematics , May , meter/metre , Mew , micro- , microscope , milli- , million , minute , Monday , Museum

N: neutron , nickel , nicotine , nine , November .

O: October , olive , once , omelet , one , opera , opium , orchestra , organism .

P: pajamas , paraffin , paradise , park , passport , patent , penguin , petroleum , phonograph , Physics , Physiology , piano , platinum , police , post , potash , President , Prince , Princess , program , propaganda, Psychology , Purr , pyramid .

Q: quack , quarter , Queen , quinine

R: radio , radium , referendum , restaurant , rheumatism , Royal , rum

S: salad , sardine , Saturday , second , September , serum , seven , sir , six , sixteen , sport , Sunday

T: tapioca , taxi , tea , telegram , telephone , ten , terrace , theatre , thermometer , third , thirteen , thirty , thousand , three , Thursday , toast , tobacco , torpedo , Tuesday , turbine , twenty-one , twelve , twenty , twice , two

U: university

V: vanilla , violin , visa , vitamin , vodka , volt .

W: Wednesday , whisky

X , Y , Z: zebra , zinc , Zoology .

12 MEDIA RECOMMENDED INTERNATIONAL WORD-LIST

1	academy	30	brave	59	dessert	88	guillotine
2	academic	31	bridge	60	diarrhea	89	gymnastics
3	accumulator	32	buffet	61	dictionary	90	hockey
4	adieu	33	bulletin	62	dilettante	91	hor d'oeuvres
5	alphabet	34	bull-dog	63	dynamo	92	hyacinth
6	alpha	35	cable	64	dyspepsia	93	imperial
7	ampere	36	cafeteria	65	economic	94	impromptu
8	apostrophe	37	cadet	66	electric	95	intelligentsia
9	atlas	38	calico	67	electron	96	interest
10	atmosphere	39	camouflage	68	element	96	iodine
11	atom	40	caravan	69	energy	97	kangaroo
12	baby	41	card	70	ensemble	98	kodak
13	bacillus	42	carnival	71	erotic	99	laboratory
14	balcony	43	catastrophe	72	eucalyptus	100	lacquer
15	banana	44	caviar	73	eugenics	101	lady
16	banjo	45	center	74	façade	102	lamp
17	barbarism	46	chaos	75	feminism	103	lancet
18	baritone	47	civilization	76	film	104	lavatory
19	bayonet	48	cocoa	77	fresco	105	league
20	benzyl	49	communist	78	flirt	106	legal
21	bicycle	50	condenser	79	freemason	107	lemon
22	billiards	51	contralto	80	frieze	108	lion
23	blonde	52	cosmopolitan	81	garage	109	lunch
24	blouse	53	crepe	82	gazette	110	lynch
25	bonbon	54	cricket	83	gentleman	111	machine
26	boss	55	crochet	84	golf	112	mademoiselle
27	bouquet	56	dahlia	85	gondola	113	magnet
28	boulevard	57	decadent	86	grammar	114	mannequin
29	bourgeois	58	demagogue	87	graph	115	manuscript

116	mash	149	pathos	182	salon	202	syntax
117	maximum	150	pessimism	183	saloon	203	syringe
118	memo	151	philosophy	184	sapphire	204	system
119	menthol	152	phonetics	185	satyr	205	tango
120	minimum	153	photograph	173	saxophone	206	technique
121	minus	154	picnic	174	Scenario	207	technology
122	modern	155	pince-nez	175	schema	208	tempo
123	monopoly	156	ping-pong	176	scout	209	tennis
124	monsieur	157	pistol	177	serenade	210	tenor
125	moral	158	plus	178	sextant	211	text
126	morphia	159	polo	179	shampoo	212	theory
127	motif	160	porridge	180	Shellac	213	thermometer
128	motor	161	pragmatism	181	silhouette	214	tournament
129	music	162	press	182	ski	215	tragedy
130	muslin	163	prima-donna	183	Summit	216	tramway
131	narcissus	164	professor	184	socialism	217	toilet
132	nature	165	profile	185	soirée	218	tomato
133	negro	166	proletariat	186	solo	219	transformer
134	nuance	167	promenade	187	soprano	220	turban
135	oasis	168	public	188	soufflé	221	turbine
136	obelisk	169	pudding	189	souvenir	222	typhoon
137	octave	170	realism	190	spectrum	223	tsar
138	option	171	register	191	sphinx	224	unicorn
139	optimism	172	rendezvous	192	staccato	225	universe
140	oracle	173	republic	193	stadium	226	utopia
141	palace	174	revue	194	station	227	vaudeville
142	palette	175	rhetoric	195	steppe	228	verandah
143	panic	176	rhythm	196	student	229	vermouth
144	panorama	177	robot	197	symbolism	230	waffle
145	paradox	178	rotor,	198	symmetry	231	waltz
146	parallel	179	roulette	199	symphony	232	whist
147	parasol	180	rucksack	200	synchronization	233	xylophone
148	parody	181	sabotage	201	syndicalism	234	zigzag

13 THOUSAND PLUS VITAL WORDS

(Advanced Learners)

Note: the meanings of the words given below are inconclusive (incomplete, lacking fullness) in meanings, therefore the reader/ learner (user of this book) is advised to look up the meanings and their proper usage comprehensively. The long list of words has been divided into sets of fifties to facilitate learning in chunks (units).

(Dr. Injeeli)

<table>
<tr><td colspan="6" align="center">SET 1 (1-50)</td></tr>
<tr><td>No</td><td>Word</td><td>Meaning / synonym</td><td>No.</td><td>Word</td><td>Meaning / synonym</td></tr>
<tr><td>1</td><td>Abate</td><td>Decrease, subside</td><td>8</td><td>abjure</td><td>Avoid, reject, deny</td></tr>
<tr><td>2</td><td>abdicate</td><td>Give up, step down</td><td>9</td><td>abomination</td><td>Sth. horrifying, disgrace</td></tr>
<tr><td>3</td><td>aberration</td><td>Irregularity, abnormality</td><td>10</td><td>aboriginal</td><td>Native</td></tr>
<tr><td>4</td><td>abet</td><td>Help, assist, support</td><td>11</td><td>abound</td><td>Full of</td></tr>
<tr><td>5</td><td>abeyance</td><td>state of temporary disuse or suspension, delay</td><td>12</td><td>abrade</td><td>Grind, rub</td></tr>
<tr><td>6</td><td>abhor</td><td>Hate, dislike</td><td>13</td><td>abridge</td><td>To make a text short</td></tr>
<tr><td>7</td><td>abhorrent</td><td>Hateful, disgusting</td><td>14</td><td>abrogate</td><td>Abolish , finish</td></tr>
</table>

15	abscond	Run away, escape	24	accrue	Grow, add, increase
16	absolve	Forgive, pardon , clear (v)	25	acculturation	Adjusting in a new culture
17	abstemious	Moderate , self-denying	26	adherent	Believer, follower, enthusiast
18	abstinent	Sober , restrained	27	adjunct	Assistant, helper
19	abstruse	Complex, puzzling	28	admonish	War, scold, get angry at sb.
20	abysmal	Terrible, very bad , awful	29	adulation	Respect, to admire
21	accede	Agree, allow	30	Adulterate(v)	Spoil, cause to become impure
22	accentuate	Emphasize, stress	31	adumbrate	to give the main points or a summary of something; to give a hint of things to come; to give only an outline of something without revealing everything about it
23	accolade	Praise, honor	32	adventitious	happening or carried on according to chance rather than design or nature, coming from outside; not native, accidental, by chance , incidental, casual

33	Advocate	(n ,v) Supporter , promoter	42	aftermath	Result, outcome
34	aesthetic	Artistic, appealing , beautiful	43	aggrandize	Exaggerate , overstate
35	affable	Pleasant, friendly, easy going	44	aggrieve	Hurt, injury , cause sadness
36	affectation	Pretending , not real	45	aghast	Horrified, amazed, shocked
37	Aficionado	Enthusiast, fan (adj.) admirer	46	alacrity	Eagerness, enthusiasm
38	affidavit	An official , legal document	47	alchemy	Experimenting
39	affinity	Closeness, relationship	48	alienate	To move or keep sb. separate
40	affliction	Sickness, misery, pain	49	allege	Claim, declare
41	affront	Insult, injury , disrespect	50	allegiance	Loyalty, faithfulness

SET 2 (51-100)

51	acerbic	Sharp, cutting, bitter	60	adduce	Offer, give, present
52	acquiesce	Agree, accept	61	ameliorate	Improve, upgrade
53	acquisitive	Greedy , grasping	62	amenable	Agreeable, willing
54	acquit	Free (v) let go , release	63	amiable	Friendly, sociable , kind
55	acrimonious	Harsh, unfriendly	64	amid	Among, in middle of
56	acronym	Short form .e.g. NASA	65	amnesty	Forgiveness, freedom
57	acumen	Wisdom, understanding	66	amoral	Dishonorable, immoral
58	acute	Strong, serious, critical	67	amorphous	Formless, shapeless
59	adage	Saying, proverb	68	anachronism	Survival of old relics

69	anagram		85	ambivalent	Unsure, undecided, hesitating
70	analogy	Similarity, comparison	86	arcane	Secret, mysterious, hidden
71	anarchy	Disorder, lawlessness	87	archetype	Model, standard, original
72	anathema	String dislike, hate	88	archives	Record of old files, documents
73	ancillary	Additional, secondary	89	arduous	Difficult, hard, tiring
74	anecdote	A short story, tale	90	arid	Land unfit for agriculture , dry
75	anhydrous		91	aristocratic	Belonging to rich , high society
76	alleviate	Lesson, decrease , relieve	92	armistice	Settlement, peace, truce
77	allocate	Distribute, give	93	arraign	Accuse, blame
78	allot	Assign, give , designate	94	arsenal	A store house of weapons
79	alloy	Mixture , blend	95	articulate	clear, fluent
80	allusion	Indirect hint , reference	96	artifact	An object or item (arts, craft)
81	altruism	Helping, serving others	97	artifice	Trick, deceive
82	amalgamate	Join, merge, combine	98	ascendancy	Control, power, going higher
83	amass	Collect in a large amount	99	ascertain	Determine, learn, find out
84	ambiguous	Unclear, confusing	100	ascetic	Sb. who avoids luxuries of life

SET 3 (101-150)

101	animosity	Hatred, enmity , dislike	119	appraise	Evaluate, judge, review
102	anomaly	Irregularity, abnormality	120	apprise	Explain, tell, describe
103	antecedent	Originator, ancestor	121	approbation	Approval, agree, praise
104	antedate	Go before a date	122	appurtenance	
105	anterior	Outer or front part	123	apropos	Right, proper, correct
106	antipathy	Opposition, hate, dislike	124	aptitude	Ability, skill, talent
107	antiquity	Ancient times	125	arbitrary	Random, chance, illogical
108	antithesis	Opposite, contrast	126	ascribe	Assign, credit (v)
109	apathy	Uncaring attitude, laziness	127	askance	Doubtfully
110	aperture	Opening, hole , gap	128	aspersion	Criticism , accusation, blame
111	aphorism	Saying , maxim, proverb	129	assail	Attack, raid
112	apocryphal	Untrue, made up	130	assert	Declare, say, affirm
113	apostasy		131	assiduous	Hardworking, diligent
114	apotheosis		132	assimilate	Mix up, join, merge , adapt
115	appalling	Awful, terrible , dreadful	133	assuage	To decrease or lessen sth.
116	appendage	Addition, add-on, extra	134	astringent	Harsh, strong, severe, sharp
117	apportion	Assign, distribute, give	135	astute	Sharp, intelligent, smart
118	apposite	Appropriate, suitable	136	atomistic	having to do with atoms

137	atrophy	Weaken, waste, deteriorate	144	auspices	Help, support
138	attenuation	Weakening, decreasing	145	auspicious	Favorable, lucky, positive
139	attest	Confirm, prove, verify	146	austere	Serious, unsmiling
140	Attribute (v, n)	Quality, characteristic	147	autonomy	Independence, self-rule
141	attrition	Cut, decrease , wearing out	148	auxiliary	Supporting, helping, backup
142	audacious	Bold, brave in rude way	149	avarice	Greed, strong desire
143	augment	enlarge, increase, expand	150	aversion	Dislike, hatred

SET 4 (151- 200)

151	avid	Strong supporter, enthusiast	161	bilateral	Two-sided , joint
152	axiom	Saying, proverb	162	bipolar	Having , relating to two ends
153	banal	Ordinary, boring, common	163	bland	Tasteless, uninteresting
154	bane	Curse, misery, annoyance	164	blandishment	Flattery, praise
155	barrage	Heavy attack, bombardment	165	blasphemy	Speaking ill of religion , God
156	belated	Delayed , overdue	166	blatant	Obvious, deliberate , rude
157	benevolent	Kind, caring, helpful	167	blueprint	Design , plan, outline
158	benign	Gentle , Kind, caring, helpful	168	brandish	Show off, display, handle
159	bequeath	Give up, leave , donate	169	brazen	Shameless, bold
160	bestow	Give, present, offer	170	brevity	Being brief, short , precise

171	brink	Edge, border	186	**ch**ronic(k)	Old, from a long time
172	bureaucracy	Official networking of a govt.	187	circumscribe	Restrict, keep in a limit
173	burnish	Polish, shine, clean	188	circumspect	Careful, cautious , prudent
174	Cajole	Persuade , encourage	189	circumvent	Avoid, by-pass , dodge, outwit
175	callous	feeling less, unkind, cold	190	clandestine	Secret, hidden , covert
176	catalyst	Sth. causing chemical reaction	191	clemency	Mercy, forgiveness, pity
177	caulk	Seal, block, plug	192	coagulate	Become thick, block, gather
178	caustic	Burning, cutting, biting	193	coalesce	Merge, mix up, join, unite
179	**c**elibacy (s)	Staying unmarried, avoiding sex	194	coda	Conclusion, ending,
180	**c**ensure (s)	Criticism , disapproval	195	codicil	Addition
181	**ch**arlatan(sh)	Sb. who makes false claims	196	coercion	Pressure , force , compulsion
182	**ch**aste/tʃ / ch	Pure, faithful , uncorrupted	197	cogent (cojent)	Forceful, convincing, strong
183	**ch**asten/ tʃ / ch	Correct (v) discipline , scold	198	cogitate/**j**/ dʒ	Think sth. deeply, consider
184	**ch**astise/ tʃ/ ch	discipline, scold, punish	199	cognizant /g/	Knowing, aware, conscious
185	**ch**imera(k)	A strange animal	200	cohesive	Joined, unified

SET 5 (201-250)

| 201 | calumny | Defaming sb. lie | 203 | candid | Open, frank, truthful |
| 202 | canard | Rumor, false information | 204 | candor | Frankness, openness |

205	capacious	Having large area, spacious	223	condescend	Show feelings of superiority
206	capitulate	Submit, surrender, give in	224	condone	Ignore, forgive, tolerate
207	capricious	Unreliable, changeable	225	confederate	United, joined
208	captivate	Fascinate, charm	226	cohort	Unite, group, gang, army
209	carcinogenic	Dangerous, poisonous	227	commensurate	Equal, appropriate
210	cardinal	Fundamental, basic , main	228	commiserate	Show, pity, sympathize
211	careen	Career, speed, travel	229	commodious	Having large space, vast
212	cartel	Union, association, gang	230	commodity	article , product of commerce
213	cartography	Study, art of making maps	231	compendium	Collection, compilation
214	cascade	Waterfall, flow	232	complement	Sth. that completes , addition
215	castigate	criticize, accuse, scold, blame	233	complicity	Involvement, support
216	concerted	Intense, determined	234	comply	Follow, obey, fulfill , carry out
217	conciliatory	settling sth. peacefully	235	comprise	Include, cover, make up
218	concise	Brief, short , summarized	236	compunction	Regret, hesitation, shame
219	concoct	Create, invent, make	237	concave	Hollow, bowl-shaped
220	concomitant	Associated, related	238	concede	Admit, confess, allow , grant
221	concur	Agree, harmonize	239	concentric	Circular , with same center
222	concurrent	joining, agreeing	240	conceptual	Related to an idea, theory

241	countenance	Face, expression, features	246	cryptic	Puzzling, mysterious, secret
242	covert	Secret, hidden, underground	247	cull	Reject, discard, remove
243	credulous	Easily believing everyone	248	culminate	End, conclude, finish, climax
244	criterion	Standard, benchmark	249	culpable	Guilty, blameworthy, at fault
245	critique	Analysis, evaluation, to assess	250	cupidity	Greed, greediness

SET 6 (251-300)

251	confer	Discuss, talk, consult	262	contentious	Argumentative, quarreling
252	configuration	Shape, outline, formation	263	contiguous	Attached, joining
253	confluence	Meeting, union, gathering	264	contingent	depending, conditional
254	confound	Confuse, mistake	265	contrite	Feeling sorry, ashamed
255	congeal	Become /make hard, solid	266	contumacious	Disobeying a legal authority
256	congruent	Consistent, similar	267	contumely	
257	conjecture	Guess, have an idea	268	conundrum	Puzzle, mystery, confusing
258	conjoin	Touch, join, be next to	269	conventional	Old, traditional, regular
259	connotation	Meaning, reference	270	converge	Met, join, come at one point
260	consternation	Anxiety, worry, alarm	271	conversant	Familiar, knowledgeable
261	construe	Interpret, understand	272	convex	Curved, curving, rounded

273	convoluted	difficult, complicated	287	deference	Respect, regard, awe
274	copious	Full of sth. plentiful	288	defunct	No more in use, out of date
275	corollary	Result, effect, outcome	289	degenerate	Break down, corrupt, decrease
276	cursory	Quick, brief, passing, hurried	290	delectable	Delicious, tasty, enjoyable
277	daunt	Discourage, scare, deter	291	deleterious	Harmful, dangerous
278	dearth	Lack, shortage, not enough	292	delineate	Describe, explain, outline (v)
279	debacle	Disaster, tragedy, loss	293	delusion	False idea, misunderstanding
280	debase	Dishonor, shame (v)	294	delve	Research, explore, study
281	debilitate	To cause sb. to become weak	295	demeanor	Manner, behavior, conduct
282	debunk	Expose, show the reality	296	demise	Death, decay, expiry
283	decimate	Destroy, demolish, ruin	297	demographics	
284	decorum	Correct manner, right style	298	demur	Object (v) protest, doubt
285	deduce	Come to a conclusion	299	demystify	Explain, clarify, translate
286	deem	Think, believe, consider	300	denotation	Meaning, suggested sense

SET 7 (301-350)

301	corporeal	Bodily, physical, worldly	303	corroborate	Support, agree, confirm
302	correlation	Link, association, connection	304	corrosive	Harsh, cutting, destructive

305	corrugated	Having rough cuts on surface	324	diffuse	wordy, of/in too many words
306	derelict	Left alone, neglected	325	dilate	Open, expand, enlarge
307	derision	Disrespect, look down on	326	denouement	Ending, conclusion
308	derivative	created from another source	327	deplete	Reduce, lessen , use up
309	derogatory	Insulting, hateful	328	deploy	Set up, send, arrange , fix
310	desecrate	Disrespect sth. / sb. holy	329	depravity	Wickedness, immorality
311	desiccate	Shrink, die after drying out	330	deprecate	Criticize, blame, find fault with
312	desist	Stop, discontinue, abstain	331	dismay	Sadness, disappointment
313	despondent	Hopeless, worried, unhappy	332	disparage	criticize, look down, make fun
314	despotic	Behave like a dictator	333	disparate	Unequal, dissimilar, unlike
315	destitute	Very poor , penniless	334	disparity	Difference , inequality
316	desultory	Aimless, random, casual	335	dispassionate	Calm, cool, unemotional
317	deter	Discourage, push back	336	disperse	Scatter, disappear , spread
318	detrimental	Harmful, damaging	337	dispirit	Discourage , cause depression
319	diaphanous	Transparent , delicate , mild	338	disproportionate	Uneven, unequal
320	diatribe	Verbal attack, criticism	339	disquiet	Anxiety, unrest, worry
321	dichotomy	Opposition, contrast	340	dissemble	Pretend, mislead
322	didactic	Moral, instructive	341	disseminate	Distribute, circulate, spread
323	diffidence	being shy, hesitate , quietness	342	dissent	Disagreement, conflict

343	disservice	Damage, harm, cause loss	347	dissonance	Disagreement , conflict
344	dissident	Rebel, who goes against sb.	348	dissuade	Discourage, put off
345	dissipate	Scatter, drive away, spread	349	distend	Sell, enlarge, expand, balloon
346	dissolution	Ending, conclusion	350	divergence	Separation, difference

SET 8 (351- 400)

351	dilatory	Slow, late, lazy, problem	363	discriminate	Separate, set apart or alone
352	dilemma	A difficult problem, situation	364	disdain	Disrespect
353	diminution	Decrease, reduction,	365	disgruntle	Displease, anger , annoy
354	disabuse	Correct sb's ideas, thinking	366	disinclination	Unwillingness, dislike
355	disambiguate	remove uncertainty or confusion of meaning	367	disinformation	False information, lie, scandal
356	disarray	Confusion, disorder, panic	368	disingenuous	Dishonest, insincere , cheat
357	discernment	Judgment, understanding	369	disinterested	Fair, impartial, neutral
358	disclaimer	Deny, not owning sth.	370	dismal	In a bad condition, dull, sad
359	disconcerting	Disturbing (adj) alarming	371	effluvia	unpleasant or harmful smell
360	discordant	Disagreeing, conflicting	372	effrontery	Boldness, arrogance
361	discrepancy	Inconsistency , difference	373	effulgent	Shining brilliantly, brilliant
362	discrete	Distinct, separate	374	effusion	Outflow, rush out, pour out

375	egalitarian	Considering all equal, fair	388	Echelon /sh/	Level, rank, class
376	divest	Deny, take away, rob	389	eclectic	Varied, extensive , wide range
377	divulge	reveal, tell, open , expose	390	edification	Learning, improvement
378	dogmatic	Strict in beliefs, unbending	391	edifice	Organization, structure
379	dormant	Quiet, asleep, hidden, inactive	392	effectual	Effective, powerful, useful
380	dross	Waste, useless, trash, junk	393	effervescent	Lively, bubbling, active
381	dubious	Doubtful, unsure, deceiving	394	efficacious	Effective, efficient, useful
382	ductility	ability to change shape, form	395	efficacy	Effectiveness , value, ability
383	duplicity	Deceiving, dishonesty	396	ephemeral	Brief, temporary, passing
384	duress	Pressure, force, threat	397	epilogue	Conclusion, end remarks
385	Ebb	Back ward flow, retreat	398	epistemology	study of nature of knowledge
386	ebullience	Enthusiasm, liveliness , joy	399	epitome	Height , soul , principle
387	eccentric	Unusual, strange, peculiar	400	equanimity	Calmness, self-control

SET 9 (401- 450)

401	egregious	obviously bad or violent	405	elocution	Expression, articulation
402	elaborate	Decorative, detailed, large	406	eloquence	Fluency with speech, fluency
403	elation	Joy, delight, enthusiasm	407	elucidate	Explain, clarify, describe
404	elicit	Draw, come to conclusion	408	elusive	Difficult to understand

409	emaciate	make ,become extremely thin	427	equivocate	beat about the bush
410	emanate	Originate , come from , born	428	erratic	unreliable, irregular
411	emancipate	To free sb, release , liberate	429	erudite	Well-educated, learned
412	embellish	Exaggerate, increase, overdo	430	eschew	Avoid, stay away from , shun
413	embody	Represent, symbolize	431	esoteric	Mysterious, secret
414	embroil	Catch, to trap, involve	432	estrange	Dissatisfy, turn off
415	embryonic	Developing, early , primary	433	ethereal	From / of outer, other world
416	eminence	Fame, reputation, renown	434	eulogy	High praise , admiring words
417	emollient	Soothing, calming	435	euphemism	Restating in milder words
418	empathy	Understanding, sympathy	436	euphoria	Joy, jubilation, excitement
419	empirical	Experimental, observed	437	evanescent	Brief, temporary , passing
420	emulate	Compete with, rival, imitate	438	evince	Show, demonstration, reveal
421	encroach	Invade, interfere , violate	439	eviscerate	Remove the guts (intestines)
422	endemic	Widespread, common	440	evoke	Bring or call to mind, arouse
423	enervate	Weaken, fail , decline, worsen	441	exacerbate	Make worse, intensify
424	enfranchise	To give power, liberty to sb.	442	excise	Remove, edit, delete , erase
425	engender	Produce , create, cause	443	excoriate	Criticize, condemn , blame
426	equipoise	equality in distribution	444	exculpate	Free, excuse, clear, let off

445	exemplary	Mode, standard , example	448	exigent	Urgent, important, crucial
446	exemplify	Represent, show	449	exonerate	Forgive, pardon , clear (v)
447	exhume	Dig up (dead body) disclose	450	exorbitant	Excessive, unreasonable

SET 10 (451- 500)

451	enigma	Problem, confusion, mystery	465	extricate	Remove, disconnect
452	enmity	Being enemy, hatred	466	extrinsic	originate from outside; external
453	ennui	Boredom, laziness	467	Façade	A false show , not real , fake
454	ensue	Follow, result(v) arise	468	facet	Face, aspect, side, feature
455	entail	Involve, need, require	469	facetious	Silly, ridiculous, improper
456	entity	Unity, body, person, part	470	fallacy	Wrong idea, error, mistake
457	entreat	Ask, beg, request ,pray	471	fanatic	Extreme, intolerant in views
458	enumerate	Count, number (v) total (v)	472	fastidious	Hard to please, choosy, picky
459	enunciate	Speak, say, state (v) declare	473	fatuous	Silly, childish, foolish, unaware
460	envision	Predict, imagine, visualize	474	fecund	Productive, fruitful, useful
461	extol	Praise, admire, worship	475	felicitous	Suitable, appropriate , fitting
462	extort	Extract, take out , squeeze	476	expedient	Convenient, practical, useful
463	extraneous	Unnecessary , irrelevant	477	expiate	make up for a loss , correct (v)
464	extrapolate	Draw conclusion , conclude	478	explicate	Explain, clarify

479	explicit	Clear, obvious , plain, open	490	germane	Useful, relevant, to the point
480	exposition	Exposition, description	491	germinate	Grow, develop, take root
481	expostulate	Disagree, object (v) complain	492	gratis	Free of charge, cost free
482	expunge	Erase, delete, clean up, cut	493	gratuitous	Costless, at no charge , free
483	extant	Present, living, existing	494	Grave	n (adj.) serious, important
484	extenuate	decrease seriousness of a crime	495	gregarious	Outgoing, sociable , friendly
485	extirpate	Root out & destroy completely	496	grovel	Plead, beg, crawl, creep
486	gamut	Extent, range, scale, scope	497	guile	Cheating , deceiving, cunning
487	garble	Confuse, jumble, twist	498	guise	A false appearance or show
488	garrulous	Talkative, chatty , chatterbox	499	gullible	Easily deceived, not clever
489	genre	Type, sort, category , class	500	Hackneyed	Out of use, old , common

SET 11 (501- 550)

501	fervent	Keen, eager, enthusiast	506	florid	Flowery, fancy, showy
502	fester	Annoy, make sb. angry	507	flourish	Decoration, show (n) display
503	fiat	Approval, agree, command	508	flout	Break, disobey , not follow
504	flagrant	Open , rude, disrespectful	509	flux	Unrest, instability, change
505	fledgling	Inexperienced, new , young	510	foment	Encourage, increase , fuel (v)

511	foray	Attack, offence , raid	525	gambit	Scheme, plan to attract sb.
512	forebode	Predict, foretell , future fear	526	haphazard	Without a plan, jumbled, messy
513	forensic	scientific criminal investigation	527	hapless	Unlucky, unfortunate
514	forestall	Expect, foresee , prevent	528	harbinger	Sb/sth that brings a news , herald
515	fortuitous	Casual , unplanned , accidental	529	haughty	Proud, arrogant
516	frenetic	Mad, wild, over excited	530	hedonistic	Lover of all kinds of pleasures
517	frivolous	Playful, jokingly, not seriously	531	hegemony	Power, control, domination
518	frugal	Very careful in spending	532	heinous	Terrible, shocking, dreadful , evil
519	fruition	Completion, fulfillment, maturity	533	heresy	Rebelling against standard beliefs
520	fulminate	Get angry at sb. strongly criticize	534	hermetic	Closed, airtight, sealed
521	fulsome	Excessive , overdone , faltering	535	heterodox	Contradictory to accepted beliefs
522	furtive	Sneaky, secretive , hidden	536	Hetero-geneous	Mixed, diverse, varied, miscellaneous , made up of variety
523	futile	Useless, pointless, worthless	537	hiatus	Pause, break, interruption
524	Gainsay	Oppose, argue, deny , contradict	538	hindrance	Interference , stoppage , hurdle

No	Word	Meaning / synonym	No	Word	Meaning / synonym
539	homage	Respect, admiration , tribute	545	Iconoclast	Reformer, free thinker , rebel
540	Homo-geneous	Similar, standard, identical , uniform , made up of similar things	546	ideology	Philosophy, belief, thought
541	hubris	Extreme pride or self-confidence	547	idiom	Saying , phrase, expression
542	hyperbole	Exaggeration, overstatement	548	Idio-syncrasy	characteristic , unique unusual features of sb's personality
543	hypocritical	Two-faced, insincere , false	549	ignominious	Embarrassing, shameful
544	hypothetical	Imaginary, supposed	550	imbroglio	Embarrassment, mess, confusion

SET 12 (551- 600)

No	Word	Meaning / synonym	No.	Word	Meaning / synonymy
551	imbue	Fill, instill	559	impetuous	Quick to act , impulsive
552	imminent	About to happen, coming up	560	implacable	Cruel, pitiless , ruthless
553	immolate	Kill, sacrifice, protest	561	implicate	Involve, link, accuse
554	immutable	Absolute, unchallengeable	562	implicit	Understood, hidden, indirect
555	impeccable	Perfect, faultless , spotless	563	implore	Request, beg, pray, appeal
556	impecunious	Poor, penniless , struggling	564	importunate	Persisting, demanding
557	impediment	Weakness, obstacle, hurdle	565	imprecation	Insult, swearword , oath
558	impervious	Resistant, damage proof	566	impromptu	Unarranged, unprepared

567	impugn	Question (v) doubt, dispute	583	ineffable	unspeakable , beyond words
568	impunity	Exemption, freedom	584	ineluctable	sure, certain, unpreventable
569	inadvertent	Unintentional , by chance	585	inert	slow, lazy, slow-moving , inactive
570	inalienable	Absolute, undeniable	586	inexorable	unstoppable, unshakeable
571	inane	Childish, silly	587	infamous	notorious, dishonorable
572	inaugurate	Establish, start, open	588	infer	conclude, assume, understand
573	incandescent	Bright, shining, glowing	589	infested	place full of harmful insects etc.
574	incarcerate	Put in jail, imprison	590	infiltrate	break into, creep into , enter
575	incarnation	Avatar, personification	591	infrastructure	building, structure, set up
576	indefatigable	untiring, determined	592	infringe	interfere with, invade, overstep
577	indelible	permanent, stubborn, fixed	593	ingenuous	inexperienced, not clever
578	indict	accuse, blame, charge	594	ingratiate	come close to sb, to get favor
579	indigenous	native, original, local, homegrown	595	inherent	natural, inborn , characteristic
580	indolent	lazy, inactive	596	innate	natural, inborn
581	indomitable	unconquerable, stubborn , tough	597	innocuous	harmless , innocent, mild , safe
582	induce	encourage, persuade , convince	598	innuendo	indirect reference, hint , suggestion

| 599 | insatiable | greedy, not possible to satisfy | 600 | inscrutable | mysterious, difficult to understand |

SET 13 (601- 650)

601	incendiary	Sth that can be burnt (fire)	615	incursion	Spread, invasion , arrival
602	incensed	Angry, annoyed , furious	616	interstices	gaps, spaces, cracks
603	inception	Start, beginning, origin	617	intervene	interfere, get involved
604	incessant	Non-stop, continual	618	intractable	stubborn ,willful, unbending
605	incidental	Related, minor, secondary	619	intransigent	inflexible, narrow-minded
606	incipient	Initial, in early stage	620	intrepid	bold, fearless, courageous
607	incisive	Keen, sharp , razor-sharp	621	intrinsic	basic, fundamental, central
608	incite	Provoke, encourage	622	introspective	thoughtful, deep thinking
609	incoherent	Confused, disjointed	623	inundate	flood, overwhelm
610	incongruous	Strange, inconsistent	624	inured	trained, used , hardened
611	Incontro-vertible	Undeniable , unquestionable	625	invective	criticize, abuse, attack
612	incorrigible	Hopeless, persistent	626	insidious	deceiving, cunning, sneaky , sly
613	increment	Increase, growth	627	insipid	dull, uninteresting, unexciting
614	inculcate	Teach, instruct, put in mind	628	insolvent	broke, bankrupt, very poor

629	insouciant	uncaringly, casual, unconcerned	640	intersperse	scatter, spread, sprinkle, intermix
630	instigate	start, provoke, bring about	641	loath	hate, dislike , unwilling
631	insular	narrow minded , limited	642	loquacious	talkative
632	insurgent	rebel , rebellious, rising against sb	643	lucid	fluent and good at speaking
633	integral	necessary, important, basic	644	ludicrous	ridiculous, stupid, silly
634	intelligible	understandable, clear, logical	645	lugubrious	sad, depressing, gloomy
635	intemperate	extreme or careless in behavior	646	luminous	shining, bright, brilliant
636	interim	temporary, short term	647	luster	shine, gloss
637	interloper	gatecrasher , uninvited , interfering	648	Magnanimous	Nobel, generous, high-minded
638	interlude	pause, break, interval, wait	649	malapropism	confusing / misusing words
639	intermittent	happening irregularly, random	650	malevolent	being mean, wicked , unkind

SET 14 (651- 700)

651	inveigh	complain, protest, abuse,	656	iridescent	shining with bright colors
652	inveterate	incurable , hardened	657	ironic	mocking, making fun of
653	invidious	unpleasant, undesirable	658	irresolute	unsure, undetermined
654	invincible	unconquerable , strong	669	irreverence	disrespect, making fun of
655	irascible	Sb. who is easily angered	660	Juxtapose	put side by side compare

661	kindle	spark, light, burn, set on fire	679	marginal	on the edge or border, little
662	kinetic	moving, mobile	680	meager	not enough, miserable, scanty
663	labyrinth	puzzle, jumble, confusion	681	meander	wander about , roam , stroll
664	laconic	brief, short, to the point	682	melee	unrest, fighting, disturbance
665	lascivious	indecent, dirty minded	683	mellifluous	smooth, sweet, pleasant
666	lassitude	tiredness, laziness	684	menagerie	zoo, farm
667	latent	hidden, covered, underlying	685	mendicant	homeless, wanderer, beggar
668	latitude	freedom, space, opportunity	686	mentor	trainer, advisor, teacher
669	laudatory	admiring, praising	687	meretricious	insincere, deceiving, false
670	lavish	overdone, wasteful, give	688	metamorphosis	transform, change
671	legacy	inheritance, heritage	689	metaphor	comparison, comparing words
672	legitimate	sincere, legal , lawful	690	metaphysical	only in theory, philosophical
673	lethargic	tired, weary, lazy	691	meticulous	careful, perfectionist
674	levity	cheerfulness , joking , fun	692	minion	follower, slave, assistant
675	libel	defaming sb. insulting	693	misanthropy	hateful, unkind towards others
676	malice	hate, meanness, cruelty	694	miserly	stingy, mean
677	malignant	evil, hateful, wicked	695	misinformation	dishonesty , wrong information
678	malleable	soft, flexible, bending	696	misogyny	hatred of women by men

| 697 | mitigate | lessen, decrease, reduce | 699 | monolithic | huge, big, solid, uniform |
| 698 | mnemonic | reminder, memory-aid | 700 | moratorium | to suspend, delay, pause, stop |

SET 15 (701- 750)

701	licentious	lustful, looking for pleasure	713	nemesis	opponent, enemy, rival
702	lionize	praise, glorify, celebrate	714	*neophyte	beginner, inexperienced, learner , (*new plant)
703	litany	prayer, request , list	715	nexus	connection, link, unity
704	litigate	court case, file legal case	716	noisome	disgusting, horrible, dangerous, foul, sickening
705	livid	very angry, furious, mad	717	notorious	infamous, with bad repute
706	liaison	link, connection, relationship	718	noxious	harmful, dangerous, deadly
707	leeway	Freedom, flexibility	719	nullify	cancel out, abolish
708	munificence	kindness, charity, generosity	720	Obdurate	stubborn, not flexible
709	nadir	base, foot, lowest point	721	obfuscate	complicate, confuse
710	narcissist	too much self-love/ praise	722	oblique	slanting, leaning
711	nebulous	unclear, not explained well	723	obliterate	destroy, demolish, abolish
712	nefarious	evil, wicked, immoral	724	obscure	unclear, confusing , doubtful

725	obsequious	obedient or serving to an extreme degree by lowering one's self like a slave	738	pandemic	disease that spreads fast
726	mordant	harsh, cutting, biting	739	panegyric (n) /ˌpanəˈjirik/	A public speech or published text in praise of someone or something
727	motility	moving, having power to move	740	paradigm	model, example, pattern
728	multifarious	of different types or variety	741	paradox	puzzle, contradiction
729	multiplicity	being of many different forms	742	paragon	model, ideal , best sample
730	mundane	ordinary, worldly, unexciting	743	parameter	limit, restriction, scope , area
731	mediocrity	of average , ordinary standard	744	paranoia	fear, distrust , doubt, suspicion
732	morose	sad, depressed, pessimistic	745	pariah	exile , outsider , alone
733	Pacify	clam, soothe , to comfort	746	parody	copy / imitate sb. to make fun
734	paean	song or expression of joy	747	parsimony	stinginess, careful in spending
735	palatable	pleasant, tasty, delicious	748	partisan	one-sided, prejudiced, unfair
736	palliate	Make (a disease or its symptoms) less severe or unpleasant without removing the cause.	749	pathology	science of the causes and effects of diseases
737	palpable	physical, sth. that can touched and felt , deep, substantial	750	pathos	sorrow, feelings of pity or sympathy

SET 16 (751- 800)

751	obstinate	stubborn, determined	764	opulent	wealthy, rich, luxurious
752	obstreperous	noisy, disorderly, disturbing	765	orthodox	traditional , following rules
753	obtrusive	obvious, unmistakable	766	oscillate	unable to decide, hesitate
754	obtuse	stupid, slow, simple minded	767	osmosis /äz'mōsis/	process of gradual or unconscious adaptation of ideas, knowledge, etc.
755	obviate	remove, avoid, prevent	768	ossify	harden , to make / turn solid
756	occlude	block, stop, shut off , close	769	ostensibly	apparently , seemingly
757	officious	bossy, self-important	770	ostentatious	showy, flashy, artificial
758	ominous	dangerous looking, worrying	771	overwrought	stressed, nervous , excitable
759	omniscient	all-knowing, wise	772	oxymoron	contradictory terms, *true lies , pretty ugly*
760	onerous	heavy, difficult, tiring	773	pervade	enter, infiltrate , cover
761	ontology	study of nature of existence	774	pervasive	prevalent, persistent
762	opaque	Solid, not able to be seen through; not transparent	775	petulant/ 'peCHələnt/	grumpy, moody, sulky or bad-tempered, childish
763	opprobrium	criticism, disapproval	776	paucity	very rare, hard to find

777	pedagogy	teaching, teaching methodology	789	perpetrator	criminal, sb. who does sth. wrong
778	pedantic	dull, concern for book learning and formal rules, too much unnecessary attention to details, deep, hidden	790	perpetuate	continue, extend , prolong
779	pedestrian	unexciting, ordinary, sb. walking along a road	791	perplex	puzzle, confuse
780	pejorative	harsh, negative , mocking	792	perquisite	privilege, bonus, extra advantage
781	pellucid	clear, bright, easily understood.	793	persevere	persist, insist, continue, endure
782	penchant	likeness, fondness , desire	794	perspicacious	wise, clear-sighted
783	penury	poverty, being hand to mouth	795	pertinent	related, relevant , appropriate
784	perfidious	disloyal, dishonest	796	perturbation	alarm, worry, uneasiness
785	perfunctory	unthinking , routine, mechanical	797	peruse	examine, check, inspect
786	peripheral	bordering , outer, marginal	798	prevail	succeed, overcome
787	permeate	fill, soak, infiltrate, seep (move) into sth.	799	prevaricate (equivocate)	act or speak in an indirect way, avoid , lie , try to escape, avoid giving straight answer, beat about the bush
788	pernicious	wicked, evil, harmful	800	proactive	active, well prepared for an action, practical, positive, ready

SET 17 (801- 850)

801	philanthropist	kind, helping others	813	pluralism	variety, of too many types
802	phlegmatic	having or showing a slow and dull temperament	814	polarize	separate, divide, oppose
803	piety	goodness of character	815	polemic	outspoken, bold, aggressive attack on or rejection of sb's opinions, belief's
804	pillory	(n) wooden framework with holes, (v) to abuse, curse	816	ponderous	weighty, heavy, awkward
805	piquant	hot spicy, tasty, pleasant	817	porous	Full of or having small holes
806	pique	anger, temper, displeasure	817	posthumous	occurring later, after sb's death (born after father's death)
807	placate	to satisfy, lessen sb's anger	818	postulate	guess, assume, suppose
808	placebo	fake (false) treatment to satisfy a patient, sample	819	pragmatic	practical, useful, realistic
809	platitude	meaningless, biased remark	820	precarious	risky, dangerous
810	plausible	believable, reasonable	821	precede	come before (sth) in time, come before in order or position
811	plethora	too much of sth. excess	822	precedent	example, model, practice
812	pliable	bendable, flexible (plastic)	823	precept	principle, teaching, rule

824	precipitous	rash, hurried, quick to act *precipitate (v) to enhance	836	prolix	using too many words , wordy
825	preclude	stop, prevent	837	promulgate	announce, enforce, spread
826	probity	justice, honor, correctness	838	propagate	
827	proclivity	liking, taste, bent, desire	839	propensity	tendency , liking, partiality
828	procrustean	relentless, merciless	840	propinquity	closeness, nearness, close relationship, convenience
829	procure	obtain, get, gain	841	propitiate	to please sb. to calm down sb.
830	prodigal	wasteful	842	propitious	
831	prodigious	extraordinary, wonderful	843	propound	Put forward (an idea, theory, or point of view) for consideration, propose, suggest , present
832	profligate	careless, wasteful	843	prosaic	simple, ordinary, unexciting
833	profuse	plentiful, generous , much	844	proscribe	ban , stop, disallow, veto, forbid
834	proliferate	increase, grow	845	protean	changeable, inconsistent
835	prolific	creative, productive, fruitful	846	protocol	rules, code of behavior, rules, The official procedure to manage affairs of state or diplomatic occasions.

| 847 | protrude | stick out, project (v) extend outward | 849 | prowess | ability, skill, competence , special talent, strength |
| 848 | provincial | local, regional, district , of province | 850 | proximity | nearness, closeness , area, range |

SET 18 (851- 900)

851	precocious	talented, gifted, advanced, intelligent spec. of a promising child (prodigy)	860	presuppose	suppose, assume, accept
852	precursor	pioneer, originator, sign	861	pretense	trick, act of deceiving , con
853	predecessor	ancestor, previous	862	quiescent	calm, slow, gentle, still motionless, inactive
854	predilection	liking, fondness, preference	863	quintessential	ideal, exemplary , essential
855	predominant	main, major, controlling	864	quixotic	idealistic, unrealistic, impractical, imaginary
856	preemptive	preventive, protective	865	Ramification	consequence, result, effect
857	preponderance	greater number, majority	866	rampant	widespread, extensive
858	prescience	ability to see or know before it happens, foresight	867	rapacious / rəˈpāSHəs/	Aggressively greedy or selfish: taking by force
859	presumptuous	rude, arrogant, bold , rash	868	rapport / raˈpôr/	connection, relationship, understanding, dealings

869	rational	sensible, having common sense , reasonable , wise	880	purported	supposed, claimed
870	rationale	basis, justification, reasoning, logic	881	putative	assumed, recognized, accepted
871	raucous	disorderly, noisy, loud, rough, wild , harsh	882	qualm	doubt, objection
872	rebuff	rejection, refusal, to deny	883	quandary	difficulty, complicated situation, dilemma , catch 22
873	rebut	show to false, deny, reject	884	quasi /kweɪzaɪ/	fake, pretending to be real, Having a likeness to something
874	recalcitrant	disobedient, unmanageable, stubborn	885	quell	crush, control, defeat, eliminate
875	recant	withdraw, take back	886	querulous	difficult, critical, hard to please
876	prudent	practical, wise, careful , cautious, sensible , planning carefully	887	retrospect	thinking about past, looking back, review, reconsideration
877	pundit(Indian)	expert, specialist, authority	888	revamp	improve look or condition of sth.
878	pungent	strong, having sharp taste , spicy	889	revulsion	disgust, dislike, horror, distaste
879	punitive	correcting by punishment , penal	890	rife	widespread, common

891	rotund	round , overweight, fat, plump	896	salient	most important, main, noticeable
892	rubric	title, heading , rule book , an established rule, tradition, or custom; guide listing specific criteria for grading or scoring academic papers, projects, or tests	897	salutary	useful, helpful, valuable
893	rudimentary	basic, fundamental , simple	898	sanction	permission, approval, agreement
894	sacrilege	speaking out bad things about a religion or holy things	899	sanguine	confident, optimistic, hopeful
895	sagacious	wise, intelligent, knowledgeable	900	satire	to mock or make fun of sth, sb.

SET 19 (901- 950)

901	recidivist	criminal, repeatedly breaking law	909	relegate	lower the position, reduce
902	recluse	sb. who stays alone , loner	910	remuneration	payment, salary, wages
903	recondite	little known , complex	911	rend	tear apart, rip apart
904	rectify	correct, repair, fix	912	renounce	refuse, refund, give up
905	redress	restore, solve a problem	913	replete	full, complete , filled
906	redundant	jobless, fired, extra, not needed anymore	914	replicate	duplicate (v) copy, imitate
907	refractory	stubborn, rebellious	915	reprehensible	wrong, shameful, bad
908	refute	contradict, deny, refuse	916	reprobate	trouble maker, no good

917	repudiate	reject, disclaim, deny	932	seamless	joined, in one piece , whole
918	repugnant	shocking, distasteful	933	sedentary	inactive, not moving, fixed , lazy
919	rescind	cancel, withdraw	934	sedulous	diligent, hardworking, keen
920	residual	remaining, left over	935	seminal	important, significant
921	resilient	strong, resistant	936	sententious	critical, moralizing, disapproving
922	resolute	firm, stubborn, definite	937	sequester	take away by force, repossess
923	respite	interval, break, relief	938	serene	calm, quiet, peaceful
924	resplendent	brilliant, stunning , shining	939	serpentine	winding, twisting , indirect
925	reticent	restraint , quiet	940	servile	behaving like a slave, too obedient (from *serve*)
926	saturnine	sad, depressed, sorrowful	941	shard	chip, piece, part
927	savory	spicy, tasty	942	simile	comparison of one thing with another with words, *as , like*
928	scant	slight, little, not enough	943	sinuous	twisting, winding, flowing
929	schism	break, division, split, separation	944	sloth	laziness, idleness
930	scrupulous	trustworthy, reliable, careful	945	slough	an area of soft, muddy ground;
931	scrutiny	analysis, careful study, search	946	solemn	sincere, serious , firm, intense

| 947 | solicit | ask, request, beg | 949 | soporific | causing sleep , calming |
| 948 | somber | gloomy, serous, | 950 | spacious | open, with much space , large |

SET 20 (951- 1000)

951	retract	withdraw, pull back, apologize	960	staid	serious, dull, calm, settled
952	specious	false, baseless	961	static	still, fixed, not moving,
953	spectrum	range, field, variety	962	stigma	shame, disgrace, dishonor
954	splenetic	dad-tempered, irritable	963	stipulate	specify, instruct, demand
955	spontaneous	quick to act, rash , at once	964	stoic	passive, not caring, unresponsive , uninterested
956	sporadic	random, irregular	965	stratagem	A plan or scheme, esp. one used to outwit an opponent or achieve an end, trick
957	spurious	false, bogus, not real	966	stratify	quiet, not talkative
958	squalid	dirty, filthy, nasty	967	stupor /'st(y)oopər/	A state of near-unconsciousness or insensibility
959	stagnant	still, not moving, motionless	968	subjugate	defeat, over power, take full control over sb./ sth.

969	subliminal	unintentional, unconscious, hidden, sending a message or information through sounds or pictures to the mind, as in advertisements	978	synopsis	outline, summary
970	subside	lessen, decrease	979	syntax	grammar, sentence structure
971	subsidize	support, sponsor, to give financial assistance	980	synthesis	mixture, blend , making sth by mixing items or materials
972	substantiate	verify, confirm, support	981	systemic	total, universal, complete, general
973	substantive	practical, basic , actual, real, considerable	982	tacit/'tasit/	silent, unspoken , understood
974	subterfuge	trick, Cheat in order to achieve one's goal	983	taciturn	quiet, not talkative
975	subtle	So slight as to be difficult to notice or describe, fine	984	tangential (tangent)	relating to or along a tangent , tangent - a line which touch a curve, but which when produced, does not cut it
976	spate	flood, wave, outbreak	985	tangible	sth. you can touch and feel, having a physical form , real, solid
977	synchronize	Harmonize, match, and cause to occur or operate at the same time or rate, Occur at the same time or rate	986	taut	firm, stiff, tense, severe

987	tawdry	cheap, flashy, showy	994	tepid	warm, not too hot, lukewarm, halfhearted, showing little enthusiasm or interest
988	tedium	tiring, boredom, dullness, without excitement	995	terse	brief, short and meaningful
989	teem	be full of, laded, crowded	996	timorous	nervous, fearful, frightened, shy, afraid
990	temerity	boldness, disrespect, being bold and brave in a very disrespectful way , challenging, rebelling	997	tirade	long angry speech or criticism
991	tenacious	stubborn, determined	998	torpid	lazy, sleepy, inactive
992	tendentious	argumentative, prejudiced, one-sided, biased, marked by a tendency in favor of a particular point of view	999	tortuous	twisting, indirect, roundabout , winding , Full of twists and turns. Excessively lengthy and complex: "a tortuous argument".
993	tenuous	weak, unconvincing, shaky, questionable	1000	tractable	easy to manage, control, obedient , ready to follow orders

SET 21 (1001- 1060)

1001	succinct	brief, to the point	1014	surreptitious	secretive , secret, sneaky
1002	suffice	sufficient , enough	1015	susceptible	at risk, Likely or liable to be influenced or harmed by a particular thing
1003	suffuse	fill up, cover	1016	sycophant	flatterer , yes man
1004	sullen	bad tempered , angry, slow moving, gloomy	1017	uninterested	uncaring
1005	sumptuous	luxurious, wonderful	1018	unkempt	messy, disorderly
1006	sunder	divide, separate , break, cut	1019	unobtrusive	modest, humble , quiet, not attracting attention
1007	superficial	artificial , only at surface	1020	untoward	unpleasant, unfortunate
1008	superfluous	extra, unnecessary, excessive	1021	upbraid	scold, blame, accuse
1009	superlative	excellent, outstanding, best	1022	utopian	ideal, idealistic, sb. who imagines of a perfect world
1010	supersede	overtake, go ahead	1023	Vacillate	hesitate, not sure , unable to decide
1011	suppress	conquer, defeat, destroy	1024	vacuity	immorality, wickedness
1012	surfeit	oversupply, excess	1025	vacuous	hesitate, not sure , unable to decide
1013	surmise	draw a conclusion , guess	1026	vapid	immorality, wickedness

1027	vehement	present everywhere, at all times, universal, global , sth. that makes its presence felt	1035	transparent	sth. you can see through
1028	veneer	hidden, secret, unknown, mysterious , Existing beyond what is obvious or admitted	1036	transpire	become known, happen
1029	venerate	one-sided, individual , independent	1037	trenchant	sharp, cutting, biting
1030	verdant	lush, green , fertile, grassy	1038	trepidation	fear, anxiety, concern, nervousness
1031	transcend	go beyond, excel (v)	1039	truculence	A nature or mood to fight, especially violently. Fiercely cruel actions or behavior. Expressing bitter opposition
1032	transient	short lived, temporary	1040	turbid	confused, unclear, disorganized
1033	transitory	passing, brief, temporary	1041	turbulence	confusion, unrest, disorder , chaos
1034	translucent	shining, bright, transparent	1042	turgid	swollen, using too difficult and unnecessary words to enhance style in language

1043	turpitude	immorality, wickedness	1052	virulent /'vir(y)ələnt/	infectious, contagious, spreading fast, powerful, poisonous
1044	Ubiquitous	present everywhere, at all times, universal, global , sth. that makes its presence felt	1053	vituperation	outburst, criticism, attack, abuse
1045	ulterior	hidden, secret, unknown, mysterious , Existing beyond what is obvious or admitted	1054	vociferous	loud, noisy, enthusiastic , crying out loudly and madly
1046	unilateral	one-sided, individual , independent	1055	volatile	in an unstable and dangerous situation or circumstances
1047	verity	truth, fact, reality, actuality, principle	1056	voluble	talkative, fluent at speaking
1048	viable	practical, worthwhile	1057	voracious	greedy, greedy for much food having a very eager approach to an activity.
1049	vicarious	Acting or done for another, indirect	1058	Warrant	certification, license, authorization
1050	vilify	criticize, accuse, speak or write about sth. / sb. in an abusive and critical manner	1059	zeal	enthusiasm, passion , strong desire
1051	virtuoso	skillful, expert, brilliant	1060	zest	passion, keenness

14 BORROWED OR LOAN WORDS IN ENGLISH

1. Scandinavian

anger, blight, by-law, cake, call, clumsy, doze, egg, fellow, gear, get, give, hale, hit, husband, kick, kill, kilt, kindle, law, low, lump, rag, raise, root, scathe, scorch, score, scowl, scrape, scrub, seat, skill, skin, skirt, sky, sly, take, they, them, their, thrall, thrust, ugly, want, window, wing

- **Place name suffixes:** by, -thorpe, -gate

2. French

- **Law and government**: attorney, bailiff, chancellor, chattel, country, court, crime, defendent, evidence, government, jail, judge, jury, larceny, noble, parliament, plaintiff, plea, prison, revenue, state, tax, verdict
- **Church**: abbot, chaplain, chapter, clergy, friar, prayer, preach, priest, religion, sacrament, saint, sermon
- **Nobility**: baron, baroness; count, countess; duke, duchess; marquis, marquess; prince, princess; viscount, viscountess; noble, royal (contrast native words: king, queen, earl, lord, lady, knight, kingly, queenly)
- **Military**: army, artillery, battle, captain, company, corporal, defense,enemy,marine, navy, sergeant, soldier, volunteer
- **Cooking**: beef, boil, broil, butcher, dine, fry, mutton, pork, poultry, roast, salmon, stew, veal
- **Culture and luxury goods:** art, bracelet, claret, clarinet, dance, diamond, fashion, fur, jewel, oboe, painting, pendant, satin, ruby, sculpture
- **Other**: adventure, change, charge, chart, courage, devout, dignity, enamor, feign, fruit, letter, literature, magic, male, female, mirror, pilgrimage, proud, question, regard, special

3. Latin

- agile, abdomen, anatomy, area, capsule, compensate, dexterity, discus, disc/ disk, excavate, expensive, fictitious, gradual, habitual, insane, janitor, meditate, notorious, orbit, peninsula, physician, superintendent, ultimate, vindicate

4. Greek (many of these via Latin)

- anonymous, atmosphere, autograph, catastrophe, climax, comedy, critic, data, ectasy, history, ostracize, parasite, pneumonia, skeleton, tonic, tragedy
- Greek bound morphemes: -ism, -ize

5. Arabic

- *via Spanish*: alcove, algebra, zenith, algorithm, almanac, azimuth, alchemy, admiral
- *via other*: Romance languages—amber, cipher, orange, saffron, sugar, zero, coffee
- *via Persian:* caravan, magazine (Arabic *makhazin*)

6. French

- **High culture**:
  ballet, bouillabaise, cabernet, cachet, chaise longue, champagne, chic, cognac, corsage, faux pas, nom de plume, quiche, rouge, roulet, sachet, salon, saloon, sang froid, savoir faire
- **War and Military**: bastion, brigade, battalion, cavalry, grenade, infantry, pallisade, rebuff, bayonet
- **Other**—bigot, chassis, clique, denim, garage, grotesque, jean(s), niche, shock
- **French Canadian**: chowder
- **Louisiana French** (Cajun)—jambalaya

7. Spanish

- armada, adobe, alligator, alpaca, armadillo, barricade, bravado, cannibal, canyon, coyote, desperado, embargo, enchilada, guitar, marijuana, mesa, mosquito, mustang, ranch, taco, tornado, tortilla, vigilante

8. Italian

- alto, arsenal, balcony, broccoli, cameo, casino, cupola, duo, fresco, fugue, gazette (via French), ghetto, gondola, grotto, macaroni, madrigal, motto, piano, opera, pantaloons, prima donna, regatta, sequin, soprano, opera, stanza, stucco, studio, tempo, torso, umbrella, viola, violin
- from Italian American immigrants—cappuccino, espresso, linguini, mafioso, pasta, pizza, ravioli, spaghetti, spumante, zabaglione, zucchini

9. Dutch, Flemish

- Shipping, naval terms—avast, boom, bow, bowsprit, buoy, commodore, cruise, dock, freight, keel, keelhaul, leak, pump, reef, scoop, scour, skipper, sloop, smuggle, splice, tackle, yawl, yacht
- Cloth industry—bale, cambric, duck (fabric), fuller's earth, mart, nap (of cloth), selvage, spool, stripe
- Art—easel, etching, landscape, sketch
- War—beleaguer, holster, freebooter, furlough, onslaught
- Food and drink—booze, brandy(wine), coleslaw, cookie, cranberry, crullers, gin, hops, stockfish, waffle
- Other—bugger (orig. French), crap, curl, dollar, scum, split (orig. nautical term), uproar

10. German

- bum, dunk, feldspar, quartz, hex, lager, knackwurst, liverwurst, loafer, noodle, poodle, dachshund, pretzel, pinochle, pumpernickel, sauerkraut, schnitzel, zwieback, (beer)stein, lederhosen, dirndl
- 20th century German loanwords—blitzkrieg, zeppelin, strafe, U-boat, delicatessen, hamburger, frankfurter, wiener, hausfrau, kindergarten, Oktoberfest, schuss, wunderkind, bundt (cake), spritz (cookies), (apple) strudel

11.Yiddish (most are 20th century borrowings)

- bagel, Chanukkah (Hanukkah), chutzpah, dreidel, kibbitzer, kosher, lox, pastrami (orig. from Romanian), schlep, spiel, schlepp, schlemiel, schlimazel, gefilte fish, goy, klutz, knish, matzoh, oy vey, schmuck, schnook,

12. Scandinavian

- fjord, maelstrom, ombudsman, ski, slalom, smorgasbord

13. Russian

- apparatchik, borscht, czar/tsar, glasnost, icon, perestroika, vodka

14. Sanskrit

- avatar, karma, mahatma, swastika, yoga

15. Hindi

- bandanna, bangle, bungalow, chintz, cot, cummerbund, dungaree, juggernaut, jungle, loot, maharaja, nabob, pajamas, punch (the drink), shampoo, thug, kedgeree, jamboree, pundit

16. Dravidian

- curry, mango, teak, pariah

17. Persian (Farsi)

- check, checkmate, chess

18. Arabic

- bedouin, emir, jakir, gazelle, giraffe, harem, hashish, lute, minaret, mosque, myrrh, salaam, sirocco, sultan, vizier, bazaar, caravan

19. African languages

- banana (via Portuguese), banjo, boogie-woogie, chigger, goober, gorilla, gumbo, jazz, jitterbug, jitters, juke(box), voodoo, yam, zebra, zombie

20. American Indian languages

- avocado, cacao, cannibal, canoe, chipmunk, chocolate, chili, hammock, hominy, hurricane, maize, moccasin, moose, papoose, pecan, possum, potato, skunk, squaw, succotash, squash, tamale (via Spanish), teepee, terrapin, tobacco, toboggan, tomahawk, tomato, wigwam, woodchuck

- (plus thousands of place names, including Ottawa, Toronto, Saskatchewan and the names of more than half the states of the U.S., including Michigan, Alabama, Texas, Nebraska, Illinois)

21. Chinese

- chop suey, chow mein, dim sum, ketchup, tea, ginseng, kowtow, litchee

22. Japanese

- geisha, hara kiri, judo, jujitsu, kamikaze, karaoke, kimono, samurai, soy, sumo, sushi, tsunami

23. Pacific Islands

- bamboo, gingham, rattan, taboo, tattoo, ukulele, boondocks

24. Australia

- boomerang, budgerigar, didgeridoo, kangaroo (and many more in Australian English)

VOCABULARY: SURVIVAL KIT

And thou shall live by the word

Material selected and adapted from some of the very old
sources and books that are now almost becoming "extinct"

Set 1: Words about the Medical Profession

1. **Gynaecologist:** The doctor treating the ailments peculiar to women alone
2. **Obstetrician:** The doctor who helps in the delivery of babies
3. **Pediatrician:** The doctor who specializes in the treatment of children's diseases
4. **Oculist:** The doctor who specializes in the treatment of eye diseases
5. **Dermatologist:** The doctor who specializes in the treatment of skin diseases
6. **Orthopaedist:** The doctor who specializes in the treatment of various deformities of the body and bone
7. **Cardiologist:** The doctor who specializes in the treatment of heart diseases
   Neurologist: The doctor who specializes in the treatment of nervous system
8. **Psychiatrist:** The doctor who specializes in the treatment of disorders of mind and emotional disturbances
9. **Internist:** The doctor who specializes in the diagnosis of internal organs
10. **Podiatrist:** The doctor who specializes in the treatment of corns
11. **Optometrist:** The specialist who is not a doctor but examines the eyes for the sole purpose of prescribing spectacles and fitting eye glasses
12. **Optician:** The person who specializes in the manufacture, making and selling of eye glasses, lenses, binoculars
13. **Orthodontist:** The person who specializes in straightening of crooked teeth
14. **Intern:** The medical graduate serving as an apprentice in a hospital taking medical training

Set 2: Names of Scientists and their field of specialization

1. **Anthropologist:** One who studies the history of development of mankind
2. **Entomologist:** One whose field of study is insects
3. **Botanist:** One whose field of study is the life of plants
4. **Philologist:** One whose field of study is language
5. **Geologist:** One who specializes in the study of earth and its composition
6. **Semanticist:** One who specializes in the study of psychological effects of words
7. **Astronomer:** One who studies the plants and the heavenly bodies
8. **Zoologist:** One whose field of study is animals of all type
9. **Biologist:** One whose field of study is all living organisms
10. **Sociologist :** One who specialize in the study of social relationships, social customs, family life etc.

Set 3: Names of different subjects and their field of study

1. **Theology:** The study of religion
2. **Philology:** The study of manuscripts or written records
3. **Linguistics:** The study of languages
4. **Geology:** The study of the earth
5. **Physics:** The study of energy
6. **Typography:** The study of the art of printing
7. **Graphology:** The study of the art of hand-writing
8. **Zoology:** The study of animals
9. **Penology:** The study of prison reform
10. **Meteorology:** The study of the weather
11. **Agronomy:** The study of farming
12. **Biology:** The study of life
13. **Seismology:** The study of earthquakes
14. **Physiology:** The study of the functions of the body
15. **Anthoropology:** The study of man
16. **Embryology:** The study of unborn babies
17. **Botany:** The study of plants
18. **Etymology:** The study of words
19. **Archeology:** The study of ancient ruins
20. **Entomology:** The study of insects
21. **Astronomy:** The science which deals with study of the heavenly bodies
22. **Astrology:** The science of foretelling events by stars

Set 4: Important words indicating the personality traits of people

1. **Ascetic:** A person who lives an austere and lonely life. He is not interested in the worldly possessions
2. **Misogamist:** A person who hates the custom of marriage and does not want to marry
3. **Misogynist:** A person who hates the women and dislikes their company
4. **Misanthrope:** A person who hates his fellowmen and the mankind
5. **Ambivert:** A person who possesses both introverted and extroverted interests
6. **Extrovert:** A person who loves the company of other people without any inhibitions. He enjoys his social contacts and possesses thoughts which are turned outward. He expresses himself freely
7. **Introvert:** A person whose thoughts are turned inward, and he never opens his heart to others
8. **Altruist:** A person who is not much interested in his own welfare but he is much interested in the welfare of the others
9. **Egoist:** A selfish person who only thinks for himself
10. **Devotee:** A person who has great devotion for religious rites
11. **Kleptomaniac:** A person who has a passion for stealing
12. **Hypochondriac:** A person who suffers, from the imaginary illness
13. **Sceptic (skeptic)** person who is a constant doubter
14. **Convivialist:** A person who is jolly, cheerful and fond of festivities
15. **Philanthropist:** A person who loves mankind

Set 5: Words describing nature of people

1. **Loquacious:** Somebody who talks a great deal
2. **Taciturn:** Somebody who keeps silent as a habit
3. **Dexterous:** Somebody who is expert and skillful in using hands
4. **Maldroit:** Somebody who is clumsy with his/her hands
5. **Sanguine:** Somebody who has red blooded cheerful nature
6. **Despondent:** Somebody who has a gloomy nature
7. **Indefatigable:** Somebody who is very hard working and never tires
8. **Indolent:** Somebody who is lazy and likes to avoid exertion or physical activity
9. **Amiable:** Somebody who has a sweet and friendly nature
10. **Irascible:** Somebody who is easily annoyed
11. **Erudite:** Somebody who has an extensive knowledge
12. **Illiterate:** Somebody who is not educated

13. **Veteran:**   Somebody who is well experienced
14. **Punctilious:**   Somebody who is very formal in etiquettes and manners
15. **Literate:**   Somebody who is educated
16. **Unceremonious:**   Somebody who is rather informal in etiquettes and manners
17. **Pacifical:**   Somebody who is inclined to make peace with the people
18. **Bellicose:**   Somebody who is very aggressive and is always looking for a fight
19. **Compunctions:**   Somebody who feels sorry for a wrong he has done
20. **Obdurate:**   Somebody who is too stubborn to admit his errors
21. **Magnanimous:**   Somebody who is generous and has exalted soul
22. **Pusillanimous:**   Somebody who has a mean and cowardly soul
23. **Credulous:**   Somebody who is ready to believe everything too quickly

Set 6: Words about important "isms"

1. **Chauvinism:**   Advocating extreme patriotism even at the cost of other countries
2. **Nepotism:**   To show extreme favoritism towards one's relatives regardless of their qualifications
3. **Epicureanism:**   To believe that the purpose of life should be eat, drink and make merry or pursuit of pleasures
4. **Individualism:**   To believe in the theory of free trade policy or laissez faire
5. **Dogmatism:**   To assert one's opinions arrogantly without sufficient evidence
6. **Fanaticism:**   To show extreme enthusiasm (narrow-mindedly) in religious matters
7. **Rationalism:**   To form an opinions by following reason and logic
8. **Stoicism:**   Being indifferent to both pleasures or pain (adj. stoic)
9. **Liberalism:**   Favoring democratic reforms and being open minded in political matters
10. **Radicalism:**   Advocating extreme changes in political matters
11. **Conservatism:**   Believing in status quo (leave it as it is) and does not want any changes in the existing order of things and opposes political changes
12. **Capitalism:**   Advocating the system of private wealth and property acquired through private enterprise
13. **Anarchism:**   Advocating lawlessness and opposing every form of government
14. **Socialism:**   Advocating that the means of production should be owned of by the state
15. **Polytheism:**   Believing in many gods (polytheist)

16. **Monotheism:**   Believing in one God (monotheist)
17. **Agnosticism:**   Not knowing whether or not God exists (agnostic)
18. **Skepticism:**   Doubting everything and asserting nothing positively
19. **Atheism:**   Believing in the non-existence of God
20. **Egoism:**   Caring only for one's selfish interests
21. **Communism:**   A system of government that is opposite to the capitalist system of government, a theory or system of social organization based on the holding of all property in common, actual ownership being ascribed to the community as a whole or to the state.
22. **Fascism:**   Believing in the overthrow of the radicals and rule by a strong dictator

Set 7: Manias and Phobias

1. **Agromania:**   A desire to live in the open country especially in loneliness
2. **Bibliomania:**   Intense desire for collecting books
3. **Dipsomania:**   An abnormal craving for drink
4. **Egomania:**   An excessive and gloomy love of oneself
5. **Megalomania:**   It is an exaggerated worship of one's own greatness
6. **Monomania:**   An obsession with one particular object or idea
7. **Nymphomania:**   Ungovernable sexual desire on the part of a woman
8. **Plutomania:**   It means a madness for money
9. **Ailurophobia:**   It means a strong fear of cats
10. **Androphobia:**   It means an irrational fear of man
11. **Claustrophobia:**   It means an excessive dread of enclosed places, deep fear of being locked in
12. **Cynophobia:**   It means a morbid fear of dogs
13. **Hydrophobia:**   It means an overpowering dread of water. It is also the name of disease resulting from the bite of a mad dog
14. **Hypsophobia:**   It means an uncontrollable fear of high places
15. **Nyctophobia:**   It means an excessive fear of night or of darkness
16. **Thanatophobia:**   It means an irrational fear of death
17. **Triskaidekaphobia:** It means fear of the number 13
18. **Xenophobia:**   It means an aversion to strangers or foreigners

Set 8: Words to flatter people around you

1. **Convivial**:   Jovial, cordial, affable etc.
2. **Indefatigable:**   Untiring
3. **Ingenuous:**   Frank, unsophisticated, innocent

4. **Industrious:**   Diligent, Hart working
5. **Magnanimous:**   Generous
6. **Versatile:**   Capable of dealing with many subjects, master of all trades
7. **Stoic:**   Indifferent to pains and pleasures, no grumbling
8. **Intrepid:**   Dauntless, fearless
9. **Audacious:**   Bold, daring
10. **Scintillating:**   Brilliant, delightful, witty
11. **Urbane:**   Cultivated, sophisticated, civilized, smooth mannered
12. **Erudite:**   A learned person
13. **Gregarious:**   Sociable, fond of company
14. **Perspicacious:**   Clear-sighted, clear-minded
15. **Popular:**   Liked by every body

Set 9: Twenty important Verbs

1. **Calumniate:**   To accuse falsely; to slander
2. **Commence:**   To begin; to originate
3. **Conjecture:**   To guess; to infer
4. **Contradict:**   To oppose by words; to deny
5. **Detest:**   To hate intensely
6. **Deteriorate:**   To make worse
7. **Emancipate:**   To set free from restraint or bondage
8. **Admonish:**   To warn; to reprove mildly
9. **Manipulate:**   To handle or manage; to turn to one's advantage
10. **Impede:**   To hinder or obstruct
11. **Disparage:**   Play down, belittle
12. **Titillate:**   Tickle, delight
13. **Adulate:**   Flatter lavishly; worship
14. **Proscribe:**   Prohibit. Forbid
15. **Obviate:**   Make unnecessary
16. **Militate:**   Work against; to fight for a cause
17. **Malign:**   Slander; spread malicious rumors about
18. **Placate:**   To conciliate; change hostility to friendliness
19. **Seduce:**   To lead astray; to entice; to induce to have sexual intercourse
20. **Singe:**   To burn on the surface; to scorch

Set 10: Twenty three important Adjectives

1. **Notorious:**   Well known for some bad quality
2. **Consummate:**   Perfect, highly skilled

3. **Incorrigible:** Beyond reform
4. **Congenial:** Suitable; to one's liking
5. **Congenital:** Existing at birth, dating from birth
6. **Chronic:** Going on for a long time, lasting a long time
7. **Psychopathic:** Mentally or emotionally diseased
8. **Unconscionable:** Without pangs of conscience
9. **Glib:** Fluent, more voluble than sincere; suspiciously fluent talker
10. **Myopic:** Near-sighted
11. **Presbyopic:** Far sighted
12. **Spasmodic:** Convulsive
13. **Eccentric:** Queer
14. **Toxic:** Poisonous
15. **Masochistic:** Enjoying cruel treatment, satisfaction of sexual impulses by endurance of pain
16. **Antiseptic:** Germ killing
17. **Sadistic**: Love of inflicting pain
18. **Aesthetic:** Fond of beauty
19. **Enigmatic** Puzzling'
20. **Sardonic:** Cynical
21. **Sycophantic:** Addicted to giving false flattery
22. **Titanic:** Huge
23. **Phlegmatic:** Not easily excited

16 FOREIGN WORDS AND PHRASES USED IN ENGLISH

The English meanings given below are not necessarily literal translations

1. **ab intio** (āb ĭ-nĭsh'ē-ō') [Lat.] from the beginning:

   E.g. I did not agree to the proposal *ab intio*.

2. **ad absurdum** (ad ab-sir'dum) [Lat.]: to the point of absurdity.

   E.g. He kept on repeating his argument *ad absurdum.*"

3. **ad hoc** (ˈad-ˈhäk) For the specific purpose, case, or situation at hand

   E.g. Professor Rozenberg was appointed *ad hoc* lecture in the department of sociology.

4. **ad infinitum** ad in-fun-eye'tum) [Lat.]: to infinity.

   E.g. The boring lecture seemed to drag on *ad infinitum*.

5. **alma mater** (al-mə-ˈmä-tər) [Lat.] a school, college, or university at which one has studied and, usually, from which one has graduated (literal meaning: gracious , nourishing mother)

   E.g. He went to visit his *alma mater* and to meet some of his old professors at the good old institute.

6. **ad interm** (ĭnˈtər-əm) [Lat.] in the meantime , a temporarily arrangement

   E.g. The speaker of the national assembly became the *interim* president after the president resigned from his office on the account of illness.

7. **ad nauseam** (ad noz'ee-um) [Lat.]: to a sickening degree.

   E.g. The politician described his achievements one after another ***ad nauseam.***

8. **aficionado** (uh-fish'ya-nah'doh) [Span.]: an enthusiastic fan.

   E.g. I was surprised at what a pop music ***aficionado*** he had become.

9. **angst** (angkst) [Ger.]: fear and anxiety.

   E.g. Judy's teenage ***angst*** was a nightmare for her parents to cope with.

10. **annus mirabilis** (an'us muh-ra'buh-lis) [Lat.]: wonderful year.

    E.g. Last year was the ***annus mirabilis*** for our company as the company made huge profits on its sales.

11. **ante meridiam** , am (an-ti-mə-ˈri-dē-əm, -dē-ˌem) [Lat.] before midday , post meridiam – after midday

    also: **diem** - day, **per diem** – per day

12. **au revoir** (ˌōr-ə-ˈvwär) [Fr.] good bye, until we meet again

    E.g. With tears in her eyes, she said ***au revoir*** to all her family members and boarded the last train to a far off destination.

13. **a priori** (ah pree-or'ee) [Lat.]: based on theory rather than observation.

    E.g. The fact that they have moved to a much smaller house is ***a priori*** that they are having financial difficulties."

14. **au courant** (oh' koo-rahn') [Fr.]: up-to-date.

    E.g. The shoes, the hair, the clothes—every single detail of her appearance, was absolutely ***au courant.***

15. **beau geste** (boh zhest') [Fr.]: a fine or noble gesture often wasted.

E.g. My colleagues often spoke ill of me to the boss but their ***beau geste*** could not deter my promotion.

16. **beau monde** (boh' mond') [Fr.]: high society.

E.g. Such graceful style would impress even the ***beau monde.***

17. **bête noire** (bet nwahr') [Fr.]: something or someone particularly disliked.

E.g. The very mention of his ex-wife is a ***bête noire,*** to him.

18. **bona fide** (boh'na fide) [Lat.]: in good faith; genuine, true.

E.g. "For his sheer excellence and command on the subject, it was clear that he was indeed a ***bona fide*** expert in her field."

19. **bon mot** (bon moe') [Fr.]: a witty remark or comment.

E.g. He amused the audience by his ***bon mot*** remarks and humorous comments.

20. **bon vivant** (bon vee-vahnt') [Fr.]: a person who lives luxuriously and enjoys good food and drink.

E.g. All his life he lived like a true ***bon vivant,*** but died as a pauper after his business crashed.

21. **bon voyage** (bōⁿ-ˌvȯi-ˈäzh, ˌbän-; ˌbōⁿ-ˌvwī-ˈäzh) [Fr.] "Good trip", or "have a good trip".

E.g. His friends shouted, "bon voyage!" as he entered the check-in lobby at the airport.

22. **carpe diem** (kar'pay dee'um) [Lat.]: seize the day.

E.g., "So today is your final interview for the job, just be confident and ***carpe die.***

23. **carte blanche** (kart blonsh') [Fr.]: unlimited power to act on one's own.

E.g. A boss may have ***carte blanche*** around the office, but at home is a slave to his family's demands.

24. **casus belli** (kay'sus bel'eye) [Lat.]: an act justifying war.

    E.g. The death of a single soldier in border crossfire proved be enough of a *casus belli* for a full-scale war between the two countries.

25. **cause célèbre** (koz suh-leb'ruh) [Fr.]: a widely known but controversial case or issue.

    E.g. The so called war on terror has now become a *cause célèbre.*

26. **caveat emptor** (kav'ee-ot emp'tor) [Lat.]: let the buyer beware.

    E.g. Before you take a hasty decision about buying that secondhand car, *caveat emptor*!

27. **comme ci comme ça** (kom see' kom sah') [Fr.]: so-so.

    E. g My opinion about this plan is *comme ci comme ça.*

28. **comme il faut** (kom eel foe') [Fr.]: as it should be; fitting

    E.g. The wanted terrorist was finally gunned down by the commandoes. His end was truly *comme il faut.*

29. **coup de grâce** (koo de grahss') [Fr.]: finishing blow.

    E.g. Winning an Oscar for his very successful movie came as *coup de grâce.*

30. **cri de coeur** (kree' de kur') [Fr.]: heartfelt appeal.

    E.g. Numerous people made a *cri de coeur* on face book to raise funds for the cancer stricken child.

31. **de rigueur** (duh ree-gur') [Fr.]: strictly required, as by etiquette, usage, or fashion.

    E.g. Manners and values that were once a *de rigueur* of cultural and social traditions in England are now slowly disappearing.

32. **coup d'etat** (kü-(ˌ)dā-ˈtä , kuːdeɪˈtɑ) [Fr.] a sudden , violent overthrow or change of an existing government by a small but well-equipped group

E.g. The military took over the country through a ***coup d'etat*** and decided to indict the president over corruption charges.

33. **deus ex machina** (day'us ex mahk'uh-nuh) [Lat.]: a forced or unconvincing method to resolve a situation. "Stretching probability

E.g. The movie concluded with a ***deus ex machina*** ending in which everyone was rescued at the last minute.

34. **dolce vita** (dole'chay vee'tuh) [Ital.]: life of physical pleasure and enjoyment

E.g. After a continuous stretch of work without vacation, he is looking for a week of ***dolce vita*** in Switzerland.

35. **de facto** *(*di-ˈfak-(ˌ)tō) [Medieval Latin]: exercising power as if legally accepted,

E.g. After the death of the president, the vice president became the de facto president.

36. **de jure** (dē-ˈju̇r-ē) [Lat.] by law, according to law; by right

E.g. He was given the possession of his father's property ***de jure.***

37. **ecce homo** (ek'ay ho'mo) [Lat.]: behold the man.

E.g. The painting depicted the common Renaissance theme, *ecce homo*—Christ wearing the crown of thorns.

38. **enfant terrible** (ahn-fahn' tay-reeb'luh) [Fr.]: a nasty and stubborn child; a terribly outspoken or bold person.

E.g. He continued to annoy all the passengers on board by his ***enfant terrible*** like behavior.

39. **entre nous** (ahn'truh noo') [Fr.]: between ourselves; confidentially.

E.g. Please don't share this information with anyone, it should remain **entre nous.**

40. **en route** (äⁿ(n)-ˈrüt, en-, in-, -ˈraut) [Fr.]

    E.g. Can you please pick some grocery for me en route the town.

41. **et cetra - etc.** (et-ˈse-tə-rə) [Lat.]: and the rest ; number of unspecified additional persons or things

42. **et tu Brute** (ɛt ˈtuː ˈbruːtɛ) [Lat.]: "Even you, Brutus*?" or* "You too, Brutus?"

    A quotation or expression used to show the utmost, extreme or the most unexpected betrayal by someone you trusted wholeheartedly

    Last words Roman emperor Julius Caesar to his friend Marcus Brutus at the moment of his assassination

    E.g. The man he had trusted with his life betrayed him at the end, and had him arrested by the police. Turning to him in handcuffs he said , **et tu Brute**

43. **eureka** (yu̇-ˈrē-kə) [Greek]: I have found

    E.g. When Archimedes finally discovered a method for determining the purity of gold, he exclaimed, **eureka!**

44. **ex-officio** (ek-sə-ˈfi-shē-ˌō,) [Lat.]: By virtue of office or position

    E.g. He made the decision ex officio

45. **exampli gratia** – *Abbr.* **e.g.** (ig-ˌzem-plē-ˈgrä-tē-ˌä, -ˈgrä-sh(ē-)ə)

46. **extempore** (ex·tem·po·re , ĭk-stĕm'pə-rē) [Lat.]: done, carried out, or composed with little or no preparation at all

    E.g. Although he gave an extempore speech he had his audience spellbound.

47. **fait accompli** (fate ah-kom-plee') [Fr.]: an accomplished fact, seemingly permanent but not necessarily.

E.g. There's no use for complaining about the delay in flight, it's a ***fait accompli***.

48. **faux pas** (foh pah') [Fr.]: a social mistake, blunder

E.g. Suddenly, he realized what silly ***faux pas*** he had committed unconsciously.

49. **glasnost** (glaz'nohst) [Rus.]: open and frank discussion

E.g. The husband and wife decided to hold a ***glasnost*** about their divorce settlement.

50. **hoi polloi** (hoy' puh-loy') [Gk.]: the common people.

E.g. Plato did not believe that the ***hoi polloi*** should have the right to vote and elect their rulers.

51. **ibidem** Abbr. **ib** or **ibid** [Lat.]: ('i-bə-ˌdem; i-'bī-dəm) In the same place, used in footnotes and bibliographies to refer to the book, chapter, article, or page ; in the same place, thing or case

52. **impasse** ('im-ˌpas) A road or passage without any exit; A situation that is so difficult that no easy or quick solution seems possible; a deadlock

E.g. The impasse between the government and the opposition has led to much unrest and tension among political parties.

53. **in camera** [Lat.]: in private or secrete

E.g. The board of directors met ***in camera*** to discuss the corruption case against the general manger of the company.

54. **in loco parentis** (in loh'koh pa-ren'tiss) [Lat.]: in the place of a parent. (***loco*** – location, place)

E.g. The court appointed Michael Jackson's mother to serve ***in loco parentis*** for his (MJ's) children.

55. **in situ** (in sit'too) [Lat.]: situated in the original or natural position.

E.g. The statue of Gandhi has been removed from the city square and placed **in situ.**

56. **in toto (**in toh-toh) [Lat.]: totally; altogether: on the whole, entirely, completely

E.g. David Copperfield's aunt decaled that she will support him ***in toto*** to provide for all his needs.

57. **inter alia** (in-tər-'ā-lē-ə , in-tur eh-lee-ah) [Lat.]: among other things

E.g. Dismissing the case, the judge remarked, inter alia, the prosecutor has failed to provide credible witnesses to support his arguments.

58. **in vino veritas** (in vee'no vare'i-toss) [Lat.]: in wine there is truth, a person speaks truth after being drunk, (also, veritable- true, real from ***veritas***)

E.g. The drunken old man spoke all about the romantic affairs of his youth at the party, thus proving - ***in vino veritas.***

59. **ipso facto** (ip'soh fak'toh) [Lat.]: by the fact itself.

E.g. A monk or a nun, ***ipso facto,*** cannot marry.

60. **laissez faire** (les-ey fair; French le-sey fer) [Fr.]:

Theory that promotes noninterference in the affairs of others, especially with reference to individual conduct or freedom of action; leave the individual alone; free trade policy

E.g. Liberals generally believe in the ***laissez faire*** policy in all the matters of an individual's life

61. **lingua franca** [Italian : lingua, *language* + franca, *Frankish (*that is, European)

(in Linguistics) a language used for communication among people of different mother tongues

E.g. English, no doubt has earned the status of lingua franca in the whole world.

62. **mala fide** (ma-lə-'fī-dē, -də , mä lä f d) [Lat.]: in bad faith – opposite of **bona fide** ; someone carrying a bad reputation , known to be a deceiver , cheater or untrustworthy person

E.g. The company declared the corrupt employee *mala fide* and dismissed him from the job.

63. **modus operandi** *Abbr.* **MO** (mō'dəs ōp'ə-rān'dē, -dĭ' , məʊdəs ɒpə'randi:) [Lat.]: the mode or method of doing something, the procedure carried out to do sth ; the way in which something operates or works

E.g. The police found out that the serial killer had adopted a new *modus operandi* for every murder he committed.

64. **mano a mano** (mah'no ah mah'no) [Span.]: directly or face-to-face in a conflict or encounter.

E.g. The ringleader of the gang warned his men not to intervene as he wanted to handle his rival *mano a mano.*

65. **mea culpa** (may'uh kul'puh) [Lat.]: I am to blame. (culprit from *culpa*)

E.g. The drunken driver pleaded *mea culpa* for the accident.

66. **nom de guerre** (nom duh gair') [Fr.]: pseudonym.

E.g. He went by his *nom de guerre* when visiting popular nightclubs.

67. **nom de plume** (nom duh ploom') [Fr.]: pen name.

E.g. Many writers use their *nom de plume* instead of revealing their real identity for their writings.

68. **nota bene** (noh'tuh ben'nee) [Ital.]: note well; take notice.

E.g. The invitation card carried a short reminder: *nota bene,* The program will start at 8:00 pm sharp.

69. **par excellence** (pär-ˌek-sə-'läⁿs) [Fr.]: up to a high degree of excellence; beyond comparison ; by the way of special distinction or prominence, being the best of a kind

    E.g. Among English plays, Shakespeare's "Romeo and Juliet" is *par excellence*

70. **per capita** (per kap-i-tuh) [Lat.] *capita* – head: Per unit of population; per person, per head , average per person

    E.g. Income per capita has been steadily rising in this country.

71. **per diem** Abbr. **p.d** (per dee-uhm , pər dē'əm) by the day; for each day, per day

    E.g. The contract employees in this company are paid their wages *per diem.*

72. **persona non grata** (per-soh'nuh non grah'tuh) [Lat.]: unacceptable, unwanted, or unwelcome person.

    E.g. A diplomat who is found spying in a country may be declared a *persona non grata* and deported to his country.

73. **prima facie** (pry'ma fay'she , prahy-muh fey-shee-ee) [Lat.]: at first sight, clear and evident, first impression

    E.g. *Prima facie,* the death of the young woman is a case of suicide but the police are treating it as a murder.

74. **post mortem** (pōs(t)-'mȯr-təm) [Lat.] an examination of the body made after the death of a person, mainly to determine the cause of death

    E.g. The post mortem report revealed that the prisoner had been poisoned to death in his prison cell.

75. **pro bono** (pro boh'noh) [Lat.]: done or donated free of charge; free.

    E.g. The retired old teacher decided to teach poor children *pro bono.*

76 **quid pro quo** (kwid' pro kwoh') [Lat.]: measure for measure; an equal exchange or return

E.g. He promised his patron (sponsor) that she would return his favors *quid pro quo* when he had the means,

77. **sans souci** (sahn soo-see') [Fr.]: carefree, without worry, free, easy going

E.g. Usually he doesn't take anything serious, so don't be surprised by his *sans souci* attitude.

78. **schadenfreude** (shah den froy'deh) [Ger.]: pleasure at someone else's misfortunes.

E.g. Some people look for schadenfreude than feeling sorry at others' hard luck and failure.

79. **sine qua non** (sin'ay kwah nohn') [Lat.]: necessary element or condition.

E.g. Spices are the *sine qua non* of Indian cuisine.

80. **sotto voce** (suh'tow voh'chee) [Ital.]: in a quiet voice, attempting not to be overheard.

E.g. Two ladies kept whispering to each other *sotto voce* while gossiping about the guests in the party.

81. **sub judice** (sub'dʒu ːdɪsɪ , sŭb jōō'dĭ-sē') [Lat.]: means that a particular case or matter is under trial or being considered by a judge or court, in process of a court trial

E.g. Since this high profile case is still *sub judice,* the press and the media have been barred from its in-depth (detailed) coverage.

82. **suo moto** (sue-oh moe-toe) [Lat.] Literally translated, *suo moto* means "on its own motion". In strict legal sense, the term refers to a situation where a judge acts without a petition being filed by either party before the court. It may well be taken as "judicial activism"

E.g. The chief justice of the supreme court took a *sue moto* action against a high government official in the corruption scandal made public by the media.

83. **via** ('vī-ə, 'vē-ə) [Lat.]: by way of, by the means of, through the medium of

E.g.

    a. He flew to Singapore *via* Bangkok.
    b. I informed him about the project *via* one of our mutual friends.
    c. She did some research *via* computer.
    d. They went home *via* a shortcut.

(also, *via media* – middle course)

84. **vice versa** (ˈvaɪsɪ ˈvɜːsə , vī-si-ˈvər-sə) [Lat.]: opposite , in the same way, opposite on the same terms, the position being reversed

    E.g. Doctors qualified to work in England are accepted in Scotland and *vice versa.*

85. **vis-a-vis** [Fr.]: (vēz-ə-ˈvē) face to face';

    E.g. The interviewee and the interviewer sat *vis-a-vis* at the table.

86. **vini, vidi, vici** (ven'ee vee'dee vee'chee) [Lat.]: I came, I saw, I conquered.

    E.g. Alexander the great was right in saying, *veni, vidi, vici,* as almost anywhere he went, he conquered without facing much resistance.

87. **verboten** (fer-boh'ten) [Ger.]: forbidden, as by law; prohibited.

    E.g. Discussing sex-related matters in public is *verboten* in many conservative (*traditional*) societies.

88. **vox populi** (voks pop'yoo-lie) [Lat.]: the voice of the people. Common opinion, view or judgment of general public (*common people*)

    E.g. Most dictators fail to regard the *vox populi* until they are finally removed by the street power of the common people.

    Also, *vox-pupil, vox dei* – the voice of the people is the voice of God/ gods

89. **viva voce [vi·va vo·ce]** (vī'və vō'sē) [Lat.]: by word of mouth : orally

    E.g. The foreman gave the instructions *viva voce.*

90. **viz** [abbreviation for *videlicet*] namely, that is to say, as follows, or , to explain something that has already been said in a more accurate and clearer way

E.g. I want to buy the early versions of some books in classical literature viz. Paradise Lost, Divine Comedy and Oedipus Rex.

91. **Zeitgeist** (zite'guyst , 'tsīt-ˌgīst, 'zīt-) [Ger.]: the thought, feeling or awareness characteristic of a particular period of time, the spirit of the age or spirit of the time

E.g. Michael Jackson's songs were a *zeitgeist* of the 80s in America.

17 COMMON ABBREVIATIONS AND ACRONYMS

I. Time and Calendar

A. Days of the Week: Sun., Mon., Tues., Wed., Thurs., Fri., Sat.

B. Months of the Year: Jan., Feb., Mar., Apr., May (no abbreviation), Jun., Jul., Aug., Sept., Oct., Nov., Dec.

1. **A.D.** =   anno Domini
2. **B.C.** =   before Christ
3. **B.C.E.** =   before the Common Era
4. **A.M.** =   ante meridiem (before noon)
5. **P.M.** =   post meridiem (after noon) (a.m. and p.m. are exception to the no-period-for-acronyms rule)
6. **CST** =   Central Standard Time
7. **DST** =   Daylight Saving Time
8. **EST** =   Eastern Standard Time
9. **MST** =   Mountain Standard Time
10. **PST** =   Pacific Standard Time
11. **c.** =   circa (approximate date)
12. **hr.** =   hour
13. **min.** =   minute
14. **sec.** =   second
15. **mo.** =   month
16. **yr.** =   year

II. Directions and Addresses

1. **Apt.** =   apartment

2. **Ave**. = avenue
3. **Blvd**. = boulevard
4. **c/o** = care of
5. **Cir**. = circle
6. **Ct**. = court
7. **Dr**. = drive (note that this is the same abbreviation as for doctor)
8. **Ln**. = lane
9. **Rd**. = road
10. **St**. = street / saint
11. **Ste**. = suite
12. **Ter**. = terrace
13. **Tpk**. = turnpike
14. **E** = east
15. **N** = north
16. **S** = south
17. **W** = west
18. **U.S.A**. = United States of America ; UK = United Kingdom
19. **Acad**. = academy
20. **Assn**. = association
21. **Corp**. = corporation
22. **Dept**. = department
23. **Div**. = division
24. **Ft**. = fort , feet
25. **Univ**. = university

III. Personal Titles

1. **Capt**. = captain
2. **Col**. = colonel
3. **Cpl**. = corporal
4. **Gen**. = general
5. **Lt**. = lieutenant
6. **Sgt**. = sergeant
7. **Dr**. = doctor
8. **L.P.N**. = licensed practical nurse
9. **R.N**. = registered nurse
10. **Esq**. = esquire
11. **Gov**. = governor
12. **Mr**. = mister

13. **Mrs.** =   missus
14. **Ms.** =   miz (miss.)
15. **Prof.** =   professor
16. **Msgr.** =   monsignor
17. **Sr.** =   sister
18. **Jr.** =   junior
19. **Sr.** =   senior

IV. Academic Degrees

1. **B.A.** =   bachelor of arts
2. **B.B.A.** =   bachelor of business administration
3. **B.S.** =   bachelor of science
4. **D.A.** =   doctor of arts
5. **Ed.D.** =   doctor of education
6. **J.D.** =   doctor of law
7. M.A. =   master of arts
8. **M.B.A.** =   master of business administration
9. **M.D.** =   doctor of medicine
10. **M.S.** =   master of science
11. **Ph.D.** =   doctor of philosophy

V. Miscellaneous Others

1. **AKA** =   also known as
2. **ASAP** =   as soon as possible (sometimes pronounced *ay-say*)
3. **ATM** =   automated teller machine
4. **FAQ** =   frequently asked question
5. **ID** =   identification
6. **IQ** =   intelligence quotient
7. **Intl.** =   international
8. **MC** =   master of ceremonies (sometimes written out as *emcee*)
9. **PIN** =   personal identification number
10. **P.S.** =   postscript
11. **RSVP** =   respondez s'il vous plaît (French for ***please reply***)
12. **RIP** =   rest in peace
13. **SPF** =   sun protection factor
14. **SOS** =   save our souls / spirits

15. **TBA** =   to be announced
16. **TBD** =   to be determined

VI. Top 50 Popular Text & Chat Acronyms:

1. **2moro** =   Tomorrow
2. **2nite** =   Tonight
3. **BRB** =   Be Right Back
4. **BTW** =   By The Way
5. **B4N** =   Bye For Now
6. **BCNU** =   Be Seeing You
7. **BFF** =   Best Friends Forever
8. **CYA** =   See Ya!
9. **DBEYR** = Don't Believe Everything You Read
10. **DILLIGAS** = Do I Look Like I Give A Sh**
11. **FUD** =   Fear, Uncertainty, and Disinformation
12. **FWIW** =   For What It's Worth
13. **GR8** =   Great
14. **ILY / ILU**= I Love You
15. **IMHO** =   In My Humble Opinion
16. **IRL** =   In Real Life
17. **ISO** =   In Search Of
18. **J/K** =   just Kidding
19. **L8R** =   Later
20. **LMAO** =   Laughing My A** Off
21. **LOL** =   Laughing Out Loud or, Lots Of Love
22. **LYLAS** = Love You Like A Sister
23. **MHOTY** = My Hat's Off To You
24. **NIMBY** = Not In My Back Yard
25. **NP** =   No Problem -or- Nosy Parents
26. **NUB** =   New person to a site or game
27. **OIC** =   Oh, I See
28. **OMG** =   Oh My God
29. **OT** =   Off Topic
30. **POV** =   Point Of View
31. **RBTL** =   Read Between The Lines
32. **ROTFLMAO** = Rolling On The Floor Laughing My Ass Off
33. **RT** =   Real Time
34. **THX / TX / THKS** = Thanks

35. **SITD** = Still In The Dark
36. **SOL** = Sheer Out of Luck
37. **SWAK** = Sealed (or Sent) With A Kiss
38. **TFH** = Thread From Hell
39. **RTM** = Read The Manual
40. **TLC** = Tender Loving Care (tables, ladders and chairs in WWE)
41. **TMI** = Too Much Information
42. **TTYL** = Talk To You Later -or- Type To You Later
43. **TYVM** = Thank You Very Much
44. **VBG** = Very Big Grin
45. **WEG** = Wicked Evil Grin
46. **WTH** = What The Heck
47. **WYWH** = Wish You Were Here
48. **XOXO** = Hugs and Kisses

VII. Common Acronyms Used in Chat

1. **AFK** = Away From Keyboard
2. **BRB** = Be Right Back
3. **BBIAB** = Be Back In A Bit
4. **BBL** = Be Back Later
5. **TTFN** = Ta Ta For Now
6. **BBS** = Be Back Soon
7. **BTW** = By The Way
8. **HAGN** = Have A Good Night
9. **KISS** = Keep It Simple
10. **KIT** = Keep In Touch
11. **EG** = Evil Grin
12. **BEG** = Big Evil Grin
13. **NYOB** = None of Your Business
14. **OMG** = Oh My God
15. **PM** = Private Message
16. **POS** = Parents Over Shoulder
17. **TTYL** = Talk To You Later
18. **LTNS** = Long Time No See
19. **IDK** = I don't know

VIII. Common Acronyms Used in Military/Government

1. **AWOL** =   Absent Without Leave
2. **JROTC** = Junior Reserve Officer Training Corps
3. **MIA** =   Missing In Action
4. **POW** =   Prisoner of War
5. **DAFB** =   Dover Air Force Base
6. **SWAT** =   Special Weapons And Tactics
7. **Navy SEALs** = Navy Sea Air Land forces
8. **APB** =   All Points Bulletin
9. **FBI** =   Federal Bureau of Investigation
10. **OSHA** = Occupational Safety and Health Administration
11. **CIA** =   Central Intelligence Agency
12. **NASA** = National Aeronautics and Space Administration
13. **USSR** = Union of Soviet Socialist Republic
14. **USA** =   United States of America
15. **NAFTA** = North American Free Trade Agreement
16. **DelDOT** = Delaware Department of Transportation
17. **DMV** =   Division of Motor Vehicles
18. **CPS** =   Child Protective Services
19. **RNC** =   Republican National Committee
20. **CSI** =   Crime Scene Investigation

IX. Common Acronyms Used in Appreciation

1. **LYLAB** = Love You Like A Brother
2. **GMTA** = Great Minds Think Alike
3. **ROFL** = Rolling On Floor Laughing
4. **TY** =   Thank You
5. **TYVM** = Thank You Very Much
6. **YW** =   Your Welcome
7. **NP** =   No Problem
8. **WTG** =   Way To Go
9. **BF** =   Boyfriend
10. **GF** =   Girlfriend
11. **GJ** =   Good Job
12. **BF** =   Best Friend
13. **BFF** = Best Friends Forever
14. **BFFL** = Best Friends For Life

15. **Gr8** =   Great
16. **FTTE** =   Friends till the end
17. **FBF** =   Face book friend

X. Common Informative Acronyms

1. **AIDS** =   Acquired Immune Deficiency Syndrome
2. **HIV** =   Human Immunodeficiency Virus
3. **DARE** =   Drug Abuse Resistance Education
4. **ADD** =   Attention Deficit Disorder
5. **ADHD** =   Attention Deficit Hyperactivity Disorder
6. **DOB** =   Date Of Birth
7. **GMT** =   Greenwich Mean Time
8. **OTC** =   Over The Counter
9. **CDC** =   Centers for Disease Control and Prevention
10. **ASAP** =   As Soon As Possible
11. **FYI** =   For Your Information
12. **EST** =   Eastern Standard Time
13. **PST** =   Pacific Standard Time
14. **CST** =   Central Standard Time
15. **PPV** =   Pay Per View
16. **SSN** =   Social Security Number
17. **JIT** =   Just In Time
18. **ADL** =   Activities of Daily Living
19. **AMA** =   Against Medical Advice
20. **MD** =   Medical Doctor

XI. Common Acronyms Used in Industry

1. **AKA** =   Also Known As
2. **BAU** =   Business As Usual
3. **DBA** =   Doing Business As
4. **DND** =   Do Not Disturb
5. **MBA** =   Masters of Business Administration
6. **OT** =   Overtime
7. **POS** =   Point Of Service
8. **DAEMON** = Disk And Execution Monitor
9. **HR** =   Human Resources

10. **POP** =   Post Office Protocol
11. **TNT** =   Tuner Network Television
12. **TBC** =   To Be Continued
13. **TBN** =   Trinity Broadcasting Network
14. **ESPN** =   Entertainment and Sports Programming Network
15. **CBS** =   Columbia Broadcasting System
16. **MTV** =   Music Television
17. **NBC** =   National Broadcasting Company
18. **ABS** =   Anti-lock Breaking System
19. **ABC** =   American Broadcasting Company
20. **PBS** =   Public Broadcasting Service
21. **UFO** =   Unidentified Flying Object

XII. Common Acronyms Used as Identity

1. **NFL** =   National Football League
2. **AFL** =   American Football League
3. **NBA** =   National Basketball Association
4. **NHL** =   National Hockey League
5. **AA** =   Alcoholics Anonymous
6. **AARP** = American Association of Retired Persons
7. **MADD** = Mothers Against Drunk Driving
8. **PG** =   (under) Parents' Guidance
9. **PGA** =   Professional Golfers' Association
10. **SWM** =   Single White Male
11. **SWF** =   Single White Female
12. **APA** =   American Psychological Association
13. **MLA** =   Modern Language Association ; Member of Legislative Assembly
14. **ACS** =   American Cancer Society
15. **AMA** =   American Medical Association
16. **ADA** =   American Dental Association
17. **FLAG** = Foreign Language Association of Georgia
18. **PAWS** = Progressive Animal Welfare Society
19. **WWE** =   World Wrestling Entertainment
20. **SPCA** = Society for the Prevention of Cruelty to Animals
21. **AAAS** = American Association for the Advancement of Science
22. **FIFA** = Federation International of Football Associations
23. **ICC** =   International Cricket Council

Difference between Bio Data, Resume and CV

Bio-Data:
Bio-Data consists the information about the individual and his attributes, hobbies, interests along with educational qualification to describe the person the best.

Resume:
A resume is a one or two page "summary" of your skills, experience and education. Generally no more longer than a page or two. It indicates candidate's professional qualification.

CV:
A Curriculum Vitae is a longer and more detailed synopsis. Generally over a couple of pages long. It indicates candidate's professional experience.

18 FRENCH WORDS AND PHRASES

Used in English

French words are generally not pronounced the way they are spelled in accordance with the English spelling and sound system; therefore, please check the correct pronunciation of the words before using them, especially in speech.
Visit, http://www.thefreedictionary.com/billet-doux
for correct pronunciation

Pronunciation Key					
ă	pat	k	**kick, cat, pique**	o͞o	boot
ā	pay	l (nēd'l)	lid, needle*	ou	**out**
â<r< td=""></r>	**care**	m	**mum**	p	**pop**
ä	father	n (sŭd'n)	**no**, sudden*	r	**roar**
b	**bib**	ng	thing	s	**sauce**
ch	**church**	ŏ	pot	sh	**ship, dish**
d	**deed**, milled	ō	toe	t	tight, stopped
ě	pet	ô	**caught, paw, for, horrid, hoarse****	th	**thin**
ē	bee	oi	noise	*th*	**this**
f	**fife, phase, rough**	o͞o	took	ŭ	cut

g	**g**a**g**	û<r< td=""></r<>	**ur**ge, t**er**m, f**ir**m, w**or**d, h**ear**d	ər	butt**er**
h	**h**at	v	**v**al**v**e		
hw	**wh**ich	w	**w**ith	**Foreign**	
ĭ	**p**it	y	**y**es	œ	*French* f**eu**, *German* sch**ö**n
ĭ	**p**ie, by	z	**z**ebra, **x**ylem	ü	*French* t**u**, *German* **ü**ber
ĭ<r< td=""></r<>	**p**ier	zh	vi**s**ion, plea**s**ure, gara**ge**	KH	*German* i**ch**, *Scottish* lo**ch**
j	**j**u**dge**	ə	**a**bout, it**e**m, edibl**e**, gall**o**p, circ**u**s	N	*French* bo**n** (bôɴ)

> In English the consonants *l* and *n* often constitute complete syllables by themselves.
>
> **Fr. = French , Eng. = English**

A

1. **À la carte:** [ɑ lə ˈkɑrt] lit. "on the menu"; In restaurants it refers to ordering individual dishes rather than a fixed-price meal.
2. **A propos:** [a-prə-ˈpō] regarding/concerning (note that the correct French syntax is à propos de
3. **Adieu:** [ə-dyo͞oˈ, əˈdyu] lit. "to God"; farewell; goodbye, until we meet again
4. **Aide-mémoire:** lit. "memory aid"; an object or memorandum to assist in remembrance, or a diplomatic paper proposing the major points of discussion
5. **Amour-propre:** "self-love", self-respect.
6. **Attaché:** [ăt'ə-shā , əˈtæʃeɪ] a person attached to an embassy
7. **Au contraire:** [oʊ kɔ̃ˈtrɛr] on the contrary.
8. **Au pair:** [(ô pârˈ, əʊ ˈpɛə] a young foreigner who does domestic chores in exchange for room and board. In France, those chores are mainly child care/education.
9. **Au revoir!** [oʊ rəˈvwar , ōˈ rə-vwärˈ] "See you later!" (to the pleasure of seeing you again).

10. **Avant-garde**: [ä'vänt-gärd , ˌævɒŋ'gɑːd] innovative movements in art, music and literature;

B

1. **Baguette:** [bæ'gɛt , bă-gĕt'] a long, narrow loaf of bread with a crisp crust, often called 'French bread'
2. **Beau geste:** [bō zhĕst' , bo ʒɛst] lit. "beautiful gesture", a gracious gesture, a kind act
3. **Belle:** (bĕl , bɛl) a beautiful woman or girl.
4. **Belles-lettres:** [bĕl-lĕt'rə , bɛl'lɛ trə] lit. "fine letters"; beautiful words , refers to writings in literature
5. **Billet-doux:** [bĭl'ā-doo' , bɪl eɪ'du] lit. "sweet note", love letter
6. **Bon appétit:** [boʊn æpeɪ'ti] lit. "good appetite"; enjoy your meal
7. **Bon mot:** [bôN mō , bɔ̃ mo] well-chosen word(s), particularly a witty remark
8. **Bon vivant:** [bôN' vē-vän' , bɔ̃ vivã] one who enjoys the good life, a pleasure-seeking person
9. **Bon voyage**: [bôN' vwä-yäzh , bɔ̃ vwajaʒ] lit. "good journey"; have a good trip!
10. **Bourgeois:** [ˌbʊə ʒwɑ ziː] member of the middle-class.
11. **Bouquet:** [boʊ'keɪ , (bō-käN] a bunch of flowers.
12. **Bric-à-brac:** ['brɪkəˌbræk , brĭk'ə-brăk] a collection of old furniture etc.
13. **Brunette:** [broo-nĕt , bru'nɛt] a brown-haired girl
14. **Bureau:** [byoor'ō] (pl. bureaux) office; originally meant "desk" in French.
15. **Bête noire:** [beyt nwahr ; Fr. bet nwar] a scary or unpopular person, idea, or thing, anything that becomes a cause of annoyance to sb.
16. **Boutique:** [boo-teek] a clothing store, usually selling designer/one off pieces In French, it can describe any shop, clothing etc.

C

1. **Cache:** [kăsh , kăsh] a collection of items of the same type (or weapons) stored in a hidden or inaccessible place
2. **Café:** [kă-fā , 'kæfeɪ] a coffee shop (also used in French for "coffee"
3. **Carte blanche:** [kärt bläNs , kɑrt 'blɑntʃ , kɑrt 'blɑ̃ʃ] lit. "white card" (i.e. blank check); unlimited authority.
4. **C'est la vie!** (Se la vi) "That's life!" or "Such is life!" or "It is what it is!" It is sometimes used as an expression to say that life is cruel but that one must accept it.

5. **Chargé d'affaires:** [shär-zhā' dē-fâr , ʃɑːʒeɪ dæ'fɛə] a diplomat left in charge of day to day business at a diplomatic mission.

6. **Chauffeur:** [shō'fər, shō-fûr' , 'ʃəʊfə ʃəʊ'fɜː] a privately hired driver.

7. **Chef d'œuvre:** [she-dœ-vruh] a masterpiece.

8. **Cliché:** [klee-shey] lit. negative; unconvincing through overuse, no more believable

9. **Clique:** [kleek , klek] a small exclusive group of friends; always used in a scornful (disrespecting, mocking) way in French.

10. **Coquette:** [kō-'ket] a flirtatious girl; a woman who tries to gain the attention and admiration of men without being sincere and honest on her own part

11. **Coup de grâce:** [koo duh grahs , ku də gras] lit. literally, blow of mercy killing of a badly wounded enemy soldiers, now more often used in a figurative context

12. **Coup de maître:** [koo duh me-truh] stroke of the master, master stroke. This word describes a planned action skillfully done.

13. **Crème de la crème:** [krem duh lah krem , krɛm də la krɛm] Best of the best, "cream of the cream," used to describe highly skilled people or objects. A synonymous expression in French is fin du fin.

14. **Connoisseur:** [kon-uh-sur] an expert in wines, fine arts, or other matters of culture; a person of refined taste.

15. **Coup d'état:** [koo dey-tah] a sudden change in government by force; literally "hit (blow) of state

16. **Critique:** [kri-teek] a critical analysis or evaluation of a work

17. **Croissant:** [krwah-sahn] a crescent-shaped bread made from a kind of a pastry.

18. **Cul-de-sac:** [kuhl-duh-sak] a dead-end street.; an impasse

D

19. **De rigueur:** [də rē-gœr , də rɪ'gɜr] required or expected, especially in fashion or etiquette

20. **Décor:** [dā'kôr', dā-kôr' , deɪ'kɔr, 'deɪ kɔr] n. the layout and furnishing of a room.

21. **Déjà vu:** [dā'zhä vōō , deɪʒæ 'vu] lit. "already seen": an impression or feeling of having seen or experienced something before.

22. **Dénouement:** [dey-noo-mahn] lit. "untying": the resolution or the very ending of a play or a short story

23. **Dossier:** [daw-see-ey , daw-syey] a file containing detailed information about a person usually involved in an illegal act

24. **Début:** [dey-bi yoo] first public performance of an entertainment or in a sport event

25. **Du jour:** [duh zhoor , duː ˈʒɔ , Fr. dy ʒur] lit. "of the day": said of something fashionable, attraction for a day that is quickly forgotten

E

26. **Eau de Cologne** [ō-də-kə-ˈlōn] a mildly perfumed (toilet) water

27. **En bloc:** [ɑ̃ blɔk , ahn blawk , Eng. en blok] as a group.

28. **Entrepreneur:** [ɑn trə prəˈnɜr] a person who undertakes and operates a new project or business and shoulders some accountability for the possible risks.

29. **En suite:** [ahn sweet] in succession; in a series or set.

30. **Exposé:** [ek-spoh-**zey**] a public exposure or revelation, as of something dishonorable, a published exposure of a fraud or scandal

F

31. **Fait accompli:** [fɛ ta kɔ̃ˈpli , fāˈtä-kôɴ-plē"] lit. an accomplished fact; something that has already happened and is thus unlikely to be reversed or changed, a done deal

32. **Faux pas:** [fō päˈ , ˌfəʊ ˈpɑː Fr. fo pɑ] lit. "false step": violation of accepted, although unwritten, social rules

33. **Femme fatale** [fem-fə-ˈtal , fam fəˈtɑːl , *English* ˈfɛm fəˈtæl] lit. "deadly woman" a woman who attracts men by an appearance of charm and mystery but mostly to the ruin of the man

34. **Fiancé/e:** engaged; lit. a man/woman engaged to be married.

35. **Forte:** [1. fawr-**tey** 2. fawrt, fohrt] a strength, a strong point, a special kill

G

36. **Gaffe:** [găf , gæf] blunder

37. **Gendarmerie**: [zhän-där m -r , zhä -där-m –r] a military body charged with police duties

38. **Genre** [ˈzhän-rə , ˈʒɒnrə or ˈdʒɒnrə] a type or class, kind" or "sort, classification

H

39. **Hors de combat:** [ôrˈ də kôɴ-bä , ɔr də kɔ̃ˈba] lit. "out of the fight or contest": prevented from fighting, usually by injury.

I

40. **Impasse:** a situation offering no escape, as a difficulty without solution, an argument where no agreement is possible, etc.; a deadlock.
41. **In lieu:** of [l o͞o] in place (of)

J

42. **Joie de vivre:** [zhwä' də vē'vrə , ʒwa də vivrə] joy of life / living

L

43. **Liaison:** ['li ə,zɒn , zən or , li'eɪ zən , lee-ey-zawn] the contact or connection maintained by communications between various units or entities , sb. who performs this task
44. **Lingerie:** [lahn-zhuh-rey , lɑn ʒə'reɪ] a type of female underwear.
45. **La belle dam sans merci:** a beautiful girl without mercy.

M

46. **Mademoiselle:** [mad-uh-muh-zel , mam-zel; French mad-mwa-zel] lit. "my noble young lady" young unmarried lady, miss.
47. **Malaise** [mə-'lāz , ma-, -'lez] a general sense of depression or unease.
48. **Milieu:** [mil-yoo] social environment; setting (has also the meaning of "middle" in French.)

N

49. **Nouveau riche:** [noo - voh reesh] lit. "newly rich", used to refer particularly to those living a lavish lifestyle with their newfound wealth

O

50. **Omelette (omelet):** [om-lit, om-uh] dish made from beaten eggs cooked quickly in a pan.
51. **Que cera cera:** (Spanish origin) [Kay-Sa-Rah, Sa-Rah] What will be, will be.

P

52. **Par avion:** [Pa Ra-vy awn , Pa Ra Vi yon] by air mail, in French, it also means, **by plane** in general.
53. **Par excellence:** [pahr ek-suh-lahns, ek-suh-lans; French pa-rek-se-LAHNS] "by excellence": ideal, exemplary
54. **Parole:** [puh-rohl]

   a. the conditional release of a person from prison prior to the end of the maximum sentence imposed.
   b. such release or its duration.
   c. an official document authorizing such a release.

55. **Précis:** [prey-see] a concise summary, an abridged book about the matter. Literally, précis means precise, accurate.

Q

56. **Quelle horreur!** [kilo hergh]
   What a horrible thing! that's terrible, how horrible, isn't that awful, how awful

R

57. **Raison d'être:** [reɪ zoʊn ˈdɛ trə , rāˈzōn dĕtˈrə] "reason for being": justification or purpose of existence.
58. **Rapport:** [ra-pawr, -pohr] relation; connection, especially harmonious or sympathetic relation: a new employee trying to establish close rapport with his colleagues
59. **Renaissance:** [ren-uh-sahns] lit. meaning rebirth, a cultural movement in the 14-17th centuries.
60. **Répondez s'il vous plait**: [rey- **pohn** - dey seel voo **pley**] (RSVP) Please reply.
61. **Rendezvous:** [**rahn**-duh-voo] lit. "go to"; a meeting, appointment reprise
62. **Résumé:** [**rez**-oo-mey] a document listing one's qualifications for employment.
63. **Risqué** [ri-**skay** , ˈrɪs keɪ] sexually suggestive , indecent

S

64. **Sa la vie / C'est la vie:** [se la vee] that's life ; such is life
65. **Sabotage:** [săb'ə-täzh' , sa bə ̗täzh] Destruction of an employer's property (as tools or materials) or the hindering of manufacturing by dissatisfied workers
66. **Sans:** [sănz] without
67. **Savant:** [să-vänt , ˈsævənt Fr. savã̃] lit. "knowing" a wise or learned person; in English, one exceptionally gifted in a narrow skill.
68. **Silhouette:** [sil-oo-et] the image of a person, an object or scene consisting of the outline and a featureless interior, with the silhouetted object usually being black.
69. **Sobriquet** [**soh**-bruh-kay , sō-bri-̗kā] an false name, a nickname

T

70. **Tête-à-tête:**[teyt-uh-teyt, tet-uh-tet; Fr. te-ta-tet] lit. "head to head"; a warm and friendly get-together or private conversation between two people.
71. **Tour de force**: lit. [toor duh fohrs] "feat of strength": a masterly or brilliant stroke, creation, effect, or accomplishment

V

72. **Vis-à-vis:** [vee-zuh-**vee**] lit. "face to face [with]": in comparison with or in relation to; opposed to
73. **Vive:** [viːv] "Long live…!"; lit. Live
74. **Voir dire** [vwahr deer] a trial within a trial, or (in America) jury selection

ACKNOWLEDGEMENT

Bibliography and Resources:

Learner's Companion Series – Vocabulary by George Davidson Learners Pub. ©2002

http://hypertextbook.com/facts/2001/JohnnyLing.shtml

Types of Nyms: Word Classes , *http://www.fun-with-words.com/nym_heteronyms. html#Capitonyms*

Word Stress: http://www.englishclub.com/pronunciation/word-stress-rules.htm

Word Formation: http://suite101.com/article/parts-of-words-a146319 http://www. prefixsuffix.com/rootchart.php , (David Crystal, *How Language Works*. Overlook Press, 2005)

Silent Letters: http://academic.cuesta.edu/acasupp/as/810.htm

Spelling Rules *international.ouc.bc.ca/pronunciation/poem01.html*

http://en.wikipedia.org/wiki/Diphthong

http://www.amity.org.uk/Training/Spelling Rules/Spelling Rules.htm

http://www.cis.doshisha.ac.jp/kkitao/library/article/test/vocab.htm

Collocation: Kenneth Beare, About.com Guide

Compounds words: Ref. http://grammar.ccc.commnet.edu/grammar/compounds. htm

www.ruf.rice.edu/~kemmer/**Words**04/structure/**borrowed**.html

http://www.k-3teacherresources.com/compound-words.html#words

Bauer, L. and I.S.P. Nation. 1993. Word families. International Journal of Lexicography 6, 4: 253-279.

Ref: http://www.phon.ucl.ac.uk/home/dick/tta/wf/wf.htm

Biber, D. 1990. A typology of English texts. Linguistics 27: 3-43.

Campion, M.E. and W.B. Elley. 1971. An Academic Vocabulary List. Wellington: NZCER.

Carroll, J.B., P. Davies and B. Richman. 1971. The American Heritage Word Frequency Book. New York: American Heritage Publishing Co.

Carter, R. and M. McCarthy (eds.) 1988.Vocabulary and Language Teaching. London: Longman.

https://academic.cuesta.edu/acasupp/as/507.HTM

http://iteslj.org/Articles/Cervatiuc-VocabularyAcquisition.html

http://www.lextutor.ca/freq/lists_download/

VI. Why Build Your Vocabulary?

http://virtualsalt.com/vocablst.htm

Ref: Building Vocabulary for College (5th Edition) By Kent Smith Houghton Mifflin ©2000

The 1062 Vital Vocabulary Words

Source: Robert A. Harris http://www.virtualsalt.com/vocablst4.htm

Nation, I.S.P., 1990, *Teaching and Learning Vocabulary*, Newbury House, New York

West, 1953, *A General Service List of English Words*, Longman, London

Xue Guoyi and Nation, I.S.P, 1984, *A University Word List*, Language Learning and Communication 3, 2:215-229

Nation, I.S.P., 1990, Teaching and Learning Vocabulary, Newbury House, New York
West, 1953, A General Service List of English Words, Longman, London
Xue Guoyi and Nation, I.S.P, 1984, A University Word List, Language Learning and Communication 3, 2:215-229

http://www.infoplease.com/ipa/A0001619.html

Instant Vocabulary by Gopal Puri

http://abbreviations.yourdictionary.com/articles/common-accronyms.html